HULL-HOUSE MAPS AND PAPERS

HULL-HOUSE MAPS AND PAPERS

A Presentation of Nationalities and Wages
in a Congested District of Chicago,
Together with Comments and Essays on Problems
Growing Out of the Social Conditions

By the
RESIDENTS OF HULL-HOUSE,
a Social Settlement

INTRODUCTION BY RIMA LUNIN SCHULTZ

University of Illinois Press
Urbana and Chicago

Library of Congress Cataloging-in-Publication Data
Hull-House maps and papers : a presentation of
nationalities and wages in a congested district of Chicago,
together with comments and essays on problems growing
out of the social conditions / by the residents of Hull-House;
introduction by Rima Lunin Schultz.
p.   cm.
Includes bibliographical references and index.
ISBN-13: 978-0-252-03134-2 (cloth : alk. paper)
ISBN-10: 0-252-03134-2 (cloth : alk. paper)
1. Social settlements—Illinois—Chicago.
2. Sweatshops—Illinois—Chicago.
3. Immigrants—Illinois—Chicago.
4. Chicago (Ill.)—Social conditions—19th century.
5. Hull-House (Chicago, Ill.)
I. Schultz, Rima Lunin, 1943–
HV4196.C4H76   2007
362.84009773′11—dc22   2006011258

Contents

Maps follow page 58.

Introduction

Rima Lunin Schultz

The year 2005 marked the one hundred and tenth anniversary of the publication of *Hull-House Maps and Papers: A Presentation of Nationalities and Wages in a Congested District of Chicago Together with Comments and Essays on the Problems Growing Out of the Social Conditions* (*HHM&P*). Hull-House residents worked on the project between 1892 and 1894, and, after a contract with Thomas Y. Crowell was negotiated with the help of Richard T. Ely in 1894, the volume was published in 1895.[1] Hull-House residents made a dramatic statement about their shared values and understanding of the nature of social science knowledge and its usages in a democratic society when they made the decision to put together a collaborative work of sociology based on their experiences as residents of Chicago's Near West Side. They were certain that publishing maps with explicit information about the wages and conditions of the working poor in the Nineteenth Ward would educate the public and lead to much-needed reforms. The belief that an enlightened citizenry could be mobilized for reform causes was part of the Progressive Era's faith in the efficacy of social science investigation to produce solutions for society's problems. *HHM&P*, the first study of its kind in the United States, directly influenced subsequent social surveys that also emanated from settlement houses rather than from universities.[2]

The volume of maps and papers is a major work of the progressive movement. Kathryn Kish Sklar calls *HHM&P* "the single most important work by American women social scientists before 1900."[3] For Leon Fink, *HHM&P* is "one of the classics of social science and muckraking journalism in this period along with Charles Beard's *An Economic Interpretation of the Constitution,* John R. Commons's *Documentary History of American Industrial Society,* Ida Tarbell's *History of Standard Oil Company,* Jacob Riis's *How the Other Half Lives,* Lincoln Steffens's *Shame of the Cities,* and W. E. B. Du Bois's *The Philadelphia Negro.* "[4]

The contents of the volume reflect the deeply political nature of settlement work in its early days and force us to rethink the ways in which Jane Addams, the head resident of Hull-House, and her colleagues have been relegated to the margins of progressive movement history and have instead been linked to developments in the field of social work or even, lately, been confined to gender studies. Reading *HHM&P* reminds us that settlement houses were key organizations in the major social and political movements of the day. Hull-House was at the cutting edge of major initiatives that collectively defined progressivism by the 1900s. It had literally and figuratively mapped those initiatives by 1893, the year the settlement celebrated its fourth birthday.

At the time Addams and the Hull-House residents began the maps and papers project the gulf between the rising, propertied classes and the working poor who lived in the slums of East London, the West Side of Chicago, or on the Lower East Side of New York threatened social order. Hull-House residents developed their settlement in the hope that by living with working-class and poor immigrants and sharing daily experiences they could find solutions to societal problems growing out of social conditions in slums. The new relationship between rich and poor avoided the humiliation and paternalism of traditional Christian charity. Addams was uncertain of the right method, but she knew that the burgeoning industrial society that offered future progress was a complex, increasingly interdependent web of social and economic relations that required the addition of what she defined as the "social function to democracy."[5]

Traditional views about the role of government and the nature of economic laws still dominated all branches of government, the political party system, and the religious and academic establishments. Social Darwinists such as the political economist and ordained Episcopal minister William Graham Sumner of Yale University rhetorically asked what the social classes owed each other. For them, the answer was "nothing." The iron law of supply and demand ruled and established wages and hours that Social Darwinists argued derived from laws as natural and unchangeable as the physical laws guiding the planets. In contrast, Addams led the settlement movement's attack on classical liberal economic thinking when she stressed "that the dependence of classes on each other is reciprocal."[6]

HHM&P should be placed in the context of the protest literature emerging from the 1870s, including Henry George's *Progress and Poverty* (1879), an inquiry into the cause of industrial depressions and the increase of poverty alongside increases in wealth. The paradox of wealth and poverty informed the Hull-House maps as it had Charles Booth's *Life and Labour of the People of London* (1889), which was accompanied by startling maps of the prevalence of poverty in London.[7] Riis's *How the Other Half Lives* (1890) was a graphic account of children who lived in poverty in New York City. The discovery that the United States was no different than Europe and that the slums in U.S. cities were comparable to the vilest quarters of the Old World so disturbed Congress that money was appropriated to study the issue.[8]

The study of urban sociology (or sociology of any topic) was in its infancy. No maps had ever been created that showed nationalities and wages household by household, and next to nothing had been written about sweatshops and child labor. Analysis of state care of the indigent sick and insane and of the poorhouse from the point of view of whether these services were being delivered appropriately—and in the best interests of inmates—was a radical departure. The maps and papers constituted an incredible effort to quantify data about the most intimate conditions of workers' lives; the amount of air, light, and space available for individuals and families in tenements; the hourly rate for making a buttonhole, or stitching hems, or pulling the basting threads; the intricate scheme of work and sleep that families and boarders were required to maintain in order to reap survival wages; the process of premature aging among breadwinners; the extent of deformities and occupational diseases in children; and the lasting effects of industrial injuries.

This book is important because it is one of the first publications that refuted conservative laissez-faire economics with statistical data on wage labor. It is one of the first publications that graphically details the plight of immigrants and documents their work ethic, blaming the economic system rather than the individual for social conditions in the slums. Its publication, however, was not an isolated occurrence. *HHM&P* was a significant and innovative work that resonated with other social theorists and social science practitioners in the new departments of sociology and economics of universities and in newly established organizations such as the American Economic Association, which was founded in 1885.[9] Their contemporaries identified Addams and other Hull-House residents as sociologists, and the Hull-House social investigations that followed on the heels of *HHM&P* were published in the *American Journal of Sociology*.[10]

The location of the maps and papers project in a social settlement rather than a university department contributed to its innovative and groundbreaking results. When it was suggested that Addams could be more useful as a chair of sociology rather than as head of Hull-House, Ely, a progressive economist and founder of the American Economic Association, replied, "If she were a professor of sociology she would be simply one professor among many others." What she was doing was "work for the nation" he contended, and "a model work for the whole country." Noting that there were many critics of Hull-House, he contended, "Miss Addams should by no means be tempted away from Hull-House; but Hull-House itself should be developed into the greatest 'People's University' on the continent."[11] It was Ely, general editor of the Library of Economics and Politics, who selected *HHM&P* as the fifth volume in the series and promoted it as an important work of sociology. For him and for many pioneers who promoted the study of social science and dissemination of social science research there was no problem or inherent contradiction in having social investigation emanate from a settlement house.

HHM&P is a work of social science whose contributors believed that sociological knowledge was the result of the integration of social investigation and advocacy, an opposite approach from the canonical model that was just beginning to emerge in the late 1890s and became by the 1920s the only acceptable way to be a professional social scientist. By the 1920s the kind of sociological investigations undertaken at Hull-House no longer fit the criteria of academic research. *HHM&P* and other studies published by Hull-House were either ignored or placed in the category of applied social science. Addams became identified as one of the founders of social work rather than as a sociologist. She argued that her position outside the academy gave her the insights and independence critical for the sociological investigations in which she engaged. Ironically, that outsider status became the major reason she was denied a place in the history of the social sciences in the United States.

Since the 1980s historians have revised the history of the social sciences in the United States and recovered the nineteenth-century American social science tradition that "joined claims of science and disinterested expertise with the democratic and humanitarian impulses associated with moral reform. Its practitioners included independent scholars, civil servants, and both male and female social reformers," including Jane Addams, Florence Kelley, and others associated with Hull-House.[12] This emerging revisionist narrative defines *HHM&P* as an important work in the field and places the Hull-House contribution in the center rather than at the margins.[13]

The recent interest in *HHM&P* is almost entirely attributable to the rich interpretive work of scholars Mary Jo Deegan, Kathryn Kish Sklar, and Dorothy Ross, who have recognized the significance of this volume in the larger project of revising the narrative of modern American history. Specifically, the work of Sklar, Deegan, and Ross has overturned the standard histories of the progressive movement and American political history from 1890 to 1920; the history of the development of the social sciences; and, particularly, the history of the development of sociological knowledge and the role of gender in the construction of the modern welfare state. The example of *HHM&P* as the "single most important work of women sociologists" has opened an entire field of inquiry. The writing of the American women sociologists and social policy theorists have begun to be reconsidered. Reclaiming the texts of women social thinkers in the Progressive Era has been enlightening and productive of new interpretations of the origins of the modern welfare state. Understanding the role women constructed for themselves as public intellectuals and as political beings forces reconsideration of civic engagement, the nature of political participation in a democratic society, and the role of professionalism and the empowerment of the academy as the site of the production of knowledge in society.

The Contributors to *HHM&P* and the Goal of the Collaboration

There were ten contributors to the volume: Florence Kelley, Alzina Parsons Stevens, Agnes Sinclair Holbrook, Isabel Eaton, Charles Zueblin, Josefa Humpal-Zeman, Alessandro Mastro-Valerio, Julia C. Lathrop, Ellen Gates Starr, and Jane Addams.[14] Only Kelley and Zueblin had university training in economics and politics. This appeared not to disturb Addams whose prefatory remarks privileged experience over specialized education. She emphasized that all the contributors had been "in actual residence in Hull-House" (46) when they wrote their articles. "'In the study of society which we call sociology,' the settlement method of living among the people and 'staying with them a long time'" Addams had explained, "was the new method 'coming into vogue.'" She described how residents studied their neighbors "'to learn their needs and their manner of thought.'"[15]

For Addams, there was no contradiction in lived experience and claiming the scientific nature of the work when seeking the nature of their neighbors' reality. "The residents of Hull-House offer these maps and papers to the public," she wrote, "not as exhaustive treatises, but as recorded observations which may possibly be of value, because they are immediate, and the result of long acquaintance" (45).[16] Addams made clear that authority for the maps and papers comes from the investigators having lived in the neighborhood, not as theoreticians or scholars but as activists engaged in constructive work. She valorized that manner of knowing the neighborhood as the hallmark of the sociological investigation undertaken by settlement houses independently of universities or government agencies.

Along the same lines, Holbrook, who worked closely with Kelley on color coding and transferring the coded data onto the maps, notes that the maps are "an attempt . . . to put into graphic form a few facts concerning the section of Chicago immediately east of the House" (53). Throughout her brief discussion of methodology Holbrook emphasizes the efforts employed to obtain facts: "The manner of investigation has been painstaking, and the facts set forth are as trustworthy as personal inquiry and intelligent effort could make them." She also bases the accuracy of the data on the experience and long residence in the neighborhood of Florence Kelley, "the expert in charge" (57). Holbrook also reiterates Addams's caution that the "aim of both maps and notes is to present conditions rather than to advance theories—to bring within reach of the public exact information . . . rather than to advise methods by which it may be improved" (58). Echoing Addams's suggestion that public awareness will result in social betterment, Holbrook writes that "merely to state symptoms and go no farther would be idle; but to state symptoms in order to ascertain the nature of disease, and apply, it may be, its cure, is not only *scientific,* but in the highest sense *humanitarian"* (58, emphasis added).

Judging from the centrality of the wages and nationalities maps and of the articles that focus on sweatshops and garment workers in the Hull-House neighborhood, the selection of the maps and many of the topics of the essays appear to have been largely a function of the investigative work being carried out by Florence Kelley from 1892 in the context of the anti-sweatshop campaign. It is hard to imagine the maps and papers project being conceived without Kelley's initiative. She brought the statistical techniques of social investigation to Hull-House and used them as a powerful tool of social reform.[17]

An extraordinary woman, Kelley knew American politics from her father, William Darrah Kelley, a member of Congress from Pennsylvania from 1860 to 1890, and women's rights activism from her grandmother, Sarah Pugh.[18] Kelley studied history and social science at Cornell University and government and law at the University of Zurich. There she met and married a Russian Jew, Lazare Wischnewetsky, who was also a medical student and a socialist. While in Europe, Kelley had her first child; translated into English a work by Frederick Engels, *The Conditions of the Working Class in England;* and joined the German Social Democratic Party. The Wischnewetskys returned to the United States and settled in New York, where the couple had two more children. It was a difficult marriage, and in 1891, after divorcing Wischnewetsky, Kelley resettled in Chicago with the three children.

The Hull-House community provided Kelley, a single mother in need of employment and child care, with the support system she desperately needed.[19] Addams was able to have her appointed as a special agent of the Illinois Bureau of Labor Statistics, and "in that capacity Kelley completed roughly one thousand forms by 'sweaters victims' in the garment industry, first by visiting them at work, then at home."[20] She found that Hull-House was "surrounded in every direction by homework carried on under the sweating system. From the age of eighteen months few children able to sit in high chairs at tables were safe from being required to pull basting threads."[21] Kelley's presence contributed to the radicalization of other Hull-House residents, who began to witness the world around them through the lens provided by her investigations. Kelley made them realize that the children who played with blunt, coarse needles for sewing bright silk into different shapes would return home to "home work" requiring the coarse, sharp needles necessary for sewing buttons on garments. Kelley wrote, "The contrast was a hideously painful one to witness, especially when the children fell asleep at their work in their homes."[22]

Florence Kelley's investigations for the Illinois Bureau of Labor Statistics were published in an influential report. Trade unions, the Illinois Woman's Alliance, and Kelley and the Hull-House community of residents and supporters, including Mary Kenney, Henry Demarest Lloyd, the Rev. Jenkin Lloyd Jones, and Abraham Bisno, a trade union organizer in the clothing industry, kept up the pressure on the politicians. The Illinois Factory and Inspection Act (also known as the Sweatshop Act) passed in 1893, a product of intense lobbying in Springfield. The act, which Kelley drafted, set sanitary standards for the workplace, prohibited the employment of children under age fourteen in manufacturing enterprises, limited the daily working hours for females to eight, and increased the enforcement powers of factory inspectors. The reform-minded governor John P. Altgeld appointed Kelley to serve as chief inspector and Alzina Stevens as assistant inspector.[23]

At the same time, Kelley collected statistics on factories and sweatshops for Illinois, Carroll D. Wright, head of the U.S. Department of Labor, appointed her to head a team of "schedule men" (government investigators) being sent to Chicago as part of a national study that Congress had commissioned of the slums of selected American cities (55). Kelley was allowed to select the area of Chicago to be studied. It was a golden opportunity to combine social investigation and advocacy, and Kelley chose Chicago's Nineteenth Ward, the port-of-entry neighborhood where Hull-House was located. She was already knowledgeable about the Nineteenth Ward, particularly the garment industry that was the neighborhood's largest employer and the "sweating system" that had infiltrated the industry, forcing down wages and increasingly bringing women and children into its employ (63–64).

Addams and the other Hull-House residents shared Kelley's interest in learning about the worst conditions that existed in the lowest sort of neighborhoods of industrial districts. As Addams had written to her sister, Mary, five months before Hull-House opened its doors, she had been "looking up different 'slums.'"[24] For the facility's college-educated residents, the area just east of Hull-House had all the characteristics of a quintessential slum.[25]

Stevens, who worked with Kelley on the child labor section of the project, was a seasoned labor leader who had served as president of the Working Women's Union Number 1, founded in Chicago in 1878. A printer by trade, she became a journalist in the 1880s but remained engaged in labor movement activities, forging coalitions with middle-class women reformers and women in the socialist and trades and labor unions. In 1893 Terrence Powderly asked Stevens, who had been active with the Knights of Labor for about ten years, to represent the Knights on the Women's Labor Committee of the World's Congress Auxiliary, the body charged with planning labor meetings at the World's Columbian Exposition. Through the committee she met Addams and leaders of the Illinois Woman's Alliance and the Chicago Woman's Club.[26]

Kelley and Holbrook were responsible for organizing the data and making the maps (55). Holbrook, young and intellectually ambitious, had moved to Chicago soon after graduating in 1892 from Wellesley College. There she completed a rigorous sequence of mathematics, chemistry, zoology, physics, and psychology and also pursued courses in the arts. She enrolled in a course in constitutional law at the University of Chicago and became a resident of Hull-House in February 1893.[27] Holbrook's background in mathematics, science, and the visual arts equipped her to translate social statistics collected for the study into a visual form—maps. Her major contribution was to color code the outline maps supplied by a Chicago surveyor, Samuel Greeley, for maps of wages and nationalities.[28] As Florence Kelley recounted, "Her accuracy, patience and deftness rendered feasible what had seemed an impossible task."

Eaton, affiliated with the College Settlements Association in New York, was in residence at Hull-House for a three-month period. Her contribution to *HHM&P* compared the conditions of the cloakmaking trade in New York and Chicago.[29] The brief article was based in part on data she obtained from interviews with Abraham Bisno and other labor leaders active in Chicago's tailoring trades (90–95).[30] After her stint at Hull-House, Eaton moved to Hartford, Connecticut, where she headed the Social Settlement of Hartford, and by 1896 the College Settlement Association subsidized her research work at the Philadelphia Settlement. During a nine-month residence she investigated African American domestic service in the Seventh Ward, resulting in an additional report that was attached to the social survey conducted by W. E. B. Du Bois.[31] Eaton's report was published in *The Philadelphia Negro* in 1899.[32] The Philadelphia survey followed many of the innovations of social investigation in the maps and papers project at Hull-House.[33]

Lathrop joined the settlement in 1890. She, like Holbrook, was from Illinois but had also ventured east for college, graduating from Vassar in 1880. Lathrop, "like so many members of the first generation of college-educated women, returned to her family after college and served as her father's secretary, read law in his office, and identified with the local Republican Party," Robyn Muncy observes, "yet none of these promised her a career. Although the doors of higher education had swung open to women, the gates to professions, business, and electoral politics for the most part remained closed. Women like Lathrop, brimming with intelligence and ambition, had to clear new paths to independence and public authority, a challenge that her generation began to meet very effectively in 1889."[34]

In 1893 Governor Altgeld appointed Lathrop to the Illinois State Board of Charities. She inspected all 102 county institutions for the sick, homeless, and insane, an investigative task she approached in a manner that reflected the philosophy and practice of Hull-House sociology. According to Addams, who wrote her biography, Lathrop looked at the institutions from the point of view of the inmates themselves.[35] She served as a member of the Board of Charities (1893–1901 and 1905–9) and as a result of that experience came to support civil service reform. She advocated filling administrative positions with experts in public administration or in the treatment of people with disabilities instead of with political appointees. It was a viewpoint developed in Lathrop's chapter in *HHM&P*.[36]

Two contributors—Mastro-Valerio and Humpal-Zeman—had edited ethnic newspapers, Italian and Bohemian (Czech), respectively. Immigrants themselves, they both were controversial figures in their communities, where they functioned as interpreters of American culture and guides for American social reformers like Addams to the transnational politics of those same communities.[37] Addams met Mastro-Valerio at the time that she and Starr were exploring possible sites to launch their experiment in settling. He took Addams on a tour of Italian neighborhoods and described his own activities including his work as a truant officer for the Chicago public schools.[38] Disturbed by the poor quality of life many Italian immigrants experienced in cities like Chicago, Mastro-Valerio saw a solution to the problems faced by immigrants in urban industrial America in agricultural colonies. In 1890 he led a small group of Italian immigrants from the Hull-House neighborhood to southern Alabama, where they established the town of Daphne near Mobile.[39] He then returned to Chicago where he and his wife, Amelie Robinson, became Hull-House residents.[40]

At the time that Mastro-Valerio contributed his article on Italians in the Nineteenth Ward for *HHM&P* he had not yet founded his newspaper, *La Tribuna,* but already had a local reputation as "a devoted friend of his fellow-countrymen . . . the Chicago Garibaldi who is trying to lead all the Italians out of the bondage of ignorance."[41] In 1895 Mastro-Valerio, with Addams's support and connections, established the Italian Institute. Basically an immigrant protection agency, it was modeled on the one in New York to provide relief and aid, a free employment bureau, and legal protection and to encourage colonization efforts. The institute had a temporary office in the Hull-House settlement, with Count Antonio Ladislao Rozwadowski, the royal Italian consul of Chicago, serving as president; Mary J. Wilmarth, a leading figure in the organized women's clubs of the city and benefactor of Hull-House, as second vice president; Addams as third vice president; and Lyman J. Gage, president of the First National Bank, Chicago, the first vice president.[42] Gage, a civic-minded businessman, had served as president of the Civic Federation of Chicago and knew Addams, who had also been involved in that organization. By 1895, only six years after opening her settlement, she was able to broker affairs between Chicago's urban elite and ethnic leaders such as Mastro-Valerio because of her acknowledged role as an interpreter of life in the Near West Side immigrant neighborhood.[43]

It is difficult to gauge, on balance, the social capital Mastro-Valerio and Addams accrued from his affiliation with Hull-House. Not everyone in Chicago's Italian communities agreed with Mastro-Valerio or thought of him as a spokesperson for Italian Americans.[44] He supported labor over capital and was a nineteenth-century liberal who espoused an "anti-Irish attitude, and militantly anti-clerical views."[45] Hull-House's reputation among conservative elements of the Roman Catholic hierarchy as an atheistic, anticlerical, and socialistic place that should be avoided by decent Catholics derived in part from Addams's association with Mastro-Valerio.[46] For Addams, a more complicated issue was involved. Her friendship with Mastro-Valerio must have been based in part on shared views on Italian nationalism and clericalism.[47] Her interest in learning about the neighborhood by experiencing it was framed, of course, in the context of her own politics.

Humpal-Zeman's relationship with Hull-House resembled Mastro-Valerio's, but she never became a partner with Addams in constructing institutional bridges between Bohemians and Hull-House. Humpal-Zeman attended the College for Women of the Western Reserve in Cleveland in the early 1890s after the death of her parents and an earlier marriage of convenience that was painfully unsuccessful. She also converted to evangelical Protestantism, in part as a result of the support she received from American women who were active in the Women's Christian Temperance Movement (WCTU). She even established a Bohemian chapter of the WCTU. She began her career as a journalist during college and supported herself in part by contributing articles to midwestern Slavic journals.[48]

Humpal-Zeman's writing brought her to the attention of leaders in the Bohemian community in the United States. She became secretary of the Bohemian Columbian Exposition Committee in 1892, withdrawing from college in 1893 and returning to Chicago, where she helped organized the Bohemian women's exhibit of the exposition. That activity brought her into contact with Addams and other Chicago reformers. Humpal-Zeman became a resident at Hull-House in 1894 and enrolled at the University of Chicago. While in residence, she began a Bohemian women's newspaper, *Zenske Listy,* one of the first Bohemian women's weeklies in the world. The first edition appeared on June 15, 1894, with articles on women's education, features on Czech literary women, and information about the Hull-House settlement.[49]

After a one-year residency, she left Hull-House and returned to Prague briefly. When Humpal-Zeman returned to Chicago, Hull-House residents voted to reject her request to return as a settlement resident. They felt "her best sphere [for activism] was in the Bohemian neighborhood." Her roots in Bohemian women's groups in Chicago and in Prague were deep and remained her primary affiliations.[50]

Humpal-Zeman found herself in conflict with different elements of the Bohemian community in Chicago. She bore the brunt of attacks leveled by community leaders critical of her evangelical Christian message, advocacy of women's rights, and too-close ties to the Hull-House settlement and American women social activists. Although *Zenske Listy* prospered, the personal attacks against Humpal-Zeman did not abate, and in 1901 she decided to step down from editorship of the newspaper. She continued, however, her career as a journalist in other venues.[51]

Charles Zueblin was born in the United States. Zueblin did his undergraduate work at the University of Pennsylvania and Northwestern University, followed by graduate work at the Yale Divinity School. While at Yale, where he was trained as a minister, he was influenced by a young biblical scholar, William Rainey Harper, who would later become the first president of the University of Chicago. Zueblin furthered his studies of the Old Testament in Leipzig, but wrote to Harper in January 1891 that he was abandoning this field for political and social science. Shortly thereafter he moved into Hull-House. The contact with Addams ultimately led to Zueblin making social settlement work one of his major interests. He was a founder of Northwestern University Settlement in 1892. Simultaneously, Harper hired him as secretary of one of the University of Chicago's extension divisions and as an instructor in sociology. He became a full professor in 1902 and remained at the University of Chicago until 1908. Mary Jo Deegan observes that his critical analysis of society, especially the role of business in it, led to Zueblin's ultimate removal from the University of Chicago.[52]

Starr, who co-founded Hull-House, appears to have had a minor role in the *HHM&P* collaboration, yet her chapter is key to understanding the complex ways in which the Hull-House residents approached the working-class neighborhood in which the settlement was located. Her chapter, along with the appendix that Addams wrote and illustrated with photographs of the interiors and exteriors of the settlement, explains the scheme the two women shared. They also establish that Starr's initial vision came from the writing of two English social theorists, John Ruskin and William Morris (132–33). Moreover, she had been influenced directly by the art and education theories of T. C. Horsfall, also British, who had introduced a way to circulate collections of pictures in Manchester, England, schools.[53]

Like Addams, Starr came from old American stock—the former from Pennsylvania settlers and the latter from a New England family—that had migrated to Illinois in the antebellum era to take advantage of the economic development of the new region. Unlike her friend Jane, whose father had become the wealthiest man in Stephenson

County, Illinois, Ellen's father never achieved economic success and eventually abandoned farming to become the proprietor of a small-town drugstore. His Granger pop-
ulism and support of education for women influenced his daughter. In addition, Eliza
Allen Starr, her father's sister, provided the unique model of an independent woman
artist and poet who functioned as an intellectual from her studio "salon" in downtown
Chicago. Aunt Eliza had also converted from the Unitarianism of her New England
upbringing to Roman Catholicism and was one of the country's leading authorities
on Christian art.[54] She encouraged her niece to attend college. Because of the family's
limited financial resources, however, Ellen was only able to complete a year at the
Rockford Female Seminary, where she and Addams met.

The two young women continued their friendship after Starr left Rockford and
began a ten-year career as a teacher, first in a small Illinois town and then in Chicago
at Miss Kirkland's School for Girls, where she taught the daughters of Chicago's elite.
The women's friendship deepened over the years, and in 1888 Addams asked Starr to
travel to Europe with her. It was that trip that solidified their resolve to establish a
settlement in a Chicago neighborhood. Starr already had an interest in art history, a
subject she knew from her aunt, Eliza Allen Starr, well known for her art history lectures. Starr also had experienced a deep, even emotional, connection to the aesthetic
power of Christian art over the course of her own spiritual development. The ideas of
the arts and crafts movement, and of the more generalized belief that great civiliza-
tions were built on the works of art that were generated from the people, formed in
Starr a horror of the loss of craftsmanship (read, art) in industrial production.

The European trip with Addams further convinced Ellen Starr that one of the
most serious problems of modern industrial society was a lack of opportunity for the
masses to appreciate and produce great art. Starr shared with others of her generation
a belief in the efficacy of great works of art to inspire people from all classes in society,
and she was passionate in her dedication to bring sculpture and paintings, even if only
good copies of great works, to people in Chicago's poorest districts. Her experience,
however, had been teaching art history and other subjects in the humanities to rich
young girls in an elite private academy in Chicago. She was able to turn that deficit
into an asset in a relatively short time. Her passion for art, vivacious personality and
wit, and knowledge of elite social circles allowed Starr to create a citywide alliance of
clubwomen, educators, and public-spirited artists such as Lorado Taft. The alliance
brought art work into public schools in the meanest, poorest neighborhoods of Chicago, starting with grammar schools closest to the Hull-House settlement.[55]

By the time Starr and Addams opened the doors of Hull-House, Starr had developed the local social and intellectual connections necessary to launch her as dissemi-
nator of the Western art tradition in an immigrant neighborhood. Because of the con-
tacts she had made at Miss Kirkland's, when Starr and Addams looked for volunteers
to run the kindergarten or sponsor a club at the settlement they naturally were drawn
to that elite circle.[56]

Addams soon became the voice of Hull-House, but in the early years Starr was the more influential of the two women in using art education in a variety of strategies to improve the quality of life for inhabitants of the Nineteenth Ward and, in conjunction with other initiatives with children, implementing theories about the role of art in the development and maturation of a child's character.[57] These ideas about the role of art in the lives of the working class were current in England during the women's visit there in 1888.

The two women imitated the English example in 1890 when a Chicago businessman and cultural philanthropist, Edward B. Butler, donated $5,000 for a new building to be constructed just south of the Hull homestead so an art gallery could be the first addition to the new settlement.[58] At the grand opening on June 21, 1891, Samuel and Henrietta Barnett of Toynbee Hall were honored guests. In addition to the exhibition and art studio space in the Butler building, there was also a lending library that was a branch of the Chicago Public Library, and Starr began to loan works of art—water colors, photographs, and reproductions—to Hull-House's neighbors.[59]

Addams played a different role in the collaboration. Although she was not the intellect behind the use of sociological data in map form, her vision of the social settlement's use of sociology was innovative. It authorized a generation of college-educated women to embark on a life of social investigation connected to social reform. Addams and Starr were among the generation of women and men formally educated in the curriculum of a traditional, preindustrial world. They came of age in the 1880s, feeling unprepared to cope with the social realities of industrialism. They had read voraciously in the transatlantic social literature of the mid-nineteenth century in their search for solutions to, as Addams would so aptly put it, the objective and subjective necessities of their age.[60]

In 1892, only three years after she and Starr "settled" on Chicago's West Side, Addams spoke for her generation at a conference held at the School of Applied Ethics in Plymouth, Massachusetts, when she proclaimed that Hull-House was part of "a certain *renaissance* going forward in Christianity" worldwide that was best expressed not by any adherence to formal creeds but by "the impulse to share the lives of the poor."[61] In Plymouth, site of a historic "settling" that had hoped to establish social and political structures able to resist the errors and corruptions of the Old World, Addams defined the new settlement movement as "an experimental effort to aid in the solution of the social and industrial problems which are engendered by the modern conditions of life in a great city."

Although Addams did not use the word *political* but instead wrote about the responsibility of her generation to redefine the boundaries of personal ethical behavior by privileging personal experience as an authoritative way of knowing about the world, she empowered her generation to seek careers and be active when engaging in social reform. In inspiring women and men to "settle" as she and Starr had, Addams unleashed a torrent of volunteers who followed her example. One of the essential elements of the collaboration that produced *HHM&P* was the voluntary nature of the

work. Addams tapped into the age's moral revulsion at the social conditions of industrial society and the terrible economic inequalities that existed at the same time that
she offered a strategy for civic engagement. She placed the maps and papers project in
the context of a larger reform enterprise emerging in the United States and in Europe.
Thus the study of the local environment was seen as being connected to many other
investigations. The social investigation undertaken for the maps and papers project
of necessity happened in the context of Addams's larger goal—creating community
and reforming society. Sociological investigation, in this context, became one of the
tools for a generation of college-educated women and men who wanted to join her in
reforming society.

As one of the leaders of a social movement that was experimental and spontaneous in its approach, Addams encouraged residents who joined her to pursue a range
of activities and initiate all manner of innovative programs. Soon Hull-House became
known internationally as a center for research and social reform. Daniel T. Rodgers
describes how Hull-House and other American settlements functioned as "hostelries"
in the cosmopolitan climate of the era, where visitors exchanged ideas, debated the latest important books and studies, and stimulated experiments.[62] Hull-House attracted
creative, daring, and intellectually aggressive individuals who had a sense of adventure,
a feeling "that to settle down to live in the slums of a great city was a piece of daring
as great as trekking across the prairie in a covered wagon," but for others, like Alice
Hamilton, who became a resident in 1897 after completing medical school, the experiences of living in the neighborhood turned "an adventure in 'slumming'" into a "deep
commitment to social justice."[63]

HHM&P and Women Sociologists

HHM&P can legitimately be classified as the product of women social scientists.[64]
Women rather than men designed and directed the project and wrote all but two of the
essays included in the volume. Addams argued forcefully for a social science different
from the model that was emerging in university settings. She and her colleagues, most
of whom were women, envisioned social science knowledge as coming from civic participation across class, race, and ethnic divisions; systematic collection of data was to be
rigorous and based on information that came from direct engagement with the subject.
An important condition for developing social knowledge was openness to learning
about the needs and circumstances of actual people. Addams believed, as did Florence
Kelley, that women had a unique contribution to make in the field of sociology.[65]

The first generation of women professionals—Grace and Edith Abbott, Sophonisba
Breckinridge, Florence Kelley, Alice Hamilton, Jane Addams, and Julia C. Lathrop—
did some of their most significant social research in the context of the social settlement movement. Even as they were able to command salaries in government work, as
writers and lecturers, and as college professors and research faculty, they found their

most creative engagement in the context of the female dominion or infrastructure whose center was the social settlement. In the 1870s and 1880s the male pioneers of the academic social sciences founded the first university departments and embraced objectivity and theory in an attempt to establish a social science modeled on the natural sciences.[66]

Women found themselves excluded from faculty positions in the new social science departments of universities, including at the University of Chicago, even when they had received their graduate training and degrees in those departments. Breckinridge, for example, received a Ph.D. in political science in 1901 and a J.D. degree in 1904 from the University of Chicago. She graduated summa cum laude in both programs but was not hired on any faculty, although male students of less standing were offered positions at colleges and universities.[67] The circumstances of Edith Abbott's professional training and career trajectory also attest to the exclusion of talented women social scientists from male-dominated academic departments.[68]

This generation of professional women also maintained some of their most productive political alliances through the clubs and organizations of women's political culture, reinforcing their ability to sustain research and political interests that the academic environment did not favor or support. *HHM&P* is the first example of how women's political culture and the social settlement provided space for intellectual maturation and development and gave women the opportunity to pursue socially relevant research without reactions from trustees and corporations whose donations to male-run institutions had significant impact on the kind of research universities pursued and the way in which a professional canon emerged.

Between 1892 and 1933 there were, Sharon Haar maintains, twenty-three investigations conducted by Hull-House residents, including *HHM&P*. Harr reports that Hull-House women investigators "worked through relationships of affinity via both the activities of the settlement house and municipal reform," whereas "the burgeoning urban sociology movement [the men of the Department of Sociology at the University of Chicago] rested on the belief in detached scientific objectivity."[69] Hull-House residents Grace and Edith Abbott, Sophonisba Breckinridge, and Alice Hamilton—the group that followed Kelley, Stevens, and Lathrop—increasingly conducted research and advocacy in several work cultures. The first generation of university-trained specialists, they also chose both investigative research and advocacy, the latter a result of their connection with Hull-House. Their careers included government service, university teaching, clinical practice, and social science investigation. Residency at Hull-House created space in which women's professional careers were encouraged, but their commitment to activism, the concrete expression of the social claim, was supported through the collective work of the house.

HHM&P and the Production of Sociological Knowledge

Looking at the *HHM&P* project through the analytic lens of gender also allows a creative evaluation of the way the production of knowledge was financed in America during the Progressive Era. Realizing that a major work of sociological investigation and analysis was produced outside the academy allows consideration of how the formative period of sociological investigation was carried on and reflection about the diversity of funding as an aspect of democratic rather than elitist models of the production of knowledge in society.

Hull-House was funded by women involved with social causes and who participated in a women's political culture separate from the political party system run by men. The women's club movement in Chicago was willing to support research and experimentation at Hull-House, especially when the questions that were being asked had to do with the rights and protections of women and children.[70] Members of the Chicago Woman's Club—the premier group of social activist women in the city—met Addams and Starr in 1889 when the two women were looking for a location for their settlement. The two were immediately endorsed for membership.[71] The club's leading activists, including Mary J. Hawes Wilmarth, soon became supporters of experiments undertaken at Hull-House. Wilmarth "was intrigued with Jane Addams's description of the settlement house she envisioned and became an early and enthusiastic supporter of both Addams and Hull-House."[72] She subsidized residents at Hull-House who could not pay their own way and generally supplied funds to keep the settlement running. Considerably older than Addams and Starr, Wilmarth helped them make connections among the wealthy and influential women who made up the network of activist clubwomen.

Many examples exist of how wealthy clubwomen underwrote the reform agenda at Hull-House. In the 1890s—a period of industrial conflict, economic depression, and protracted, severe unemployment—the plight of unemployed women in the Nineteenth Ward made a lasting impression on the Hull-House residents who were determined to experiment with a "model lodging house and workshop." The Chicago Woman's Club (CWC) provided the funds.[73] Several years later the Chicago Woman's Club and Hull-House, along with several reform-minded jurists, coalesced to lobby the state legislature for a separate court system for juveniles. When the juvenile court system was inaugurated in 1899, the first court of its kind in the United States, the CWC provided funds to pay the salaries of probation officers and continued to do so for almost a decade before the Illinois legislature assumed responsibility for the costs. In 1909 Hull-House and the CWC established the Juvenile Protective Association (JPA) to monitor the court and ensure that the founding philosophy be implemented. The JPA office was located in one of the settlement's buildings. Louise de Koven Bowen, Hull-House's treasurer and one of the major benefactors of the settlement, served as the JPA's president. Bowen used her wealth and connections among rich clubwomen to finance research and publications, occasionally writing studies herself.[74]

Women's marginalization within academia is a complicated issue that cannot be reduced to the simple explanation that men excluded them. Men who challenged the assumption that advocacy threatened the scientific standing of the social sciences also found themselves marginalized or excluded. Such men as Henry Carter Adams at Cornell in 1886, Ely at Wisconsin in 1893, and Edward W. Bemis at the University of Chicago in 1894, faced being fired or were threatened with firing for advocating "radical ideas."[75] Ely was put on trial by the University of Wisconsin Board of Regents in 1894, just at the time that he was encouraging Florence Kelley and Jane Addams to publish the *HHM&P.* Sklar writes that Ely "typified the accommodationist response to this threat when he recanted his radicalism during . . [the] trial" and declared that he was "a conservative rather than a radical," thereby disavowing his early vision of political science as incorporating advocacy and moral reform.[76]

After the Bemis case, John Dewey—a friend of Addams who served as a trustee of the settlement and acknowledged its influence on his thinking—became cautious. "In an essay on academic freedom published at the end of his tenure at Chicago," Robert Westbrook maintains, "Dewey advised colleagues in the social sciences that the injection of moralism and an inflammatory tone into criticism of the established order would get them into hot water."[77] Addams understood the freedom that Hull-House's independence afforded her and the social scientists, men as well as women, who joined in the maps and papers project.

Hull-House, unlike many settlement houses that either were affiliated with religious denominations or universities or had boards of directors of a conservative bent, initially existed with few formal rules. The money contributed appears to have been given without strings attached. Helen Culver, however, owner of the Hull homestead and surrounding lots, was an exception who placed conditions on her gifts. She stipulated that Hull-House be incorporated under state law and that she be a lifetime trustee of its board.[78] These conditions were written into a property agreement in 1895, and Culver remained on the Hull-House board until 1920.[79] Addams relied on Hull-House's architect, Allen B. Pond, and William Colvin, a businessman and supporter of Hull-House, to negotiate with Culver.[80] Addams did not look forward to Culver's increasing influence and, approaching the legal incorporation stipulated by her landlady, she wrote to her confidant, Mary Rozet Smith, that "the fatal moment has arrived when we must incorporate."[81]

Addams did manage to keep Hull-House "independent," that is, with no affiliation to a university or religious association. She did, however, have to negotiate or mediate the settlement's interests with Culver, who went on to create an endowment fund for Hull-House in 1906 and who, in her gifts of property and money, was one of the settlement's major philanthropists.[82] It is not clear whether Culver ever influenced policy; indeed, there is no evidence that she imposed her will regarding Addams's political or policy decisions or even second-guessed her development plans. Addams may have been wistful about the loss of the original spontaneity of the settlement with incorporation rather than anxious about any potential constraints she might personally experience. A look at the arrangements makes it clear that the small group of trustees and officers were there to support Addams's leadership, not hinder it. She held, after all, the offices of president and treasurer. In fact, the trustees and officers of the new Hull-House Association were a friendly, almost ingrown, group that offered almost unconditional support for Addams and her agenda. The original trustees were Addams, Helen Culver, William H. Colvin, Mary Hawes Wilmarth, Mary Rozet Smith, and Allen B. Pond. Edwin B. Smith served as the legal adviser. Officers were Addams, president; Wilmarth, vice president; Pond, secretary; Addams, treasurer; and Colvin, auditor. Gertrude Barnum, a Hull-House resident, was assistant treasurer.[83] This small group retained control of Hull-House during the first twenty years, with only the addition of Louise de Koven Bowen, John Dewey, and William R. Hutchinson.[84]

Culver was a businesswoman, and her desire to oversee financial aspects of the settlement may be seen as different from the more typical female philanthropists who supported Hull-House. The other two major Hull-House donors, Louise de Koven Bowen and Mary Rozet Smith, combined a hands-on volunteer participation in the settlement with generous personal financial contributions. Although there were male philanthropists who gave money to Hull-House, the key women donors—Bowen, Smith, and Culver—provided the preponderance of funding. Two men who gave extensively—Charles Mather Smith and Joseph T. Bowen—were the father and husband respectively of Smith and Bowen. In addition, Bowen and Addams engaged in fundraising campaigns for Hull-House. They used their social and political connections, including the sizeable women's reform infrastructure, to secure funding through private donations. The two women preferred private funding and were reluctant to accept contributions from foundations, charities, or the government.

The Maps and Papers

Inspired by Charles Booth's *Life and Labour of the People* (1886–1903), the Hull-House residents compiled detailed maps that illustrated the nationalities and wages of the largely immigrant population in one of the most congested industrial sections of Chicago. In addition, there were ten essays about the maps, the district's sweatshops, wage-earning children, cloakmakers, immigrant neighborhoods in the vicinity of the social settlement, Cook County Charities, the role of art in working-class districts, and the settlement's role in the labor movement. An appendix containing photographs illustrating the settlement's programs and physical expansion in the neighborhood provided a summary of Hull-House's accomplishments.

The maps are innovative and pioneering expressions of urban sociology, but little has been said about the ten essays that constitute the rest of the volume. It has, however, been suggested that they convey more reliable information about the settlement's day-to-day life than about the larger city.[85] The inclusion of photographs of interior and exterior images of the Hull-House complex and the absence of any photographs of the neighborhood is a graphic statement that *HHM&P* is about the settlement's reform agenda. No correspondence or notes have been found to explain what appears to be an idiosyncratic selection of topics, especially in regard to the ethnic groups discussed in depth. Why, for example, is there not a chapter on the Irish in the Hull-House neighborhood? Agnes Holbrook remarks that the Irish "although pretty well sprinkled" were more numerous in the better section of the neighborhood near Hull-House (60).

Situated closer to Hull-House than the Bohemian community of Pilsen, Holy Family parish, which Ellen Skerrett calls "the most highly organized English-speaking parish in Chicago," had a communicant strength of twenty thousand Irish—men, women, and children. "What possible reasons," Skerrett asks, "could there be for neglecting the neighborhood's largest and oldest ethnic group? Perhaps after living in the area for five years, Addams and Starr believed that the Irish did not need—or want—their help or that there were more deserving ethnic groups in the immediate neighborhood."[86]

The answer may be that the volume of maps and papers came together in the aftermath of a victorious antisweatshop campaign, when Hull-House resident Florence Kelley, as chief factory inspector, opened her office in Hull-House and began, with her assistant inspectors, to enforce the new law. Jews, Bohemians, and Italians, not the Irish, were the victims of the sweating system. Moreover, Humpal-Zeman, the leading feminist in the Czech community, also resided at Hull-House during the maps and papers project. Already acknowledged as a journalist by her community, especially Czech American women's organizations, Humpal-Zeman was in the right place at the right time.

The Maps and Map Notes and Comments

The multicolor maps in this volume show wages and nationalities of the population living in a third of a square mile near Hull-House. They also represent a major volunteer effort on the part of the Hull-House residents. Four schedule men returned completed schedules daily to Florence Kelley from April 6 to July 15, 1893, and before a form was sent to the commissioner of labor in Washington, D.C., it would be copied by a Hull-House resident—the nationality of each individual, his or her wages when employed, and the number of weeks she or he was idle during the year beginning April 1, 1892 (55). The information was then color-coded and transferred to maps. Holbrook, comparing her maps with Charles Booth's, emphasized the "greater minuteness" of the Chicago survey and predicted that this precision "will entitle it to a rank of its own, both as a photographic reproduction of Chicago's poorest quarters on the west, and her worst on the east side of the river, and as an illustration of a method of research" (57). The Booth maps covered the whole of London, each street colored according to the class of its residents and no effort made to describe or quantify ethnicity and race.[87]

To the modern eye, the nationalities map seems a tapestry of colors signifying that a mix of ethnic groups lived on almost every street. The Hull-House residents acknowledged that phenomenon, stating that the nationalities map illustrated a strong pattern of ethnic "intermingling" in the one-third of a square mile under scrutiny. Hypothetically, a map that covered all of Chicago might have shown a pattern that supported the popular view that foreigners lived in distinct, separate enclaves. The map contradicts the popular notion of colonies, however, and shows that foreigners on Chicago's Near West Side were "more or less intermingled" (60). But, Kelley and Holbrook insisted, "A decided tendency to drift into little colonies is apparent" (60).

The three chapters that examine the Bohemians in Chicago, the Italian colony on the Near West Side, and the Jewish ghetto reinforce this idea of separate ethnic enclaves. The chapters describe geographic sections of the city near Hull-House but not in the area included in the maps. There was no effort to map these sections.[88] The chapters also include uneven information about spatial clustering. Only the statistical information that Zueblin, a sociologist, offers on Jews addresses the issue of intermingling versus clustering. Zueblin's interest in such statistics is pertinent because the Jewish quarter is perceived in the popular imagination as the quintessential ghetto or ethnic colony that is the most ingrown, isolated, and resistant to assimilation. Zueblin finds, however, that "only in the small or 'lesser Ghetto'" found in the Seventh Ward do Jews dominate the population. In the greater ghetto, "an area of about a square mile, and a population of perhaps seventy thousand," there are only "twenty thousand Jews" (97). Zueblin also contends that the population of Jews in Chicago had been greatly overestimated and that "the physical characteristics of the Ghetto do not differ materially from the surrounding districts" (97). Yet Zueblin persists in using the concept of a separate foreign colony and goes even further by employing an Old World term—*ghetto*—that misrepresents the actual fluidity and relative ease of Jewish geographic mobility in the United States.

The persistence of the use of a foreign colony or quarter as a way of making sense of the residential patterns of immigrants must be something other than a spatial and demographic phenomenon. It is more about cultural markings and insider-outsider perceptions than actual numerical percentages or homogeneous residential patterns.[89] The only exception to this generalization is the way in which ghettoes were created in northern cities for African Americans. This is evident in the nationalities map, which identifies "Negroes"—natives of the United States and English-speaking—as clustered almost entirely in a small area "wedged in Plymouth Place and Clark Street" east of the Chicago River (60). Thomas Philpott suggests that "the authors did not seem to appreciate the significance of the evidence that had been compiled so painstakingly," and that "the Hull-House residents themselves spoke of immigrant 'colonies' as if they were spatial entities which could be pinpointed on a map."[90]

The "nationalities" mapped are actually classes or categories that have been constructed by the Hull-House residents and represent a political and cultural "mental map" about race and ethnicity. Holbrook explains that the map is not a simple enumeration of "people from so many corners of the earth" but rather a classification of them. At least twenty-five different nations are represented in the eighteen classifications in addition to African Americans, a non-national group (59–60). Rather than eighteen different nationalities, the nationalities map arranges the population into eighteen different color codes that reflect a blend of categories, including race, country of birth, language group, and religion. The color white, for example, represents English-speaking people, including English, English Canadians, Scots, all Americans of native parentage, and children born in the United States of foreign parents. The youngsters had to be more than ten years of age or, if younger, attend public schools (59).

Many cultural and political assumptions underlie the English-speaking classification. Those children under ten, and whose parents had been born outside the United States, who attended parochial schools, presumably were aggregated with the nationality group of their parents. The Roman Catholic parochial school system in the Nineteenth Ward was extensive. Its leaders believed the church was doing the work of citizenship training by "diffusing culture and teaching civilization" through religious training, schools, and agencies.[91]

The residents at Hull-House appear to reflect the Progressive Era's anxiety about the influence of Roman Catholicism in the formation of new citizens when they included only children attending public schools in the English-speaking group. They were also reacting, perhaps, to the use of foreign languages in some parochial schools as well as English.[92] Given the pervasive race thinking of Americans during this period, including those who were progressive reformers, it is not surprising that Hull-House residents created a separate category for African Americans even though they properly identified them as "natives of the United States" who spoke English (59).[93] Holbrook noted that there were only "two colored people . . . west of the [Chicago] river, while large numbers [were] wedged in Plymouth Place and Clark Street" (60). Given the patterns of housing segregation taking hold in northern cities in the 1890s it is not surprising that most blacks lived in a small area that held a dense population.

The Irish (represented by the color green) were also separated from the English-speaking classification. Holbrook explains that "at first sight" the Irish would appear to belong to the English-speaking group, but they "form so distinct and important an element in our politics and civic life that a separate representation has been accorded them" (59).[94] Hull-House residents were already becoming aware of the influence Irish American politicians in their ward.[95] They began their first campaign against Johnny

Powers, the Nineteenth Ward alderperson, in 1895, having challenged the system of patronage in the ward over garbage collection.

There are other problems with the nationalities map. The map does not indicate exactly where inhabitants lived. Holbrook colored in a lot in a predetermined order that did not show who lived in what building. Moreover, the map did not indicate the precise location of various nationalities with the lots containing multiple dwellings but rather applied the colors in square or rectangular blocks, following a consistent sequence described by Holbrook: "The white portions representing the aggregate numbers of English-speaking people found in the house or houses on each city lot, including American-born children (often belonging to a dozen different families), are uniformly placed next to the street-front, so that the eye readily determines the proportion in any street or block, as well as in the space covered by one lot. The green (Irish) come next behind; the yellow (Bohemian) follow; and the blue (Italian), red (Russian), and red stripe (Polish) occupy the rear of the lot in the order named; while the other colors there maybe hover between the two extremes" (60).

Holbrook also explains that "in so small a map of two dimensions to represent accurately the position of the tenements occupied by members of various nationalities when the houses are two, three, and four stories high, the arrangement of colors is designed to suggest the mass, rather than the location, of the various peoples indicated by them" (60). Aware of its limitations, Holbrook suggests that "there is a certain correspondence between the disposition of colors and the location of tenants thereby represented, when many born in different countries occupy rooms and houses on the same lot" (60). The map also reveals the potential complexity of cultural interactions in a small area of a large city where on a daily basis immigrants and their children had to overcome a multitude of cultural and linguistic barriers.

On the wage map, which covered the same area as the nationalities map, the colors indicate income by dwelling place. Six categories, ranging from less than $5 a week to more than $20, were marked by different colors. Most households fell in the $5 to $10 range (blue); the poorest category (black) represented an average weekly family income of $5 or less and included old people (62).[96]

There are also spaces colored white on the wage map. These are found east of the river and indicate brothels. Residents classified them separately "both because their numbers and whereabouts are of importance, and because it would be unfortunate to confuse them with laboring-people by estimating their incomes in the same way" (62).

The wage map uses the family rather than the individual as the unit for representation. Head, wife, children, and such parents, brothers, cousins, and other relatives as live in the same dwelling are scheduled as one household (61). The wage map includes every boarder, and each member of the family who paid board was defined as a self-supporting individual and, in terms of the wage map, classed as a separate wage-earner (61). Holbrook explained that to accord a single man the same representation as was given "his father with six, eight, or ten children or other dependents whom he must support [might] seem at first sight misleading" but made sense in the Nineteenth Ward "since a wife and children were sources of income as well as avenues of expense" (61).

Families with a weekly average income of $5 ($105 in 2005 dollars) or less were unable to aggregate $260 ($5,460) dollars a year. The Italian employed on the railroads from twenty to thirty weeks of the year at $1.25 ($26) a day received $150 ($3,150) to $225 ($4,725) a year on average (21). The largest class in the district—an area colored blue on the map—represented families earning from $5 ($105) to $10 ($210) a week (62).[97]

The map shows that the district was a combination of multiple land uses: residential, factory, warehouse, and rail yard as well as stores and brothels. Most people lived in about thirty small blocks between Halsted and the river; east of the river were five residential blocks adjacent to the vice or brothel district.

The Papers

Americans who read Kelley's two chapters "The Sweating System" and "Wage-Earning Children" (written with Alzina Stevens) probably had read journalistic accounts of sweatshops before the publication of *HHM&P.* Kelley was known in Chicago and the rest of Illinois for her outspoken attacks on the conditions in tenement workshops. Yet people still argued that there were benefits to be derived from "homework." It was, some defenders insisted, a great aid to widows with children. Such work, they argued, allowed mothers an income from sewing that could be done without leaving their young children. Other arguments were made for the valuable skills that children learned when they, too, engaged in sewing at home. Kelley's dissection of the sweating system demythologized homework and instead described how an increase in the numbers of sweatshops and households engaged in homework was undermining the entire garment industry. Not only were workers in sweatshops being exploited, but the spread of sweatshops as a way of reducing the costs to manufacturers who owned factories was also weakening the position of skilled factory workers. Every worker in the garment industry suffered from the introduction of the sweating system.

"The Sweating System" lays out a comprehensive overview of what has happened in the garment industry. On the one hand, the evolution of capitalism toward large-scale manufactoring had made it possible for labor union organization and better conditions for workers in the clothing factories or "inside" shops. Workers, most of them American-born and English-speaking, had been able to make gains in wages and improvements in conditions as they had been empowered through trades unions. They had even been the beneficiaries of state regulation of work places. On the other hand, the introduction of the sweating system had worsened conditions for a group of unorganized workers, less skilled, foreign-born, and not fluent in English. These workers were found in the "outside" shops (sweatshops) located in work rooms rented by "sweaters." Very little capital was required to begin operations; sweaters rented cheap workrooms in tenements and found immigrant workers willing to do piece-work for very low wages.

Kelley made it clear that no amount of industriousness and thrift by workers could overcome the inherent exploitative conditions under which they labored. Kelley told of a diligent worker who had begun work at age fourteen and by thirty-four was an old man, unfit to work any longer. During those twenty years his earnings had ranged from $260 to $300 each year. In ordinary years of merely average prosperity, workers were inevitably applicants for relief to supplement, during three to five months, the earnings made during the busy season (68).

It was the sweating system that was the culprit. Only its demise and the growth of large-scale manufacturing and union organization could change the outcomes for the thousands of workers in the garment trade. Kelley broke down myths that were current and described horrific conditions, yet at the same time her detailing of the dehumanizing effect of the sweating system did not strip the workers of their humanity. Kelley also was careful that her writing did not descend into sensationalism as she informed readers that the clothes they purchased could not be guaranteed to be free from disease.[98]

With two exceptions, every manufacturer of garments in Chicago gave out clothing to be made in tenement houses. Yet Kelley indicted the approximately eight hundred sweaters licensed by the city under the new factory inspection law for the sweating system. They had no organization; were separated by differences of religion, nationality, language, and location; and as individuals they haggled with the manufacturers, undercutting each other and calculating profits on their ability to reduce the pay of employees below the pay that manufacturers might reduce theirs. Sweaters made their profits by investing whatever capital they could in unfinished garments and through a process of getting workers to complete the work as quickly as possible and for as low a rate of pay as could be achieved. Sweaters' victims—the workers in the outside shops—worked far into the night, often disregarding Sunday and all the holidays.

Kelley's ability to write convincingly and authoritatively about the garment industry in Chicago was the result of her position as chief factory inspector under the factory and workshop inspection act of 1893. She wrote compellingly about the long-term outcomes of child labor in the sweatshops: "During the effort to remove them [children] from these shops, there were found boys whose backs have been made crooked for life by continuous work at heavy machines, and boys and girls unable to speak English, and equally unable to read or write in any language" (66).

Kelley explained how sweaters were found in all parts of the city. She also pinpointed one of the key ironies of the system. Sweaters, recent immigrants themselves, were tenants who rented by the week or month. They were one or two steps ahead of their victims in the struggle to achieve success in the United States. In the Nineteenth Ward, the sweaters were Russian Jews and Bohemians whose employees were of the same nationality. Russian Jews and Bohemians worked in tenement shops, while home finishers—those who worked in their own tenement apartments—were exclusively Italians, the wives and daughters of street-sweepers and railroad gang hands. Conditions and wages for home-finishers were no better than for those who worked in tenement shops, although defenders of homework emphasized its benefits for mothers with small children. Kelley did not think it possible to make headway in reforming work conditions in the garment trades, however, until all manufacturing in any tenement was prohibited by law (67).

Kelley and Stevens's "Wage-Earning Children," a stark depiction of child labor in the Nineteenth Ward, demolishes any lingering argument for the potential value of children's work in the garment trades. "Nothing in our work," they observe, "has been more of a revelation than the migratory method pursued by the children, which forever disposes of the only argument in favor of child-labor that before seemed valid; namely, that the work afforded a sort of industrial education for the boy or girl who must depend upon manual labor for livelihood in adult years" (84).

Instead of "schools" for the future, sweatshops and factories were breeding grounds for future ill health and a work career of increasing instability. "It is a matter of the rarest occurrence to find a set of children who have been working together two months in any factory," Kelley and Stevens maintain. "They are here to-day and gone to-morrow; and, while their very instability saves them from the specific poison of each trade, it promises an army of incapables, to be supported as tramps and paupers" (84).

Kelley and Stevens anticipated the studies of industrial toxicology pioneered by Alice Hamilton in the Hull-House neighborhood a decade later as she described the dire effects of arsenic and mercury, nicotine poisoning, and skeletal disorders resulting from long hours spent at old-fashioned sewing machines, cheaper than more modern ones, that still required foot power (84).

Children were employed, they concluded, not because there were technical requirements of the industries themselves that required children's participation but because their fathers could not make enough money working long hours in unorganized trades (86). Moreover, they asserted, "It [was] a consequence of the premature disablement of the men upon whom the support of the children would normally fall" (86). What Kelley and Stevens learned was that where a trade was well organized through trade unionism few children were to be found at work in it. Child labor was more prevalent where women workers were unorganized.[99]

Their solution to the child-labor question was the enforcement of school attendance to the age of sixteen, including the radical notion of the state providing subsidies for the poorest of working children so that they could remain in school. In addition, Kelley and Stevens advocated a minimum age for work at sixteen, compulsory school attendance to age sixteen, and a system of factory inspectors and truant officers. These men and women, equipped with adequate salaries and traveling expenses, would be charged with the duty of removing children from mill and workshop, mine, and store and placing them at school. Finally, her recommendations included ample provision for school accommodations and money supplied by the state through school authorities "for the support of such orphans, half orphans, and children of the unemployed as are now kept out of school by destitution" (89).

In their analysis of the cause and cure for child labor Kelley and Stevens put forward radical proposals that challenged the deepest, core values of conservative laissez-faire capitalism. They rejected all conventional arguments in support of child labor and called upon the state to provide whatever subsidies were needed to ensure that children would remain in school until they were sixteen, a recommendation that has still not been met entirely although the federal government endorses the slogan "no child left behind." Kelley's vision informed the coalition of women and men progressives who fought, without success, for a federal amendment prohibiting child labor.

Isabel Eaton's chapter on Chicago and New York cloakmakers tells a familiar story. It is a tale of workers toiling long hours but never being able to achieve financial security. In the case of the cloakmakers, the situation was particularly appalling because these workers were skilled and had begun to organize themselves into unions. Unfortunately, Eaton's brief "Receipts and Expenditures of Cloakmakers in Chicago, Compared with Those of That Trade in New York" does not probe the reasons why the cloakmakers made so little progress. Eaton was only at Hull-House for three months, and she relied on Abraham Bisno for most of her Chicago statistics. Bisno, a cloakmaker for ten years, was appointed a state deputy factory inspector under the factory and workshop inspection law of 1893. The material he made available to Eaton was from the wage record books that he kept as an inspector (91). She also relied on statistics based on one hundred records gathered in 1894 by Hull-House investigators. Her conclusion was shocking. Even though the relatively skilled Chicago cloakmakers toiled long hours, "'every man [was] in debt'" (94). They did, however, have better dwellings than cloakmakers in New York with regard to size, light, and ventilation. Rents were also higher in New York. The cloakmakers in both cities paid too high a proportion of their wages to rent (95).

Julia Lathrop's contribution is not about the garment industry directly, yet it is closely related because she sought long-term outcomes of the sweating system for families in the Hull-House neighborhood. Lathrop's position on the State Board of Charities expanded her understanding of the way in which a political system riddled with patronage—coupled with a minimalist philosophy of government's role in society and framed in the moralistic discourse of nineteenth-century charity organizations—was woefully inadequate for meeting the social and economic realities of industrialism.

Why do people end up in the county institutions? Lathrop in 1895 had not freed herself from the traditional concepts of worthy and unworthy poor. At the same time she advocated improving public institutions through professionalism and removal of political patronage she was still disturbed with "the lack of system and classification among the beneficiaries of the infirmary and the county agency for outdoor relief. We are shocked," she added, "by the crudeness of the management which huddles men, women, and children, the victims of misfortune and the relics of dissipation, the idle, the ineffective criminal, the penniless convalescent, under one roof and one discipline" (129). Lathrop wanted to separate "that small remnant of blameless poor for whom we can surely make more dignified provision without pauperizing society." She found it painful to see the worthy poor "die disgraced by the association of a public poorhouse" (129)

Lathrop blamed an uncaring and isolated public that had no personal experience with public institutions and had never visited them. "How many persons in the city of Chicago whose incomes make them safe from the possibility of a personal interest in these places ever visit them, or perhaps know where they are?" she asked (129). Holding the progressives' faith in the efficacy of public knowledge and attention, Lathrop contended that studies such as hers had a salutary effect.

There are three chapters that concern ethnic groups in the vicinity of Hull-House and are written by Humpal-Zeman, Zueblin, and Mastro-Valerio. Mastro-Valerio and Humpal-Zeman's experiences as individuals whose geographic and cultural relationships were complicated by insider-outsider roles allow a glimpse of the social dynamics between Hull-House residents and their neighbors. Zueblin was the only one of the three who wrote as an outsider to the community. His residency provided the young sociologist with an opportunity to benefit from the research agenda set by Florence Kelley, and he used Board of Health statistics and data from the Employment Bureau run by the United Hebrew Charities and his personal observations to write about Jews in the Maxwell Street neighborhood. In "The Chicago Ghetto" Zueblin articulates opinions about the most recent Jewish immigrants from Eastern Europe, ideas held by most assimilated German Jews. That group had been in the United States from the eighteenth and nineteenth centuries and had adapted successfully to American culture. They identified overwhelmingly with American middle-class values, and Reform Judaism offered a religious expression compatible with civic engagement in the American democracy. In Chicago, Rabbi Emil G. Hirsch, leader of the Reform Congregation Sinai, and prominent laymen including Julian Mack and Julius Rosenwald were active in liberal religious circles and advocated Progressive reforms. Zueblin, a liberal, Social Gospel Protestant, held similar ideas with Reform Jews about the role of religion in society. Agreeing with the Reform Jewish community, his chapter praises those institutions in the Maxwell Street neighborhood that encouraged assimilation and considers the Orthodox Jewish institutions and way of life to be a drawback.

Orthodoxy, Zueblin maintained, perpetuates the isolation or separation of Jews from mainstream American society. Assimilating institutions such as the Jewish Training School, the Maxwell Street Settlement, and even socialism, he said, were modernizing elements with positive outcomes. "It remains to be seen," Zueblin wrote, "whether external forces will teach him [the ghetto Jew] to expand both his personal and social horizon, or lead him, as in the past, to draw himself within his shell." For Zueblin, the best that could happen to the ghetto "is its annihilation" (105).

Zueblin's use of the word *ghetto* is problematic. Jewish neighborhoods in the United States were not ghettos in the European sense of the word. Zueblin argues that the physical characteristics of a ghetto did not differ materially from surrounding districts and even "race differences" are "not too apparent to the casual observer" (97). He also cites statistics to demonstrate that Jews had a lower death rate than other immigrants in the city, comparing death rates in three Chicago wards, one of which had a population that was primarily Jewish (98). "Whether it is due to his religious observances or his exclusiveness, the vitality of the Jew is incontestable," Zueblin concludes, but he also is concerned about the ability of the United States to absorb "these foreign elements" in its cities (98–99). Ironically, the qualities that come from group cohesiveness—religious observances and ethnic solidarity—become worrisome to reformers like Zueblin, who are concerned about the ability of different subcommunities to engage in the civic life of the nation.

Humpal-Zeman's "The Bohemian People in Chicago" focuses on gender and discusses the differences between men and women as well as differences between Bohemian women and other Slavonic women. She idealizes Bohemian women and family life, explaining that immigrants initially were men of cultivation and high social standing who sought political freedom in the United States. "Bohemia has never sent her 'slums,'" she maintains, "but only the more energetic and able-bodied" (108). Chicago's Bohemian community had an elaborate infrastructure of self-help, religious, education, and cultural institutions, and those of all classes invested in property. Bohemian building and loan associations flourished; from 1885 to 1893 the five major associations accumulated almost $700,000 (109). By 1895 there were about twenty-three labor organizations in the Chicago Bohemian community, accounting perhaps for the high percentage of working-class property ownership. Bohemian workers joined the eight-hour movement and campaigned against child labor.

Given her idealization of the Bohemian family, Humpal-Zeman had to deal with the inherent contradiction posed by the numbers of Bohemian children who worked in factories. "It is a great temptation to all foreigners to sacrifice the children," she observed, "for the little ones can often get work when grown people, slow to learn a new language, are forced to be idle" (111). Bohemian women workers had not organized in a similar manner to male trade unionists, and thousands of girls were left unorganized and uninformed.

Humpal-Zeman always uses the transnational context to explain the behavior of Chicago's Bohemians. Food was better and more plentiful in Chicago, she asserts, but Bohemians missed the free garden concerts available in almost every large city in Bohemia, as well as Sunday walks, reading rooms, and various holiday feasts. Thus they yearned for more social life and, in the context of American popular culture, created substitute entertainments that were "not always wholesome" (110).

Regardless of the richness of the Bohemian communial infrastructure, Humpal-Zeman concludes, assimilation is the path for most immigrants and their children in her community. The pull of transnational loyalties and alliances, potentially threatening to Americans concerned with civic engagement among all groups, was not nearly as strong a factor in the lives of the Bohemian community as the popular culture of urban America. The new "Bohemian-American" was "entirely original" and "unlike the real Bohemian, and foreign to the American" (110).

Adopting the role of the insider who interprets his people's situation in the United States to the American public, Mastro-Valerio attempts to explain how "such a noble people as the Italians" seem willing to live in squalor in American cities (121). He does so by juxtaposing their longing to return to the land of their birth and to the idyllic, pastoral countryside with their ability to sustain seemingly unendurable conditions in order to gain money for the eventual return. He says, for example, that Italians are perceived as having filthy homes, but life in crowded tenements, along with lack of ventilation and proper municipal sanitation, forced otherwise clean-living people to adjust to terrible conditions. In Italy, he notes, even the houses of the poorest people are made clean in the countryside. His passionate attachment to Italian culture and shame at the behavior of many of his compatriots in the United States create the dynamic tension in his chapter. Italians work hard to survive in the United States. Women work to add to the family income and ignore housekeeping. Maestro-Valerio is conflicted, wanting to both criticize and valorize the "greed of gain" he sees in the illiterate peasants who want only to return to Italy with money they have saved so they can become property owners. These unskilled, urban tenement-dwellers, however, also disappoint him. They spend money like water, adopt aspects of vulgar American popular culture, and even send their children into the streets to work. Beneath this new identity, he maintains, they are skilled agriculturalists who have been alienated from the land. Maestro-Valerio argues that the "only means for the regeneration of the Italian immigrants from the state in which they nowadays find themselves in the crowded districts of the American cities is to send them to farming" (117).

The final chapters in *HHM&P* are by Ellen Starr and Jane Addams, the latter doing double duty by writing the volume's appendix, a review of the achievements of the settlement thus far. The appendix includes photographs noteworthy for the choice of subject matter. That the camera is used to illustrate the growth of Hull-House both physically and programmatically rather than to add visual "data" about ethnic neighborhoods or even record the best examples of the worst sweatshop conditions provokes questions about the subject matter of the volume. It is possible to learn a great deal more about how Hull-House viewed the world around the settlement than about immigrant life in Chicago—or, for that matter, about the larger metropolitan area in which the thirty or so blocks so thoroughly depicted in the nationalities and wage maps form a small corner.

Ellen Starr's chapter on art and labor is a mixture of derivative ideas about art taken from her reading of English theories of art's critical civilizing effect and her knowledge of recent efforts in London to bring art to the masses. Seemingly unaware, or perhaps dismissive, of the arts and crafts produced by European immigrants in the ethnic, religious, and cultural institutions they sustained in neighborhoods near Hull-House, Starr worried that such work was disappearing in working-class areas. The basic economics of survival were so great that she questions whether it was "worth the cost to try to perpetuate art under conditions so hopeless" (130). Believing that authentic art derived from free people and a just society, she argued that a settlement like Hull-House was in a unique position. It "must work with all energy and courage toward the rescue of those bound under the slavery of commerce and the wage law" (137) and at the same time bring art to the neighborhood. Starr postulated a future world when a "social state" would "finally supplant" present conditions of industrial warfare and art would flourish (137). Starr's comments on the necessity of liberating workers so they may have the freedom to create their own art forms prefigures her personal journey toward radical activism in solidarity with exploited workers.[100]

Addams's "The Settlement as a Factor in the Labor Movement" defines her position on that issue and also argues that the settlement, a relatively new entity in industrial society, had a duty and right to take part in disputes between capital and labor. From the trade union point of view, it might seem presumptuous for Addams to make such an argument for Hull-House (and, implicitly, for the settlement movement). Remarkably, she established herself in the role of mediator through her efforts on behalf of the Civic Federation of Chicago during the Pullman Strike in 1894, when she tried unsuccessfully to arbitrate the strike as a member of the Federation's Industrial Committee.[101]

"A settlement," Addams writes, "accepts the ethics of its contemporaries that the sharing of the life of the poor is essential to the understanding and bettering of that life; but by its very existence it adopts this modern code somewhat formally. The social injury of the meanest man not only becomes its [the settlement's] concern, but by virtue of its very locality it has put itself into a position to see, as no one but a neighbor can see, the stress and need of those who bear the brunt of the social injury" (138).

Addams makes it clear that although residents had come to Hull-House five years earlier with generalized support for the organization of workers, the positions they now took in support of trade unions and legislation to limit hours for women and prohibit child labor were based on what they learned from daily experiences with garment workers in the neighborhood. They had witnessed the "process of extermination" of those victims of sweatshops. It was a process of "starvation and suffering" and ended with in "desperate moral disintegration," knowledge that "entails a social obligation" (139). Because capital is organized and has influence to secure legislation on its behalf, labor must do likewise, and the settlement's role is to encourage and aid in efforts to organize labor. Hull-House, Addams explained, had opened its doors to workers and welcomed the efforts to organize. The settlement's burden extended beyond encouraging labor to organize, however. It had a duty to reject class warfare and awaken in the labor movement "a consciousness of its historic development," accentuating "the ultimate ethical aims of the movement" (149).

Conclusion

HHM&P is a stinging indictment of industrial capitalism. A shared commitment to reform society is the implicit raison d'etre of the volume, and any discussion of *HHM&P* has to deal with the passion and zeal of social investigation inspired by the discovery of inequality and social injustice. The volume is the work of engaged social activists who privileged their personal experiences as residents of a settlement house situated in a slum district of a great city above all other qualifications. It stands as a testament to their collective faith in the democratic system, especially in the belief that citizens, when presented with the facts, will become motivated to reform the social system. The contributors assumed that the maps and chapters would have an educative function that would then lead to action and change. As the young, idealistic Agnes Sinclair Holbrook commented about the maps, to be ethical, the scientific and humanitarian agendas were inseparable (58).

The chapters by Addams, Lathrop, Kelley, and Starr reveal the Hull-House agenda as it developed during the social settlement's first five years. These texts document the first attempts at making sense of what the group learned from daily experiences in the neighborhood. By the presidential campaign of 1912, Addams, Kelley, Starr, and Lathrop would be leading figures in reform and labor movement circles in the United States. Within the next four years Addams had staked her claim as a pacifist and begun the process of organizing an international social movement of feminists interested in peace and justice—a new internationalism; Starr had run for the Chicago city council on the Socialist Party ticket and on the national level engaged Samuel Gompers in a debate over the nature of trade unionism and the role of women workers in the labor movement; and Lathrop had served four years as chief of the Children's Bureau in the federal Department of Commerce and Labor and, from that point of power and authority, brought the agenda of the progressive child welfare movement to the center of federal policy decisions, culminating in the passage of the Sheppard-Towner Maternity and Infancy Act in 1921. In 1899 Kelley, who had earlier worked closely with clubwoman Ellen Henrotin in organizing an Illinois Consumers' League, became the secretary of the newly formed National Consumers' League (NCL), a position she held until her death in 1932. Headquartered in New York, the NCL became "the nation's leading promoter of protective legislation for women and children."[102]

The work published in 1895 in this innovative volume demonstrates that Hull-House's women residents had implicitly and explicitly determined that the state in industrial society must expand its functions. That is easy to detect in Kelley's forceful writing, yet the message is apparent even in Starr's "Art and Labor," at first glance a peculiar selection for the book. Toward the end of her chapter Starr makes it clear that a struggle is occurring in the world and workers are fighting for their lives. The settlement "must work with all energy and courage toward the rescue of those bound under the slavery of commerce and wage-law; with all abstinence it must discountenance wasting human life in the making of valueless things; with all faith it must urge forward the building up of a state in which cruel contrasts of surfeit and want, of idleness and overwork, shall not be found" (137). Starr's rhetoric is imprecise, and her use of the word *state* does not connote advocacy for the expansion of state powers in the way in which Kelley, Addams, and Lathrop had already begun to envision. Yet hers is an emotional plea that indicates rejection of the way in which the propertied few ignore the well-being of the masses of workers, and it matches Kelley's critique of the sweating system, Lathrop's dissection of the state's inadequate role in meeting the needs of the weakest members of society, and Addams's description of the "extermination" of the workers in the Hull-House district through starvation and suffering at the hands of the sweaters.

Regardless of the virtue and self-help institutional structures within immigrant communities, the basic message of *HHM&P* is that the vast majority of unskilled and semiskilled immigrant workers need the arm of the state and cannot survive by their own means or by efforts, however well-meaning and organized, of their own communal agencies. Kelley contends that conditions will not truly improve until the state outlaws sweatshops. Julia Lathrop summed things up when she began her essay, "As the study of these maps reveals an overwhelming proportion of foreigners, and an average wage-rate so low as to render thrift, even if it existed, an ineffective insurance against emergencies, we are led at once to inquire what happens when the power of self-help is lost" (120). Even the hoped-for empowerment by workers through the agency of strong trade unions would not be adequate to provide for the less-skilled and weakest members of industrial society, Lathrop argues. "The preponderance of unskilled labor necessarily means the weakness of trade unions and mutual benefit societies; in short, the inability to organize and co-operate" (120).

Contributors to *HHM&P* brought enthusiasm, passion, and reform goals to the volume. They also brought prejudices and biases. We begin to see the limitations of the social settlement movement's progressive vision in its approach to the immigrants and former slaves and their children who migrated to northern cities. Acknowledging that race was the Achilles heel of the progressive movement and that progressive reformers included anti- and pro-immigration activists, Addams and Hull-House were examples of the liberal wing of the movement, decidedly supportive of immigrants and immigrants' rights and philosophically integrationist if not openly engaged in promoting integration in the neighborhood in which the settlement was located.

One of the major tasks of the *HHM&P* was to introduce immigrants in the vicinity of Hull-House to a general audience of English-speaking, presumably middle-class, educated, and well-meaning U.S. citizens—the privileged, propertied people whom

Addams was dedicated to educating and transforming. She saw their lack of engagement and separation from the masses as a danger to democracy and the greatest social problem of the day. Hull-House was established in part as a site where people from different backgrounds and conditions could mingle. Addams believed wholeheartedly that social progress in all arenas of national life could only come after all classes of society understood their mutuality and accepted responsibility for each other's well-being. All the programs described in the appendix to *HHM&P*—a fine public relations piece written and illustrated by Addams, who was an adroit and skillful publicist—were intended to bring the upper crust and educated of Chicago to an immigrant neighborhood where those on both sides of the great gulf would have a chance to learn respect for each other's humanity.

Within the neighborhood, Addams designed activities that increased the visibility and engagement of multiple ethnic groups. Her hope was that by staging a Greek play the Greeks, Italians, and Jews in the neighborhood as well as clubwomen and business leaders could come to a better understanding and appreciation of each other. Chicago sculptor Lorado Taft's review of the Hull-House production of *Odysseus* was published in the *Chicago Record* on December 13, 1899. The review was in such agreement with Addams's understanding of theater as a cultural mediator that she reprinted it in the *Hull-House Bulletin* in 1900.[103]

Taft wrote that the hall in which the play was staged at Hull-House "was packed too closely for comfort with the most cosmopolitan crowd I have ever seen. Everybody that I know was there or had been on the previous evenings, and there were several hundred present variously from the Lake Shore drive and the Nineteenth Ward whom I did not know. For a couple of hours all distinctions were forgotten—the millennium was here . . . we were all brothers and sisters again." The actors, Greek immigrants from the neighborhood, were "the real sons of Hellas chanting the songs of their ancestors." "What distinction it gave them!" Taft exclaimed. "They seemed to feel that they had come into their own. They were set right at last in our eyes." Taft realized that those in the audience, like himself, who saw the Greek actors from the neighborhood would "never think of them again in quite the same way as before."[104] That was exactly what Addams had hoped would happen.

Can *HHM&P* risk portraying the settlement's immigrant neighbors as noble sons and daughters of Hellas, of Jerusalem, or of ancient Rome and still make the argument that industrial capitalism must be regulated by an expanded, progressive state? The first ninety pages of *HHM&P* include no positive images of family life in the slum district near Hull-House. Although the intention is not to dehumanize further the already demoralized and dehumanized victims of the sweating system, there are no images of motherly love, parental sacrifice, or even victims' political activity against the invidious sweatshops. There are, in fact, none of the voices of the protesting socialists, anarchists, and trades unionists who were already rising in anger against their conditions. Only Isabel Eaton quotes Abraham Bisno and other officials of the Chicago Cutters' Union to illustrate the dire straits in which cloakmakers found themselves.

Equally significant, the investigation dealt with the larger problem of slums in America. In the minds of most middle-class Americans, slums were the places where immigrants lived. Before renting the Hull home on Halsted Street, Addams visited another "slum" area, Chicago's North Side, where Italians had settled. She found it "exactly as if we were in a quarter of Naples or Rome" and "immensely more attractive . . . than the Irish neighborhood" she visited the week before. She was surprised by the density of population, "more crowded that [she] imagined people ever lived in America," but she found the Italians to be "affectionate and gentle, the little babies rolled up in stiff bands and the women sitting about like mild eyed Madonnas."[105]

At the entry level of the project, the social investigation carried out under a congressional mandate and paid for by government funds required that the area to be studied must qualify as a slum. Carroll D. Wright admitted, "[I]n every [slum] district there are to be found people of the highest respectability, people of means, living in good houses, etc. They have all been considered as inhabitants of the slum districts, and necessarily so, because the enumerators or agents engaged in collecting the facts could not be expected in each case to draw the line."

The designation of "slum" in the characterization of immigrant neighborhoods was problematic for Lathrop. In her chapters about county charities, she describes the "slum" that the maps illustrate as "foreign and mal-adjusted" but differentiates the immigrants who live in slums as people with "their own shops and churches and theatres and saloons" (120). She also stresses the isolation of the immigrant from the social life of American society, a point Addams frequently made in writing about immigrants and their children.[106] Ironically, the strength of the immigrant community is also a cause for concern because it is a form of separateness and clannishness that directly challenges assimilationist goals. Even progressives such as Addams, whose respect for the ancient cultures of Greece and Italy was expressed through the performing and visual arts at Hull-House, preferred to have immigrants and their children honor their European heritage in the context of the nonsectarian social and cultural space constructed by the settlement. Her goal was to encourage civic engagement of diverse groups that might even require activities that were ethnically and racially segregated in the settlement, which was, in her mind, the nearest thing to a public square for modern industrial society.[107]

From the perspective of the anti-sweatshop and anti-child labor movements, Florence Kelley's key position provided an ideal opportunity to gather data to advocate reforms. Her selection of the blocks to be investigated was motivated, it would seem, out of concern to remedy the extreme hardships of people in the worst sections of the district. From the point of view of an investigation that could cut through stereotypes about the immigrants who had arrived in the United States since the 1880s and thereby counteract rising nativism and calls for immigration restriction, the constraints on what blocks could be included in the study had serious implications.

Had investigators been able to include the west side of Halsted Street, where the Hull-House settlement was located, and some of the blocks just beyond the limits of the map ("Forquer Street, which is a shade better than Ewing or Polk"; "the western edge of the section, the poorer members of a large and well-to-do French colony"; or "the better streets toward the corner of Twelfth and Halsted, extending south and west beyond the limits of the map") (60) there would have been opportunity to include data on immigrants' social and geographic mobility and identify the roles of entrepreneurship and home ownership as sources of positive or negative economic and social choice.[108]

The chapters by Humpal-Zeman, Mastro-Valerio, and Zueblin provide a balance. They present some of this information about social and geographic mobility for Bohemians, Italians, and Jews.[109] Mastro-Valerio, whose personal biases are evident, records instances of "Italians who have grown with the town" and "are in prosperous circumstances." These are, with few exceptions, immigrants from the north of Italy. He is horrified, however, by their accumulation of wealth because "they are neither *entrepreneurs* nor producers. They have not been identified with the wonderful, intelligent progress of the city; but they have grown rich with it from the increase in value of real estate, or from their business of selling fruit" (117).

Humpal-Zeman has the advantage of presenting data that demonstrate change in the lives of Bohemian immigrants and their children, in part because Bohemians had settled in Chicago longer than the other ethnicities studied in *HHM&P*. Investigation of the Irish and Germans on the Near West Side would have provided an important perspective or context for evaluating the more recent experiences of Jews and Italians.

The problem of the boundaries of the map is more profound when one considers the influence this approach to studying urbanism and immigration has had in sociology and urban studies research. The boundaries imposed by the use of the slum as a category placed an artificial grid on the study of urban culture. Had there been a more open-ended approach to defining what spatial unit best expressed the immigrant communities near Hull-House, perhaps the complexity of choices as the immigrants struggled to succeed in America would have included their lived experiences more authentically.

There is danger of being too harsh in criticizing the maps and papers. The world of the sweatshop victims on Chicago's Near West Side was documented with accuracy and great attention to detail and with an urgency to end the worst abuses of the system. That remains an extraordinary feat.

Hull-House residents were optimists. They saw their exposé as a form of early intervention because it seemed that solving urban problems was possible in a young city than was rapidly changing and growing and was more malleable than a tradition-bound civilization. As Holbrook wrote, "The possibility of helping toward an improvement in the sanitation of the neighborhood, and toward an introduction of some degree of comfort, has given purpose and confidence to this undertaking" (57). They also shared the optimism of progressive reformers who banked on the power of an educated and awakened citizenry.

The Hull-House residents also were optimists in their genuine interest in and hospitality toward the immigrants they had chosen to be their neighbors. It was a period, after all, in which immigration restriction and quota laws were debated and passed.[110] From the 1900s through the 1920s between seven and nine thousand adults and children came to Hull-House every week. The maps and papers published in 1895 never raise the question of whether the United States should continue to open its doors to foreigners. The assumption underlying the social investigations undertaken by Hull-House residents is that industrial democracy in the United States depended on how willing Americans were to provide rights and protections to immigrants and industrial workers. The community of Hull-House residents eagerly took up the challenge.

Notes

I am grateful for comments on a draft of this introduction by Ellen Skerrett. Her invaluable insights about the importance of interpreting maps and images for the study of urban history have enriched my understanding of Hull-House and its neighborhoods. I also thank Margaret Strobel for a careful reading of an earlier draft.

1. Kathryn Kish Sklar, *"Hull-House Maps and Papers:* Social Science as Women's Work in the 1890s," in *Gender and American Social Science: The Formative Years,* edited by Helene Silverberg (Princeton: Princeton University Press, 1998), 146.

2. These include *The City Wilderness: A Settlement Study* (1898) undertaken by Robert A. Woods, head resident of the South End House in Boston, and the *Pittsburgh Survey* (1909–11) organized by Paul U. Kellogg. Sklar contends that "neither these [improved color-coded maps in Woods's 1903 edition] nor the maps in the six volumes of the Pittsburgh Survey, published between 1909 and 1911, approached the sophistication and detail of the maps in *HHM&P"* (*"Hull-House Maps and Papers,"* 153n38).

3. Sklar, *"Hull-House Maps and Papers,"* 127.

4. Leon Fink, *Progressive Intellectuals and the Dilemmas of Democratic Commitment* (Cambridge: Harvard University Press, 1997), 18.

5. Addams opened her lecture entitled "The Subjective Necessity for Social Settlements," which she delivered at the School of Applied Ethics in Plymouth, Massachusetts, during the summer of 1892, with a definition of the work at Hull-House: "It is an effort to add the social function to democracy. It was opened on the theory that the dependence of classes on each other is reciprocal; and that as 'the social relation is essentially a reciprocal relation, it gave a form of expression that has peculiar value.'" Jane Addams, *Philanthropy and Social Progress,* edited by Henry C. Addams (New York: Thomas Y. Crowell, 1893), 1–2. Shannon Jackson observes that "to attach the word *social* to an organization or movement during this era—social justice, social settlement, social Christianity, social philosophy—was to announce an ethical commitment to human interaction and to 'real' world issues." Jackson, *Lines of Activity: Performance, Historiography, Hull-House Domesticity* (Ann Arbor: University of Michigan Press, 2000), 43.

6. Addams, "The Subjective Necessity," 1.

7. Harold W. Pfautz, "Introduction," in Pfautz, *Charles Booth on the City: Physical Pattern and Social Structure* (Chicago: University of Chicago Press, 1967), 28–30, 53.

8. Carroll D. Wright, "Introduction," in Wright, *The Slums of Baltimore, Chicago, New York, and Philadelphia* (1894, repr. New York: Arno Press, 1970), 12.

9. Mary Jo Deegan argues that the Chicago School of Sociology at the University of Chicago in its early days was influenced by the work undertaken at Hull-House and that the early men of the Chicago School had the "same ideal, to bring sociological knowledge to everyday life to enable people to make intelligent decisions." Deegan, *Jane Addams and the Men of the Chicago School, 1892–1918* (New Bruns-

wick: Transaction Books, 1990), 41. See also Richard T. Ely, "The Hull-House Work," [June 13, 1895], news clipping in Hull-House Scrapbook 3, folder 508, Hull House Collection, Special Collections, University Library, University of Illinois at Chicago (hereafter UIC, JAMC, HHC).

10. In terms of how the general public viewed Hull-House residents, a minor contributor to *HHM&P,* Alzina Parsons Stevens, known as one of the leading women labor leaders in Chicago, was defined as a sociologist in her obituary: "Mrs. A. P. Stevens Dead: Sociologist Passes Away Suddenly at Hull House" (*Chicago Tribune,* June 4, 1900, 4). Ely's collegiality toward Addams and her writing is apparent in his encouragement of new assignments for her and his appreciation of her work. He praised her work on the subject of municipal corruption and mailed her a copy of "Religion as a Social Force," "thinking that it may have some interest for you." Ely to Jane Addams, Feb. 3, 1898, series 1, reel 3–0955, Jane Addams Collection, Swarthmore College Peace Collection, Swarthmore College, Swarthmore, Pa. (hereafter SCPC, JAC).

11. Ely, "The Hull-House Work." Ely surely is referring to Walter Besant and his People's Palace in East London. Addams had visited both Toynbee Hall and the People's Palace during her European trip in 1888. Both she and Starr had read Besant's novels. The People's Palace was of great interest to Americans. Jane Addams to Sarah Alice Addams Haldeman, June 14, 1888, Haldeman-Julius Family Papers, reel 3–0968–0973, UIC, JAMC; Jane Addams to Sarah Alice Addams Haldeman, July 1888, Haldeman-Julius Family Papers, reel 2–0977–0978, UIC, JAMC.

12. Silverberg, "Introduction," *Gender and American Social Science,* 3.

13. Ellen Fitzpatrick, *Endless Crusade: Women Social Scientists and Progressive Reform* (New York: Oxford University Press, 1990). The standard history of the American Social Science Association overlooks women and gender: Thomas L. Haskell, *The Emergence of Professional Social Science: The American Social Science Association and the Nineteenth Century Crisis of Authority* (Urbana: University of Illinois Press, 1977) even though women had a major role in the ASSA and composed 20 to 30 percent of the membership. Rosalind Rosenberg, *Beyond Separate Spheres: Intellectual Roots of Modern Feminism* (New Haven: Yale University Press, 1982).

14. Kelley wrote "The Sweating-System" and, with Alzina Parsons Stevens, "Wage-Earning Children." Stevens, one of Kelley's assistant factory inspectors, had knowledge of the conditions of child labor in the sweating-system. Holbrook worked on the maps with Kelley and wrote "Map Notes and Comments." Eaton had come from the College Settlements Association in New York and contributed "Receipts and Expenditures of Cloakmakers in Chicago, Compared with Those of That Trade in New York," taken from material collected during three months' residence at Hull-House. Zueblin wrote the article "The Chicago Ghetto," on the Eastern European Jews who lived in the Maxwell Street neighborhood near the Hull-House settlement. Born in Bohemia, Humpal-Zeman resided at Hull-House and wrote the article on her ethnic community, "The Bohemian People in Chicago." Mastro-Valerio contributed "Remarks Upon the Italian Colony in Chicago." Lathrop wrote the article "The Cook County Charities." Cofounder of Hull-House, Starr contributed the article "Art and Labor." Addams was author of the "Prefatory Note," the article "The Settlement as a Factor in the Labor Movement," and the appendix, "Hull-House: A Social Settlement."

15. Quoted in Dorothy Ross, "Gendered Social Knowledge: Domestic Discourse, Jane Addams, and the Possibilities of Social Science," in *Gender and American Social Science: The Formative Years,* edited by Helene Silverberg (Princeton: Princeton University Press, 1998), 243.

16. This seems an overblown claim and out of character for Addams, whose prose is generally understated. Only she and Starr had been in residence since 1889; Lathrop arrived in 1890, Kelley at the end of 1891, Holbrook in February 1893, Eaton in 1893 and 1894, and Zueblin in 1891. Many may not have stayed longer than a year. Mastro-Valerio and Humpal-Zeman, of course, were immigrant "neighbors," with the former being a resident for several years but the latter living at the settlement for about a year.

17. For a detailed analysis of Kelley's role in the *HHM&P* project, see Sklar, *"Hull-House Maps and Papers,"* 127–55.

18. Kathryn Kish Sklar, "Kelley, Florence," in *Women Building Chicago: A Biographical Dictionary*

1790–1990, edited by Rima Lunin Schultz and Adele Hast (Bloomington: Indiana University Press, 2001), 461.

19. Sklar, "Kelley, Florence," 462–63.

20. Ibid., 463.

21. Florence Kelley, "I Go to Work," *Survey Graphic,* June 1, 1927, 272.

22. Kelley, "I Go to Work," 272.

23. Ibid.

24. Jane Addams to Mary Catherine Addams Linn, March 13, 1889, Stephenson County Historical Society, reel 2–1043, Jane Addams Papers Project (hereafter, JAPP).

25. According to Carroll D. Wright, "The slums of cities, according to the dictionaries, are dirty back streets, especially such streets as are inhabited by a squalid and criminal population; they are low and dangerous neighborhoods" ("Introduction," 13). But, Wright adds, "In every district there are to be found people of the highest respectability, people of means, living in good houses, etc. They have all been considered as inhabitants of the slum districts, and necessarily so, because the enumerators or agents engaged in collecting the facts could not be expected in each case to draw the line. The results, however, of such comprehensive inquiry are shown in the classification of occupations, earnings, etc." "A Social Settlement: Miss Addams Describes 'Hull House' in Chicago Slums," *Boston Transcript,* July 30, 1892, 9, indicates that three years before *HHM&P* was published the settlement was associated with the idea of the slums in American cities.

26. Ann D. Gordon, "Stevens, Alzina Ann Parsons," in *Women Building Chicago: A Biographical Dictionary 1790–1990,* edited by Rima Lunin Schultz and Adele Hast (Bloomington: Indiana University Press, 2001), 843.

27. Diane Dillon, "Agnes Sinclair Holbrook" at http://uic.edu/jaddams/hull/urbanexp.

28. Ibid.

29. In 1893 and 1894 Eaton was a Dutton Fellow of the College Settlements Association. *Chicago Commons* 1 (Nov. 1896): 14.

30. Eaton's article, however, did not receive much attention. After her work at Hull-House she studied "the industrial status of Negro people" in Philadelphia as a College Settlement Association fellow at the Philadelphia Settlement. She was head of a settlement in Hartford, Connecticut, around 1896. *Chicago Commons,* vol. 1 (1896 Nov), 14.

31. Isabel Eaton, "Special Report on Negro Domestic Service in the Seventh Ward Philadelphia," in W. E. B. Du Bois, *The Philadelphia Negro* (New York: Lippincott, 1899), (pt. 1), 425–26.

32. Robert E. Woods and Albert J. Kennedy, *Handbook of Settlements* (New York: Charities Publication Committee, 1911), 27, 267. In the Ginn and Company edition, Eaton is listed as coauthor, with Du Bois, of *The Philadelphia Negro* (Boston: Ginn, 1899).

33. Eaton, "Special Report on Negro Domestic Service," 425–26.

34. Robyn Muncy, "Lathrop, Julia Clifford," in *Women Building Chicago: A Biographical Dictionary 1790–1990,* edited by Rima Lunin Schultz and Adele Hast (Bloomington: Indiana University Press, 2001), 490.

35. Muncy, "Lathrop, Julia Clifford," 491.

36. Ibid.

37. Thomas Guglielmo, *White on Arrival: Italians, Race, Color, and Power in Chicago, 1890–1945* (New York: Oxford University Press, 2003), 89; Humbert Steven Nelli, "The Role of the 'Colonial' Press in the Italian-American Community of Chicago 1886–1921," Ph.D. diss., University of Chicago, 1965, 38–40; Julia E. Noblitt, with Alena Zárasová, "Humpal-Zeman, Josefa Veronika," in *Women Building Chicago 1790–1990: A Biographical Dictionary,* edited by Rima Lunin Schultz and Adele Hast (Bloomington: Indiana University Press, 2001), 417–20.

38. Jane Addams to Mary Catherine Addams Linn, March 13, 1889, Stephenson County Historical Society, reel 2–1044, UIC, JAMC.

39. Guglielmo, *White on Arrival,* 89.

40. "Hull-House Residents 1889–1929" is a list compiled by the Hull-House Association in 1929 that attempted to be inclusive of all persons who had lived there; it also listed occupations and current addresses around 1929. Resident's Lists, ser. 8, box 1, folder 294, UIC, JAMC, HHC.

41. Nelli, "The Role of the 'Colonial' Press," 38–40; Nora Marks, "Two Women's Work: The Misses Addams and Starr Astonish the West Siders," *Chicago Tribune,* May 19, 1890, 1.

42. Marks, "Two Women's Work," 1.

43. Ibid.

44. Plans for the Italian Institute fell through. Wealthy Italians in Chicago were not forthcoming, and organizers of the institute blamed the pastor of the Italian Roman Catholic Church of the Assumption, who refused to have anthing to do with "a movement emanating from Hull house, a refusal persisted in even after Archbishop Feehan [of Chicago] had become a donor and had consented to act on the executive committee." "For Want of Encouragement," *Record,* Aug. 23. 1895.

45. Nelli, "The Role of the 'Colonial' Press," 40.

46. "Is Hull-House All?" *New World,* Oct. 24, 1903, 17.

47. Jane Addams, *Twenty Years at Hull-House, with Autobiographical Notes,* edited by James Hurt (Urbana: University of Illinois Press, 1990), 150, 244–45.

48. Addams, *Twenty Years at Hull-House.*

49. Ibid., 419.

50. Minutes, special residents' meeting, May 11, 1896, n.p., Hull-House Collection, box 1, folder 295, UIC, JAMC, HHC; Noblitt, with Zárasová, "Humpal-Zeman, Josefa Veronika," 417.

51. Ibid.

52. Deegan, *Jane Addams and the Men of the Chicago School,* 19.

53. Ellen Gates Starr, untitled brochure, Oct. 29, 1892, Hull-House Scrapbook 2, folder 507, UIC, JAMC, HHC.

54. "Eliza Allen Starr: Career of the Well-Known Pioneer Art Teacher of Chicago," *Chicago Evening Post,* July 5, 1890, 3; "Life and Works of Eliza Ellen [*sic*] Starr," *Chicago Tribune,* Sept. 9, 1901, 7; "Eliza Allen Starr," *Album of Genealogy and Biography, Cook County, Illinois* (Chicago: Calumet Book Company, 1897), 664–66.

55. Chicago Public School Art Society, *A List of Pictures and Casts for Use in Schools* (Chicago: n.p., Sept. 1897), in Art Resources in Teaching Records, box 46, folder 472, UIC, JAMC, HHC; "To Teach Children to Observe: Open Meeting of the Chicago Public School Art Society," *Chicago Inter-Ocean,* Nov. 9, 1895, 7; "To Foster Art in Public Schools," *Chicago Tribune,* Nov. 7, 1895, 12; Starr, untitled brochure, Oct. 29, 1892, 3–7.

56. For example, Jennie Dow, the first volunteer in the kindergarten at Hull-House, and her friend, Mary Rozet Smith, both attended Miss Kirkland's School for Girls.

57. Jane Addams, "The Art-Work Done by Hull-House, Chicago," *Forum* 19 (July 1895): 614. Addams notes that the direction of the effort "to make the aesthetic and artistic a vital influence in the lives of its neighbors . . . naturally fell into the hands of Miss Starr."

58. "Art for Poor People: Formal Opening of Hull House," *Chicago Herald,* June 21, 1891; Addams, "The Art-Work Done by Hull-House," 616–17; "Chicago's Toynbee Hall," *Chicago Tribune,* June 21, 1891, 6; "Pictures for the Poor," *Chicago Inter-Ocean,* June 21, 1891, 7; "Thrown Open to the Public," *Chicago Tribune,* June 21, 1891, 6.

59. "Art for Poor People."

60. Victoria Bissell Brown, *The Education of Jane Addams* (Philadelphia: University of Pennsylvania Press, 2004), provides the best analysis of the social and biographical factors that prepared Jane Addams for leadership in the Progressive Age. Jane Addams, "A New Impulse to an Old Gospel," *Forum* (Nov. 1892), a version of "The Subjective Necessity for Social Settlements."

61. Addams, "The Subjective Necessity," 17.

62. Daniel T. Rodgers, *Atlantic Crossings: Social Politics in a Progressive Age* (Cambridge: Harvard University Press, 1998), discusses the exchange of ideas among Europeans and Americans interested in reform across a wide spectrum.

63. Alice Hamilton, *Exploring the Dangerous Trades: The Autobiography of Alice Hamilton, M.D.* (1943, repr. Beverley, Mass.: OEM Press, 1995), 60. Hamilton became a resident in 1897. She conducted innovative scientific research in the Hull-House neighborhood and invented what is now the field of industrial toxicology. Barbara Sicherman, "Working It Out: Gender, Profession, and Reform in the Career of Alice Hamilton," in *Gender, Class, Race and Reform in the Progressive Era,* edited by Noralee Frankel and Nancy S. Dye (Lexington: University Press of Kentucky, 1991), 134.

64. Sklar has called *HHM&P* "the single most important work by American women social scientists before 1900" ("Hull-House Maps and Papers," 127).

65. Sklar quotes from an article written by Kelley in 1882: "In the field of sociology there is brain work waiting for women which men cannot do" (Ibid., 127). For Addams's position, see Ross, "Gendered Social Knowledge," 243.

66. Mary Furner, *Advocacy and Objectivity: A Crisis in the Professionalization of American Social Science, 1865–1905* (Lexington: University Press of Kentucky, 1975); Dorothy Ross, *The Origins of American Social Science* (New York: Cambridge University Press, 1991).

67. Fitzpatrick, in *Endless Crusade,* examines the lives of four female social scientists at the University of Chicago, including Breckinridge.

68. Lela Costin, *Two Sisters for Social Justice: A Biography of Grace and Edith Abbott* (Urbana: University of Illinois Press, 1983).

69. Sharon Haar, "Location, Location, Location: Gender and the Archeology of Urban Settlement," *Journal of Architectural Education* 55, no. 3 (2002): 154.

70. Kathryn Kish Sklar, "Who Funded Hull-House?" in *Lady Bountiful Revisited: Women, Philanthropy, and Power,* edited by Kathleen McCarthy (New Brunswick: Rutgers University Press, 1990).

71. Meeting minutes of the Chicago Women's Club, April 10, 1889, recommending Jane Addams and Ellen Gates Starr for membership, Chicago Woman's Club Board Minutes, 1876–91, vol. 10, Manuscript Collection, Chicago Historical Society.

72. Lila Weinberg, "Wilmarth, Mary J. Hawes," in *Women Building Chicago 1790–1990: A Biographical Dictionary,* edited by Rima Lunin Schultz and Adele Hast (Bloomington: Indiana University Press, 2001), 984.

73. Antoinette V. H. Wakeman, "Model Lodging House," *The Gate City* (Calif.), May 16, 1895, Hull-House Scrapbook 3, folder 29, UIC, JAMC, HHC; "The Model Lodging House," unidentified 1895 newspaper clipping, Hull-House Scrapbook 3, 29, UIC, JAMC, HHC.

74. Louise de Koven Bowen, *Growing Up with a City* (1926, repr. Urbana: University of Illinois Press, 2002), 103–41. Clubwomen supported the research undertaken by the Immigrants' Protective League, also a spin-off of Hull-House and located at the settlement. Considering the research undertaken by the School of Civics and Philanthropy, the Institute for Juvenile Research (originally located at the Mary Crane Nursery, Hull-House), and studies done with data collected by the IPL and the JPA, it is clear that clubwomen influenced the course of sociological and educational investigations outside the boundaries of academe. There were even more if public health, occupational (workplace), and nutritional studies that were undertaken by the settlement are included. Such endeavors received significant support by women who can be associated directly with the women's political culture.

75. Sklar, "Hull-House Maps and Papers," 130; Robert B. Westbrook, *John Dewey and American Democracy* (Ithaca: Cornell University Press, 1991), 91. Dewey concluded, Westbrook relates, that Bemis was dismissed from teaching for political reasons.

76. Ibid. Sklar adds that Ely withdrew from the American Institute of Christian Sociology, which he had helped found in 1893. The incident is also covered in Furner, *Advocacy and Objectivity,* 163–204.

77. Westbrook, *John Dewey,* 91.

78. Peggy Glowacki, "Culver, Helen," in *Building Chicago 1790–1990: A Biographical Dictionary,* edited by Rima Lunin Schultz and Adele Hast (Bloomington: Indiana University Press, 2001), 203.

79. Minutes of April 25, 1895, Board of Trustee Minutes, March 1895–Oct. 1924, folder 1–22, HHC.

80. Jane Addams to Mary Rozet Smith, March 3, 1894, series 1, reel 2–1505–1508, SCPC, JAC. Colvin

undertook fundraising for Hull-House. Jane Addams to Mary Rozet Smith, Feb. 3, 1895, reel 2–1647–1652, SCPC, JAC.

81. Jane Addams to Mary Rozet Smith, March 26, 1895, ser. 1, SCPC, JAC.

82. Allen Pond to Helen Culver, April 18, 1906, (pp. 1–3) and Helen Culver to Jane Addams, Oct. 19, 1920, both in "Financial Records," UIC, JAMC, HHC. In 1920 Culver was persuaded to donate, during her lifetime, $250,000 in bonds (an amount later revealed to be worth $175,000) to Hull-House, the largest single donation to the settlement. She died in 1925. Her nephew, Charles Hull Ewing, served as a trustee and advisor to Addams and the settlement even after the death of its founder in 1935.

83. Minutes for April 25, 1895, Board of Trustee Minutes, March 1895–Oct. 1924, folder 2, UIC, JAMC, HHC.

84. Minutes for April 13, 1899, UIC, JAMC, HHC; *Hull-House Bulletin* 3 (Nov.–Dec. 1899): 4; HHA Minutes for April 14, 1903. Louise Bowen was elected treasurer to replace Addams, who had held the position since 1895 (Minutes for Oct. 15, 1907, UIC, JAMC, HHC). Wilmarth resigned as trustee, and Charles L. Hutchinson was elected to fill her vacancy (Minutes for Jan. 27, 1908, UIC, JAMC, HHC). Butler and Hutchinson were trustees of the Art Institute of Chicago. Colvin was extremely important to Addams when she first launched Hull-House. "Mr. Colvin helps. . . . like the saint that he is," she wrote to Mary Rozet Smith on February 4, 1895 (series 1, reel, 2–1658, SCPC, JAC). His early death was a great blow to her. Allen Pond, an architect working in the arts and crafts style, whose firm was responsible for the twelve buildings that were added to the settlement from 1890 to 1907, encountered Addams when she was meeting civic and reform-minded Chicagoans in 1889. He remained a staunch advocate for the rest of his life and spent years as a Hull-House trustee.

85. Sklar, "Hull-House Maps and Papers," 136.

86. Ellen Skerrett, "The Irish of Chicago's Hull-House Neighborhood," in *New Perspectives on the Irish Diaspora,* edited by Charles Fanning (Carbondale: Southern Illinois University Press, 2000), 191, 215.

87. Pfautz, *Charles Booth on the City,* 28–29.

88. The maps were conceived to use data from an earlier project concerned with delineating the slum districts of several U.S. cities. They were not constructed to show immigration patterns on the near West Side of Chicago, although many people have thought of the maps as doing just that.

89. The notion of "Jew Town" on Chicago's Near West Side and "Greek Town" continued long after Jews and Greeks were living in the suburbs with only a small percentage of proprietorship of some commercial properties in the historically identified "colony" and "ghetto" of an earlier period. When the University of Illinois at Chicago began to buy land adjacent to its campus that had once been the prosperous Maxwell Street Market, suburban Jews long absent from the old neighborhood displayed strong antagonism to the spread of the university and exhibited intense nostalgia for a romanticized golden age.

90. Thomas Lee Philpott, *The Slum and the Ghetto: Neighborhood Deterioration and Middle-Class Reform, Chicago, 1880–1930* (New York: Oxford University Press, 1978), 23.

91. "Is Hull House All?" 17.

92. "It would be misleading," Holbrook writes ("Map Notes and Comments," 15) "to include children under ten years of age living in a foreign colony, not in attendance upon schools where English is sure to be used, speaking a foreign language, and, although born in this country, ignorant of American life, manners, people, and of the English tongue."

93. Elizabeth Lasch-Quinn, *Black Neighbors: Race and the Limits of Reform in the American Settlement House Movement, 1890–1845* (Chapel Hill: University of North Carolina Press, 1993); Michael McGerr, *A Fierce Discontent: The Rise and Fall of the Progressive Movement in America, 1870–1920* (New York: Free Press, 2003), esp. ch. 6.

94. Skerrett examines the parochial schools of Holy Family parish and issues of culture, refinement, and art in "The Irish of Chicago's Hull-House Neighborhood" (189–222).

95. Addams's experiences at the local ward level, first as garbage inspector and then as a leading voice opposing Alderman John Powers in 1898 and 1899, were eye-opening. By 1900 she could critique reformers as well as ward politicians, seeing the issue of local politics in a more complex way than had been

possible when she first encountered "the boss." "Jane Addams Wears a Star: Appointed to the Force of Garbage Inspectors by Commissioner Kent," *Chicago Record,* April 25, 1895, 6; Jane Addams to Henry Demarest Lloyd, Dec. 22, 1895, State Historical Society of Wisconsin, Henry Demarest Lloyd Papers, reel 2–1829–1830, JAPP; "Two Women and a Man—Jane Addams, Amanda Johnson and John Powers: Remarkable Results Achieved by Womanly Influence against Overwhelming Odds in the Nineteenth Ward," *Chicago Times-Herald,* Jan. 30, 1898, 25; Jane Addams, "Why the Ward Boss Rules," *Outlook,* April 2, 1898, 881–82.

96. Holbrook, "Map Notes and Comments," 22–23. Black indicates an average weekly family income of $5 or less, including many paupers and old people who lived "with their friends." Blue indicates $5 to $10 a week; red, $10 to $15; green, $15 to $20; yellow, anything over $20; and mauve indicates the unknown, chiefly peddlers, street players, and many of the very poor. In income, the mauve designation would likely fall under either the black or blue classifications.

97. Adjusted to 2005 dollars, less than $5 equals less than $105; $5 to $10 indicates $105 to $210; $10 to $15 equals $210 to $315; $15 to $20, $315 to $420; and more than $20 is the equivalent of more than $420.

98. "The unsanitary condition of many of these tenement houses, and the ignorance and abject poverty of the tenants, insure the maximum probability of disease; and diptheria, scarlet-fever, smallpox, typhoid, scabies, and worse forms of skin siseases have been found in alarming proximity to garments of excellent quality in process of manufacture for leading firms." Kelley, "The Sweating System," 34.

99. "Where there were women workers who were unorganized, which was the case overwhelmingly, the women neither keep the children out of the shops nor demand and obtain wholesome conditions of work. This [was] conspicuously true in the garment trades, in which women and children outnumber the men by two to one; while hours are longer, sanitary conditions are inferior, and the amount of work required disproportionate to the strength of the workers, to a greater degree than is true in any other occupation." Kelley and Stevens, "Wage-Earning Children," 73.

100. Gertrude Barnum, "The Story of the Garment Workers' Victory: How the Big Strike Has Been Supported," *Morrison's Chicago Weekly,* Jan. 26, 1911, 14–15; Jennifer Bosch, "Starr, Ellen Gates," in *Women Building Chicago: A Biographical Dictionary 1790–1990,* edited by Rima Lunin Schultz and Adele Hast (Bloomington: Indiana University Press, 2001), 838–42.

101. Victoria Bissell Brown, "Advocate for Democracy: Jane Addams and the Pullman Strike," in *The Pullman Strike and the Crisis of the 1890s: Essays on Labor and Politics,* edited by Richard Schneirov, Shelton Stromquist, and Nick Salvatore (Urbana: University of Illinois Press, 1999), 130–58. Brown argues that "Addams defined an independent position on the labor question precisely because she was the 'impassioned advocate' of a cause: the cause of mediated conflict through democratic process" (132).

102. Sklar, "Florence Kelley," 464.

103. "Hull-House Retrospect," *Hull-House Bulletin* 4, no. 1 (1900): n.p., at http://uiuc.edu/jaddams/hull/urbanexp.

104. Ibid.

105. Wright, "Introduction," in *The Slums of Baltimore, Chicago, New York, and Philadelphia,* 13.

106. Jane Addams, "The Foreign-Born Children in the Primary Grades," *Journal of Proceedings and Addresses* 36 (1897): 104–12.

107. Jane Addams, "Recreation as a Public Function in Urban Communities," *American Journal of Sociology* 17 (March 1912): 615–17. Here Addams examines the way in which parks and recreation centers can function as mediating, respectful environments where immigrants and their children can gain mutual understanding and a new form of patriotism can evolve.

108. According to Diane Dillon, the schedule men included the block where the Hull-House settlement was located, but the Greely-Carlson base maps that the company supplied to the settlement did not include the block. Dillon's hypothesis is that this was the reason for the the exclusion of Hull-House from the project. Page 11 of Dillon, "Cartography in a Kaleidoscope: The Art and Science of the Hull-House Maps," draft manuscript, April 2002, Urban Experience in Chicago Website Project, Jane Addams Hull-House Museum, University of Illinois at Chicago.

109. Humpal-Zeman and Zueblin provide important statistical data along with their impressions; Mastro-Valerio's is the most impressionistic of the three chapters.

110. Roger Daniels, *Guarding the Golden Gate: American Immigration Policy and Immigrants since 1882* (New York: Hill and Wang, 2004), 3–26.

HULL-HOUSE MAPS AND PAPERS

Prefactory Note

The word "settlement" is fast becoming familiar to the American public, although the first settlement, Toynbee Hall in East London, was established so late as 1885. Canon Barnett, the founder, urged as the primal ideal that a group of University men should reside in the poorer quarter of London for the sake of influencing the people there toward better local government and a wider social and intellectual life.

Since 1889 more than twenty settlements have been established in America. Some of these are associated with various institutional features, but the original idea of a group of "residents" must always remain the essential factor.

The residents of Hull-House offer these maps and papers to the public, not as exhaustive treatises, but as recorded observations which may possibly be of value, because they are immediate, and the result of long acquaintance. All the writers have been in actual residence in Hull-House, some of them for five years; their energies, however, have been chiefly directed not towards sociological investigation, but to constructive work.

The colors in Charles Booth's wage maps of London have been retained; and, as in his appended essays, each writer is responsible for the statements appearing over his own signature.

After this explanation it is needless to add that the following papers do not deal with settlement methods or results, but simply record certain phases of neighborhood life with which the writers have become most familiar.

The appendix to the volume is a mere cursory review of the present activities of Hull-House.

Jane Addams
335 So. Halsted Street, Chicago.
January, 1895

SCHEDULES

Used in the district between Halsted Street and the Chicago River, Polk and Twelfth Streets, Chicago. United States Department of Labor Investigations, April to August 1893.

These schedules formed the basis from which the charts were colored. See chapter 1, "Map Notes and Comments."

(D. L. — 268.)

UNITED STATES
DEPARTMENT OF LABOR.
1893.

....
Special Agent Expert.

SOCIAL STATISTICS OF CITIES.

City of ....

TENEMENT SCHEDULE.

1. Enumeration district.	2. Ward.	3. Number of dwelling-house in order of visitation.	4. Number of tenement in order of visitation.	5. House number and street.

6. Stories in house ?..

7. Tenements in house ?..

8. In which story is this tenement ?..

9. Number of rooms in this tenement ?...

10. Number of families in this tenement ?...

11. Number of persons in this tenement ?..

12. Weekly rent of this tenement ?..

13. Bath-room in this tenement ?..

14. Water-closet in this tenement ?...

15. Privy with this tenement ?..

16. Yard with this tenement ?..

17. Size of yard ?...

18. Where is washing hung to dry ?...

19. Light and air ?...

20. Ventilation?..

21. Cleanliness?..

22. Outside sanitary condition ?..

THE HOME.

INQUIRIES.	ROOM No. 1.	ROOM No. 2.	ROOM No. 3.	ROOM No. 4.	ROOM No. 5.	ROOM No. 6.
23. Use						
24. Dimensions						
25. Outside windows						
26. Occupants, at night						

A1 22-93 — 10000

UNITED STATES DEPARTMENT OF LABOR, 1893.

City of ....

FAMILY SCHEDULE.

.... *Special Agent Expert.*

INQUIRIES.		PERSONS IN THE FAMILY.				
		1	2	3	4	5
7	Christian name and middle initial?					
8	Surname?					
9	Relationship to head of family?					
10	Sex?					
11	Age at nearest birthday?					
12	Conjugal condition?					
13	Mother of how many children?					
14	Number of them living?					
15	Race?					
16	Place of birth?					
17	Place of birth of father?					
18	Place of birth of mother?					
19	Years in the United States?					
20	Fully naturalized?					
21	Naturalization papers taken out?					
22	Months in school during the year?					
23	Public, parochial, or what school?					

1. Enumeration district.

2. Ward.

3. Number of dwelling-house in order of visitation.

4. Number of family in order of visitation.

5. Number of persons in this family.

6. House number and street.

A1. 1-93—5000.

	Inquiries.	Persons in the Family.				
		1	2	3	4	5
24	Able to read native language?					
25	Able to write native language?					
26	Able to read English?					
27	Able to write English?					
28	Able to speak English?					
29	Sick with acute or chronic disease?					
30	Number of days sick?					
31	Wanting or defective in mind, sight, hearing, speech; maimed or deformed?					
32	Profession, trade, or occupation?					
33	Place of work at above profession, trade, or occupation?					
34	Average weekly earnings while employed at above profession, trade, or occupation?					
35	Daily hours of work from Monday to Friday?					
36	Daily hours of work Saturday?					
37	Daily hours of work Sunday?					
38	Weeks unemployed at above profession, trade, or occupation during the year?					
39	Weeks employed at any other profession, trade, or occupation during the year?					
40	Name of such other profession, trade, or occupation?					
41	Place of work at such other profession, trade, or occupation?					
42	Average weekly earnings while employed at such other profession, trade, or occupation?					
43	How subsisted when unemployed?					

I

MAP NOTES AND COMMENTS

Agnes Sinclair Holbrook

I. General Comments

The present work is the result of an attempt on the part of some of the residents of
Hull-House to put into graphic form a few facts concerning the section of Chicago
immediately east of the House.

The boundaries of the district are Halsted Street on the west and State on the east,
Polk on the north and Twelfth Street on the south; and the inhabitants, as the maps
show, are chiefly foreigners. From Halsted to State is one mile, from Polk to Twelfth,
one third of a mile. This third of a square mile includes east of the river a criminal
district which ranks as one of the most openly and flagrantly vicious in the civilized
world, and west of the same stream the poorest, and probably the most crowded section of Chicago. At the extreme northwest of the whole, on Halsted, near Polk, is
situated Hull-House, within easy walking distance of the densely populated network
of streets and alleys on the west side, claiming our chief attention.

A string of small shops, the best sides of two or three factories, and a few rather
pretentious brick store fronts form an outer fringe on Halsted and Twelfth Streets,
and give one the impression of a well-to-do neighborhood. The main thoroughfares
running parallel with Halsted and the river between Polk and Twelfth are semi-busi-
ness streets, and contain a rather cheap collection of tobacco-stands, saloons, old-iron
establishments, and sordid looking fancy-shops, as well as several factories, and occasional small dwelling-houses tucked in like babies under the arms of industry. The
cross streets running parallel with Polk between Halsted and the river are filled with
dwelling-houses, built for one family, but generally tenanted by several, and occasionally serving as bakery, saloon, or restaurant as well as residence. The back doors of
large establishments give glimpses of the inwardness of factory life, and bent figures
stitching at the basement windows proclaim that the sweater is abroad in the land.
Furnished rooms for rent are numerous; Italian rag and wine shops abound; dressmakers', calciminers', and cobblers' signs in Bohemian, German, and Russian are not
infrequent; while the omnipresent midwife is announced in polyglot on every hand.

Enumeration shows eighty-one saloons west of the river, besides a number of "delicatessen," "restaurationen," and cigar-stands where some liquor is sold. The proportion of wooden buildings to brick is approximately two to one throughout this part of the section; but on the south side of Polk Street it is about four to one, and on Ewing more than five to one. These figures include only houses fronting on the street, and in the case of large brick blocks assume that each portion covering a city lot is a building. Structures of mixed brick and wood are counted in with the brick buildings, and a few stone fronts form an exclusive, if inconsiderable, class, by themselves. The only one of interest is No. 137 DeKoven Street, the site of the outbreak of the great Chicago fire.

It is a striking fact that where the better houses prevail, as on DeKoven, Bunker, Taylor, and Forquer Streets, the street is almost solidly built up; while on Clinton, Jefferson, and Des Plaines the more scattered houses are veritable shells. One feels very clear, however, after long acquaintance with the neighborhood, and after visits to many of the homes, that the poorest of the tiny wooden houses, damp and unwholesome as they may be, offer nothing to compare with the hideousness shut up in the inside rooms of the larger, higher, and to the casual eye the better tenements of more pretentious aspect. The smart frontage is a mere screen, not only for the individual houses, but for the street as a whole. Rear tenements and alleys form the core of the district, and it is there that the densest crowds of the most wretched and destitute congregate. Little idea can be given of the filthy and rotten tenements, the dingy courts and tumble-down sheds, the foul stables and dilapidated outhouses, the broken sewer-pipes, the piles of garbage fairly alive with diseased odors, and of the numbers of children filling every nook, working and playing in every room, eating and sleeping in every window-sill, pouring in and out of every door, and seeming literally to pave every scrap of "yard." In one block the writer numbered over seventy-five children in the open street; but the effort proved futile when she tried to keep the count of little people surging in and out of passage-ways, and up and down outside staircases, like a veritable stream of life.

One can but regard the unpaved and uncared for alleys as an especially threatening feature in all this unpleasing picture; and yet between Polk and Ewing Streets, and also between Ewing and Forquer, where there are no alleys, the condition of the rear tenements is the most serious.

It is customary for the lower floor of the rear houses to be used as a stable and outhouse, while the upper rooms serve entire families as a place for eating, sleeping, being born, and dying. Where there are alleys the refuse and manure are sometimes removed; where there are none, it would seem they accumulate undisturbed. In front of each house stand garbage-receivers,—wooden boxes repulsive to every sense, even when as clean as their office will permit, shocking to both mind and instinct when rotten, overfilled, and broken, as they often are. Fruit-stands help to fill up the sordid streets, and ice-cream carts drive a thriving trade. One hears little English spoken, and the faces and manners met with are very foreign. People are noticeably undersized and unhealthy, as well to the average observer as to the trained eye of the physician.

Especially do the many workers in the tailoring-trades look dwarfed and ill-fed; they walk with a peculiar stooping gait, and their narrow chests and cramped hands are unmistakable evidence of their calling. Tuberculosis prevails, especially in diseases of the lungs and intestine, and deformity is not unusual. The mortality among children is great, and the many babies look starved and wan.

A Special Investigation of the Slums of Great Cities was undertaken, the spring of 1893, by the United States Department of Labor, by order of Congress; and as Mrs. Florence Kelley, the Special Agent Expert in charge in Chicago, resided at Hull-House while conducting the investigation, the information collected by the government officials was brought within the very doors.

The entire time of four government schedule men from the 6th of April till the 15th of July, 1893, was devoted to examining each house, tenement, and room in the district, and filling out tenement and family schedules, copies of which are printed at the beginning of this chapter. These schedules were returned daily to Mrs. Kelley; and before they were forwarded to the Commissioner of Labor at Washington, a copy was made by one of the Hull-House residents, of the nationality of each individual, his wages when employed, and the number of weeks he was idle during the year beginning April 1, 1892.

In recording the nationality of each person, his age, and in the case of children under ten years of age the nationality of his parents and his attendance at school, were taken into account. All under ten years of age who were not pupils in the public school, and who were not of American extraction, were classified with their parents as foreigners.

In estimating the average weekly wage for the year, first the number of unemployed weeks in each individual case was subtracted from the number of weeks in the year, the difference multiplied by the weekly wage when employed, and the result divided by fifty-two; then the amounts received by the various members of each family, thus determined, were added together, giving the average weekly income of the family throughout the year.

These records were immediately transferred in color to outline maps, made from the Greely and Carlsen survey, and generously prepared for the present purpose by Mr. Greely. These charts, with the street names and house numbers, enable the reader to find any address, the lots being colored to indicate, in one case the birthplace of each individual, in the other the wage of each family. Keys attached to the outlines explain the symbols, some of the same colors being used in the two cases with different meanings.

The mode of filling out the diagrams is slightly complex, owing to the fact that an effort is made to give the location of each family and individual, as nearly as may be. In the main, the basis of representation is geographical, each lot being entirely colored over, whether occupied by one person or one hundred. When people of different nationality or wage income, however, live in the same house, or in houses on the same lot, the space given to each on the charts is proportionate, not to the size of their houses or rooms, but (in the birthplace map) to the number of individuals, and (in the wage map) to the number of families. Thus the geographical relations are preserved, except within the lot, where each individual in the one case, and each representative of a family in the other, receives equal recognition, whether he shares with half a dozen others a room in the rear of the third story, or occupies in solitary state the entire ground floor.

No clew to the density of population is therefore given, except indirectly, in such a case as occurs on the corner of Polk and Clark Streets, where one might reasonably infer large numbers from the presence of negroes, Italians, Chinamen, Russians, Poles, Germans, Swiss, French-Canadians, Irish, and Americans in one house. In general, however, the solid blue blocks of Italians on Ewing Street, and the black phalanx of negroes on Plymouth Place represent more people to the square inch than any other lots—a fact which is in no way indicated on the diagrams.

The United States Department of Labor states the exact figures as part of the report on *The Slum Investigation,* and all the statistics relating to this subject are officially published. But the partial presentation here offered is in more graphic and minuate form; and the view of each house and lot in the charts, suggesting just how members of various nationalities are grouped and disposed, and just what rates of wages are received in the different streets and sections, may have its real as well as its picturesque value. A comparison of the two sets of outlines may also be of interest, showing in a general way which immigrants receive the highest, and which the lowest rates, and furnishing points for and against the restriction of immigration.

The poor districts of Chicago present features of peculiar interest, not only because in so young a city history is easily traced, but also because their permanence seems less inevitable in a rapidly changing and growing municipality than in a more immovable and tradition-bound civilization. Many conditions have been allowed to persist in the crowded quarters west of the river because it was thought the neighborhood would soon be filled with factories and railroad terminals, and any improvement on property would only be money thrown away. But it is seen that as factories are built people crowd more and more closely into the houses about them, and rear tenements fill up the few open spaces left. Although poor buildings bring in such high rents that there is no business profit in destroying them to build new ones, the character of many of the houses is such that they literally rot away and fall apart while occupied. New brick tenement houses constantly going up replace wooden ramshackle ones fallen into an uninhabitable state. The long, low house on the northeast corner of Taylor and Jefferson cannot last long. No. 305 Ewing is in a desperate condition, and No. 958 Polk is disintegrating day by day and has been abandoned. Other cases might be cited, and disappearances one after another of the old landmarks are not infrequent. As fast as they drop away their places are filled, and the precarious condition of many old dwellings renders a considerable change in the aspect of the neighborhood only a question of a decade or so.

Where temporary shanties of one or two stories are replaced by substantial blocks of three or four, the gain in solidity is too often accompanied by a loss in air and light which makes the very permanence of the houses an evil. The advantages of indifferent plumbing over none at all, and of the temporary cleanliness of new buildings over old, seem doubtful compensation for the increased crowding, the more stifling atmosphere, and the denser darkness in the later tenements. In such a transitional stage as the present, there is surely great reason to suppose that Chicago will take warning from the experience of older cities whose crowded quarters have become a menace to the public health and security. The possibility of helping toward an improvement in the sanitation of the neighborhood, and toward an introduction of some degree of comfort, has given purpose and confidence to this undertaking. It is also hoped that the setting forth of some of the conditions shown in the maps and papers may be of value, not only to the people of Chicago who desire correct and accurate information concerning the foreign and populous parts of the town, but to the constantly increasing body of sociological students more widely scattered.

The great interest and significance attached to Mr. Charles Booth's maps of London have served as warm encouragement; and although the eyes of the world do not centre upon this third of a square mile in the heart of Chicago as upon East London when looking for the very essence of misery, and although the ground examined here is very circumscribed compared with the vast area covered by Mr. Booth's incomparable studies, the two works have much in common. It is thought the aim and spirit of the present publication will recommend it as similar to its predecessor in essential respects; while the greater minuteness of this survey will entitle it to a rank of its own, both as a photographic reproduction of Chicago's poorest quarters on the west, and her worst on the east of the river, and as an illustration of a method of research. The manner of investigation has been painstaking, and the facts set forth are as trustworthy as personal inquiry and intelligent effort could make them. Not only was each house, tenement, and room visited and inspected, but in many cases the reports obtained from one person were corroborated by many others, and statements from different workers at the same trades and occupations, as to wages and unemployed seasons, served as mutual confirmation.

Although experience in similar investigation and long residence in the neighborhood enabled the expert in charge to get at all particulars with more accuracy than could have attended the most conscientious efforts of a novice, it is inevitable that errors should have crept in. Carelessness and indifference on the part of those questioned are undoubtedly frequent, and change of occupation as well as irregularity of employment entail some confusion and uncertainty. Then, too, the length of time covered by the investigation is so great—one year—that neither buildings nor tenants remain the same throughout.

West of the river the great majority of the dwellings are wooden structures of temporary aspect and uncertain moorings; and almost any day in walking through a halfdozen blocks one will see a frame building, perhaps two or three, being carried away on rollers to make room for some factory to be erected on the old site. Suburban cottages of remote date, with neither foundations nor plumbing, travel from place to place, and even three-story tenements make voyages toward the setting sun. Like rank weeds in a fresh soil, these unsubstantial houses sprang up in Chicago's early days; and now they are being gradually supplanted by the more sturdy growth of brick blocks for industrial purposes. When thus thrown out, they find a precarious foothold in some rear yard that is not entirely filled up with stables and outhouses, or move into one of the rare vacant lots, generally farther out from the business centres. Frequent house-movings of this sort alter the face of the district more or less within a year, and some neighborhoods put on a smarter look, while increased crowding continues in all.

Families also move about constantly, going from tenement to tenement, finding more comfortable apartments when they are able to pay for them, drifting into poorer quarters in times of illness, enforced idleness, or "bad luck." Tenants evicted for non-payment of rent form a floating population of some magnitude, and a kodak view of such a shifting scene must necessarily be blurred and imperfect here and there.

But special details vary while general conditions persist; and in spite of undetected mistakes and unavoidable inaccuracies, the charts paint faithfully the character of the region as it existed during the year recorded.

These notes and comments are designed rather to make the maps intelligible than to furnish independent data; and the aim of both maps and notes is to present conditions rather than to advance theories—to bring within reach of the public exact information concerning this quarter of Chicago rather than to advise methods by which it may be improved. While vitally interested in every question connected with this part of the city, and especially concerned to enlarge the life and vigor of the immediate neighborhood, Hull-House offers these facts more with the hope of stimulating inquiry and action, and evolving new thoughts and methods, than with the idea of recommending its own manner of effort.

Insistent probing into the lives of the poor would come with bad grace even from government officials, were the statistics obtained so inconsiderable as to afford no working basis for further improvement. The determination to turn on the searchlight of inquiry must be steady and persistent to accomplish definite results, and all spasmodic and sensational throbs of curious interest are ineffectual as well as unjustifiable. The painful nature of minute investigation, and the personal impertinence of many of the questions asked, would be unendurable and unpardonable were it not for the conviction that the public conscience when roused must demand better surroundings for the most inert and long-suffering citizens of the commonwealth. Merely to state symptoms and go no farther would be idle; but to state symptoms in order to ascertain the nature of disease, and apply, it may be, its cure, is not only scientific, but in the highest sense humanitarian.

(NORTH)

NATIONALITIES MAP No.1.– POLK STREET TO TWELFTH,
HALSTED STREET TO JEFFERSON, CHICAGO.

(SOUTH)

Colored

Chinese

Scandinavian

Bohemian

French Canadian

French

Swiss

Italian

Polish

Russian

Dutch

German

Irish

English Speaking
(Excluding Irish)

LOTS UNCOLORED ARE OCCUPIED BY FACTORIES, STORES ETC., NOT BY DWELLINGS.

(NORTH)

NATIONALITIES MAP No.2.- POLK STREET TO TWELFTH,
JEFFERSON STREET TO BEACH, CHICAGO.

(SOUTH)

NATIONALITIES MAP No.4.- POLK STREET TO TWELFTH, PACIFIC AVENUE TO STATE STREET, CHICAGO.

(NORTH)

WAGE MAP No. I,—POLK STREET TO TWELFTH,
HALSTED STREET TO JEFFERSON, CHICAGO.

(SOUTH)

THESE FIGURES REPRESENT THE TOTAL EARNINGS PER WEEK OF A FAMILY.

UNKNOWN

OVER $20.00

$15.00 TO $20.00

$10.00 TO $15.00

$5.00 TO $10.00

$5.00 AND LESS

(NORTH)

WAGE MAP No.2.- POLK STREET TO TWELFTH,
JEFFERSON STREET TO BEACH, CHICAGO.

THESE FIGURES REPRESENT THE TOTAL EARNINGS PER WEEK OF A FAMILY.

$5⁰⁰ AND LESS

$5⁰⁰ TO $10⁰⁰

$10⁰⁰ TO $15⁰⁰

$15⁰⁰ TO $20⁰⁰

OVER $20⁰⁰

UNKNOWN

(SOUTH)

WAGE MAP No.3.- POLK STREET TO TWELFTH,
BEACH STREET TO PACIFIC AVENUE, CHICAGO.

$5⁰⁰ AND LESS

$5⁰⁰ to $10⁰⁰

$10⁰⁰ to $15⁰⁰

$15⁰⁰ to $20⁰⁰

OVER $20⁰⁰

UNKNOWN

THESE FIGURES REPRESENT THE TOTAL EARNINGS PER WEEK OF A FAMILY.

W. POLK   ST.   BRIDGE   POLK   BUIL   ST.

DIAMOND STONE WORKS   73

EWING   ST.

ELLSWORTH

RIVER

OF CHICAGO

86

85

C.ST.P. & K.C.R.R.
FREIGHT HOUSE

W.C.R.R.
FREIGHT HOUSE

BUILT

FIFTH

103

104

SHERMAN

FREIGHT HOUSE

P.&P.U.R.R.

C.R.I.&

CHICAGO   ROCK   ISLAND

74   DOCK

CHICAGO   DOCK

CO.

W. TAYLOR   ST.   BRIDGE   TAYLOR   ST.

75   78
CHICAGO   SUGAR   REFINERY

SOUTH BRANCH

DOCK AS BUILT

DOCK AS BUILT

C.R.I.&P.R.R. FREIGHT HOUSE AND VIADUCT ABOVE

105

FREIGHT HOUSE

DE KOVEN   ST.

PRIVATE

76
EMPIRE SLIP
FOR THE SOLE BENEFIT AND USE

77
OF THIS SUBN

ALLEY
ENGINE HOUSE

COAL
SHED

BEACH

STOWELL ST.

106

(CANAL SLIP FILLED)

C. R.I.&

W. 12TH   ST.   BRIDGE   12TH   VIADUCT   ST.

(NORTH)

WAGE MAP No.4.—POLK STREET TO TWELFTH,
PACIFIC AVENUE TO STATE STREET, CHICAGO.

THESE FIGURES REPRESENT THE TOTAL EARNINGS PER WEEK OF A FAMILY.

BROTHELS $5.00 AND LESS $5.00 TO $10.00 $10.00 TO $15.00 $15.00 TO $20.00   OVER $20.00   UNKNOWN

II. Comments on Map of Nationalities.

In classifying the people from so many corners of the earth, an effort has been made to distinguish between the groups forming different elements in social and industrial life, without confusing the mind by a separate recognition of the people of every country.

The English-speaking class (white) embraces English, English-Canadians, Scotch, all Americans of native parentage, and such children born in this country of foreign parents as are over ten years of age, or, if younger, are in attendance upon any public school. It would be misleading to include children under ten years living in a foreign colony, not in attendance upon schools where English is sure to be used, speaking a foreign language, and, although born in this country, ignorant of American life, manners, people, and of the English tongue. *West* of the river the English-speaking element is composed of American-born children, rarely over twenty years of age, whose parents are foreigners, and who bear so plainly the impress of the Old World that they may more truly be designated as second-generation immigrants than first-generation Americans. *East* of the river the majority of the white lots are filled with genuine Americans, most of them men and girls under thirty, who have come to Chicago from towns and country districts of Illinois, and from Wisconsin, Michigan, and other neighboring States, most of whom lead irregular lives, and very few of whom are found in families.

One English-speaking nation has been marked off from the class to which it would seem at first sight to belong, and allotted peculiar recognition and the color of the Emerald Isle. The Irish (green) form so distinct and important an element in our politics and civic life that a separate representation has been accorded them.

The negroes (black) are natives of the United States, a great number coming from Kentucky.

The Bohemians (yellow) are very numerous in the southwestern part of the district under consideration.

The Scandinavians (yellow stripe) include Swedes, Norwegians, and Danes.

The Russians (red) and Poles (red stripe) are closely related, and uniformly Jewish; a few Roumanians are found among the former.

The Germans (mauve) are re-enforced by a not inconsiderable number of Hungarians and Austrians; but neither they nor the Dutch (mauve stripe) are found in large numbers.

The remaining divisions of the classification according to birthplace are:—

ITALIAN	(blue).
SWISS	(blue stripe).
FRENCH	(brown).
FRENCH CANADIAN	(brown stripe).
GREEK	(olive).
SYRIAN	(olive stripe).

CHINESE   (orange).
ARABIAN   (orange stripe).
TURK   (white crescent on red).

Eighteen nations are thus represented in this small section of Chicago. They are more or less intermingled, but a decided tendency to drift into little colonies is apparent. The Italians are almost solidly packed into the front and rear tenements on Ewing and Polk Streets, especially between Halsted and Jefferson, and outnumber any single class in the district. The Russian and Polish Jews cluster about Polk and Twelfth Streets, on the edge of the "Ghetto," extending south beyond Twelfth. The Bohemians form the third great group, and occupy the better streets toward the corner of Twelfth and Halsted, extending south and west beyond the limits of the map.

The Irish, although pretty well sprinkled, are most numerous on Forquer Street, which is a shade better than Ewing or Polk. A few French pepper the western edge of the section, the poorer members of a large and well-to-do French colony, of which the nucleus is the French church near Vernon Park. Only two colored people are found west of the river, while large numbers are wedged in Plymouth Place and Clark Street.

The Italians, the Russian and Polish Jews, and the Bohemians lead in numbers and importance. The Irish control the polls; while the Germans, although they make up more than a third of Chicago's population, are not very numerous in this neighborhood; and the Scandinavians, who fill north-west Chicago, are a mere handful. Several Chinese in basement laundries, a dozen Arabians, about as many Greeks, a few Syrians and seven Turks engaged in various occupations at the World's Fair, give a cosmopolitan flavor to the region, but are comparatively inconsiderable in interest. Americans of native parents are almost entirely confined to the part of the district east of the river; and it should be borne in mind that the white patches on the west side represent children who are as foreign, in appearance at least, as their Neapolitan or Muscovite parents.

The white portions representing the aggregate numbers of English-speaking people found in the house or houses on each city lot, including American-born children (often belonging to a dozen different families), are uniformly placed next the street-front, so that the eye readily determines the proportion in any street or block, as well as in the space covered by one lot. The green (Irish) come next behind; the yellow (Bohemian) follow; and the blue (Italian), red (Russian), and red stripe (Polish) occupy the rear of the lot in the order named; while the other colors there maybe hover between the two extremes. Since it is impossible in so small a map of two dimensions to represent accurately the position of the tenements occupied by members of various nationalities when the houses are two, three, and four stories high, the arrangement of colors is designed to suggest the mass, rather than the location, of the various peoples indicated by them.

In some respects, however, there is a certain correspondence between this disposition of colors and the location of tenants thereby represented, when many born in different countries occupy rooms and houses on the same lot. Italians, if present, are invariably found in the rear tenements, and the same is true of Russian and Polish Jews; however, in most cases where one apartment contains Italians or Jews, the whole tenement house is given over to them; for the arrival of either one is followed by the prompt departure of all tenants of other nationality who can manage to get quarters elsewhere, in much the same way that the appearance of a cheap money is the signal for a scarcity of dearer coins. It is rare that one will find Italians and Jews in the same house, moreover; for the lofty disdain with which the *Dago* regards the *Sheeny* cannot be measured except by the scornful contempt with which the *Sheeny* scans the *Dago*. Further discussion of these two important factions, and of the Bohemians, is found in separate chapters devoted entirely to their consideration.

III. Comments on the Wage-Map.

In turning from the nationality-map to the wage-map, the difference between the bases of representation in the two may again be called to mind. While in the former case the individual is the unit, in the latter it is the family,—head, wife, children, and such parents, brothers, cousins, and other relatives as live in the same dwelling, and are scheduled as one household. It is not easy to say just what constitutes "family life" in this connection. It is not a common table—often enough there is, properly speaking, no table at all. It is not even a common cooking-stove, for several families frequently use the same. The only constant factor in the lives of the members of such a circle, beyond the tie of kinship, is the more or less irregular occupancy of the same tenement, at least at night. Every boarder, and each member of the family who pays board, ranks as a self-supporting individual, and is therefore classed as a separate wage-earner. East of the river almost everybody boards, and a large proportion of the families on the west side keep boarders and lodgers; while there are also frequent boarding and lodging houses containing large numbers of people. At the time of scheduling sixty men sleep every night in one basement room at No. 133 Ewing Street; and similar instances of less serious crowding are found.

It may seem at first sight misleading to call each single man of over twenty-one a "family," and accord him the same representation as is given his father with six, eight, or ten children or other dependants whom he must support. But in this neighborhood, generally a wife and children are sources of income as well as avenues of expense; and the women wash, do "home finishing" on ready-made clothing, or pick and sell rags; the boys run errands and "shine"; the girls work in factories, get places as cash-girls, or sell papers on the streets; and the very babies sew buttons on kneepants and shirt-waists, each bringing in a trifle to fill out the scanty income. The theory that "every man supports his own family" is as idle in a district like this as the fiction that "every one can get work if he wants it."

A glance at the black lots on the map, representing an average weekly family income of $5.00 or less, will show roughly the proportion of families unable to get together

$260 dollars a year. The Italian, who is said to derive his nickname, "Dago," from his characteristic occupation of digging on the *ferra via,* is, as a rule, employed on the railroads from twenty to thirty weeks in the year at $1.25 a day; that is, he receives $150.00 to $225.00 a year on the average. The fact that this is not an income of $4.32 a week, or even $2.88 a week, throughout the year, but of $7.50 a week half the year, and nothing the other half, makes it more difficult for the laborer to expend wisely the little he has than if the wages were smaller and steady. This irregularity of employment, whether caused by the season, weather, fashion, or the caprices of the law of supply and demand, affects not only the unskilled, but to a considerable degree the employee of the manufactories, and the artisan. The poorest suffer from intermittent work, of course, the most. Many paupers, and old people living "with their friends," are found among these black spots in darkest Chicago.

The next class is colored blue, and embraces families earning from $5.00 to $10.00 a week, including $10.00. This is probably the largest class in the district.

Red indicates $10.00 to $15.00, including $15.00; green, $15.00 to $20.00, including $20.00; and yellow, anything over $20.00. Mauve signifies unknown.

The wage-earners proper are confined largely to the first four classes. The fifth (yellow) is largely composed of land and property owners, saloon and shop keepers, and those in business for themselves. All such propertied people are included in the fifth class, even if they declined to make a statement as to their income, it being reasonable to suppose them well-to-do. Members of the sixth class are chiefly peddlers, occasionally musicians and street-players, and almost invariably live from hand to mouth, keeping up a precarious existence by irregular and varied occupations. Most of this class are very poor indeed, and in point of income would probably come under one of the first two classes; that is, they generally receive less than $10.00 a week, many less than $5.00.

The white lots that are so numerous east of the river indicate brothels. These houses are separately classed, both because their numbers and whereabouts are of importance, and because it would be unfortunate to confuse them with laboring-people by estimating their incomes in the same way. Usually the schedules contain no information as to the amount of money taken in; but, according to the few entries made, the gains vary widely, from $5.00 to $50.00 a week. The most interesting fact brought out by the investigation in this connection is that the brothels in this section are almost invariably occupied by American girls. A comparison of the nationality-map with the one under consideration will make this plain. Few of the girls are entered on the schedules as Chicago-born, and the great majority come from the central-eastern States. There are many colored women among them, and in some houses the whites and blacks are mixed. Only such places as report themselves brothels are so entered in the maps, the many doubtful "dressmakers" in the same region being classified as wage-earners, according to their own statements. There are no declared brothels in the region west of the river.

II

THE SWEATING-SYSTEM

Florence Kelley, State Inspector of Factories
and Workshops for Illinois

The sweating-system is confined in Chicago to the garment trades, which employ some 25,000 to 30,000 people (as nearly as we can estimate), among whom this system is found in all its modes and tenses. The manufacture of garments is in the hands of wholesale firms. Their factories are grouped in the first ward of the city, within a radius of four blocks, where they have large, well-lighted, fairly wholesome workrooms, in which the garments for the entire trade are cut. The cutters, having a strong organization, refuse to work except under conditions more or less equal with the conditions of work usual in the well-organized trades. The hours and wages prevailing in the cutters' shops, therefore, do not differ much from the hours and wages usual in the well-organized trades. Some of the wholesale manufacturers have not only the cutters' shops, but also large workrooms, in which all the processes of clothing manufacture are carried on. These latter are known as "inside shops," or garment factories; and in them the employees work under conditions vastly better than are imposed upon the sweaters' victims, though still farther than the cutters below the standard of hours and wages maintained in the well-organized trades.

In the inside shops the sanitary conditions are fairly good; and power is frequently, though by no means uniformly, furnished for running machines. The same division of labor prevails as in the smaller shops; and the garment, after being cut, goes to the operator, who stitches the scams, to the buttonholer, the finisher, and the presser. In the inside shop the presser is usually also a skilled cleaner, and adds to his function of pressing the garment made on the premises the duty of removing grease and other soils from the garments returned from the sweaters' shops. There are also usually employed in these shops both basters and girls who pull bastings out of the finished garments. Formerly the operator was often an "all around worker," who received the garment from the cutters, and handed it finished to the examiner; but the competition of the sweaters has led to a very general introduction of hand-girls, one of whom works with each operator, doing the hand-finishing on the garment as it comes from the operator. The sweating-system has affected disastrously the condition of the employees in the inside shops, since any demand of the inside hands for increased wages or shorter hours is promptly met by transfer of work from the inside shop to a sweater; and the cutters alone remain secure from this competition.

A very important functionary inside the clothing shops is the examiner, who receives finished garments both from the inside hands and the sweaters, and passes upon the satisfactoriness of the work. Incidentally, it is a painful duty of the examiner to find and destroy the vermin commonly infesting garments returned from outside workers.

Children are not employed to any considerable extent in the inside shops, and the employees are usually English-speaking workers, though comparatively few native Americans are left in the garment trades, even in the inside shops. The organizations of employees are feeble, both numerically and financially, except the cutters' union; and wages in the best inside shops are far below the rates common in well-organized trades, and are rapidly and steadily falling.

With two exceptions, every manufacturer of garments in Chicago gives out clothing to be made in tenement houses. This is true of white underwear and custom-made outer wear, quite as much as of the ready-made clothing ordinarily associated in the public mind with the sweating-system. There are three common variations in the manner of giving out goods. Many manufacturers have closed their inside shops, and retain only their cutting-rooms. These give garments directly to large numbers of individual employees, who make them up in their dwellings; or to sweaters, or to both. Manufacturers who retain their inside shops commonly give out garments in both these ways; and many of them also make a practice of requiring employees who work by day to take home garments at night, and on Saturday, to be made at home on Sunday.

Every manufacturer keeps a list of the names and addresses of the people to whom he gives out garments to be made up, and is required by law to show this list on demand to the factory and workshop inspectors.

It is the duty of the inspectors to follow up these lists, and examine the surroundings amidst which this work is done; and they report that the conditions in which garments are made that are given out from the inside shops for night work and Sunday work differ not a jot from the tenement-house shops and the sweaters' home finishers' dwellings. Thus, a recent night inspection of work given out from one of the largest cloak manufactories in the West resulted as follows: The garment maker was found in his tenement dwelling in the rear of a factory. With his family, a wife and four indescribably filthy children, he occupies a kitchen and two bedrooms. The farther bedroom could be entered only by passing through the other rooms. This farther bedroom, where the man was found at work, was $7 \times 7 \times 8$ feet, and contained a bed, a machine, one chair, a reeking lamp, and two men. The bed seemed not to have been made up in weeks; and in the bed, in a heap, there lay two overcoats, two hats, a mass of bed-covers, and nine fine tan-color capes trimmed with ecru lace, a tenth cape being on the machine in process of stitching. The whole dwelling was found to be crawling with vermin, and the capes were not free from it.

The manufacturers hold their outside workers responsible for the return of the goods; and sweaters have been prosecuted for larceny, and have been followed even beyond the borders of the State, and brought back for prosecution under the criminal law for failing to return goods intrusted to them. But the manufacturers do not hold themselves responsible for the dealings of the outside workers with their victims. Thus, a sweater extradited from another State, and prosecuted here for larceny of unfinished garments, is subject merely to a civil suit on the part of his employees for hundreds of dollars of wages due them; while the manufacturer is in no degree responsible for the payment of these wages for work done upon garments belonging to him. Such cases have not been rare; and the manufacturers disclaim all moral responsibility to the unfortunate victims, as they disclaim all responsibility to the purchasing public for disease carried in garments made in the sweaters' victims' infectious homes.

The Sweaters.

The name of the sweaters is legion. More than a thousand of their shops have been inspected, and more than eight hundred licensed by the city; while it is an open secret that these numbers fall far below the total actually existing. It is well-nigh impossible to keep perfect lists of sweaters; since a man may be an operator to-day, a sweater on a small scale next week, may move his shop in the night to avoid the payment of rent, and may be found working as operator in an inside shop at the close of the season.

The sweaters differ from the cutters in their relation to the manufacturers, in that the sweaters have no organization, and are incapable of making any organized demand for a standard of prices. They are separated by differences of religion, nationality, language, and location. As individuals they haggle with the manufacturers, undercutting each other, and calculating upon their power to reduce the pay of their employees below any point to which the manufacturers may reduce theirs; and as individuals they tyrannize over the victims who have the misfortune to work in their shops. There has never been, and there is not now, in Chicago any association of sweaters of any kind whatsoever. There is, therefore, no standard price for the making of any garment, either for the sweater or his victim. With every change of style, there is a change of price, and the tendency of the change is always downward. The fashion and the change of seasons are an ever-ready excuse for the manufacturers, who constantly aim to concentrate the work of the year into the shortest possible season. There are two reasons for this: In a short season the turn-over of the capital invested is quick and comparatively sure; and a more sinister consideration is the fact that sweaters who have long been without work, and whose coming season threatens to be very short, are ready to take work upon any terms offered them. The consequence of the concentration of the manufacture of garments into short, recurrent seasons is an extreme pressure upon the contractor for the speediest possible return of the garments given him; and, hitherto, this pressure has forced the sweaters' victims to work far into the night, and to disregard Sunday and all holidays. It is the belief of the sweaters' victims as well as of the inspectors, that a rigid enforcement of the eight-hour law within these shops will compel the sweaters to increase the number of employees, enlarge their shops, and so create groups numerically too strong to submit to conditions easily imposed upon ten or a dozen very poor people.

By persistent prosecutions of sweaters found employing children under the age of fourteen years, the practice has been to some extent broken up. During the effort to remove them from these shops, there were found boys whose backs have been made crooked for life by continuous work at heavy machines, and boys and girls unable to speak English, and equally unable to read or write in any language.

The sweaters are found in all parts of the city. They are of nine nationalities, speak nine different languages, and are of several religions. The employees ordinarily follow the nationality and religion of the sweater; though Swedes are sometimes found employing Bohemian children, and Russian Jews are found with employees of various nationalities. In general, however, the language of the shop is the language of the sweater, and follows the nationality of the colony in which it is located.

The Nineteenth Ward.

In the nineteenth ward the sweaters are Russian Jews and Bohemians; and their employees in the shops are of the same nationality, while their home finishers are exclusively Italians,—the wives and daughters of the streetsweepers and railroad gang hands, who form so large a part of the population of the ward. The garments made here are principally coats, cloaks, trousers, knee-pants, and shirts. There are one hundred and sixty-two shops, employing men, women, and children.

The shops are, without exception, in tenement houses or in the rear of tenement houses, in two-story buildings facing alleys that are usually unpaved and always noxious with the garbage and refuse of a tenement-house district. If the sweater's shop is in a tenement house, it is sometimes—but very rarely—in the ground floor front room, built for a store and lighted by large store windows. But far more commonly it is a basement, or an attic, or the flat over a saloon, or the shed over a stable. All the tenement houses selected either for shops or home finishers are of the worst and most crowded description. The staircases are narrow, and are used in common by tenants and garment workers, so that infectious diseases breaking out among the swarming children can scarcely fail to be communicated to garments anywhere under the same roof, because the utmost laxity prevails in the matter of isolation. The unsanitary condition of many of these tenement houses, and the ignorance and abject poverty of the tenants, insure the maximum probability of disease; and diphtheria, scarlet-fever, smallpox, typhoid, scabies, and worse forms of skin diseases, have been found in alarming proximity to garments of excellent quality in process of manufacture for leading firms.

There is not in the whole ward a clothing-shop in any building erected for the purpose; and in no case is steam-power supplied, but the use of foot-power is universal. In but one case known to me within this ward has a sweater acquired means sufficient to own the premises on which his shop is carried on. Employers of this class are usually tenants, who rent by the week or month, and move upon the shortest notice. To illustrate: There is at 165 West Twelfth Street a crowded tenement house, with a Chinese laundry in the ground floor front, and swarming families above. In the ground floor rear is a Jewish butcher-shop, where sausage (not of pork) is made during part of the year; but at midsummer, meat is roasted to supply the demand of a large surrounding colony of Russian Jews. Over this butcher-shop is a tailor-shop, into which the fumes and heat of the wholesale roasting below rise in the most overpowering manner. This shop possesses an irresistible attraction to sweaters of several varieties. It was occupied last summer by a firm of cloakmakers. When they were required to vacate by reason of its unsanitary condition, the shop stood empty but a short time, when two coat-making partners moved in with a large body of victims. As the landlord could not be induced to make any improvement, these also were required to move; and the shop is now occupied by a veteran knee-pants maker, who moved into it when required to separate his shop from his dwelling as a sanitary measure!

Under a clause of the law which prohibits the use of any bedroom or kitchen for the manufacture of garments by any person outside of the immediate family living therein, the inspectors are waging war upon contractors who employ help in kitchen or bedroom, or in any room accessible only by going through the living-rooms of the family. The law is loosely drawn, the difficulties are many, and progress is slow towards an entire separation of shop and dwelling. Nor will such separation ever be complete until all manufacture in any tenement house is prohibited by law.

Meanwhile, every tenement-house shop is ruinous to the health of the employees. Basement shops are damp, and entail rheumatism. They never afford proper accommodations for the pressers, the fumes of whose gasoline stoves and charcoal heaters mingle with the mouldy smell of the walls and the stuffiness always found where a number of the very poor are crowded together. The light in basement shops is bad, and they are colder in winter and hotter in summer than workrooms in ordinary factories.

Attic shops are hot in summer, and usually foul by reason of the presence of closets to which the water does not rise. As these shops are often on the fifth floor of crowded tenement houses, with narrow wooden stairs, no fire-escapes, and no sufficient water supply, the danger of death by fire is greatly aggravated by the omnipresent presser's stove. Shops on the middle floors are ill-lighted, ill-ventilated, and share the smell from the kitchens and drains of surrounding tenement flats.

The dye from cheap cloth goods is sometimes poisonous to the skin; and the fluff from such goods inhaled by the operators is excessively irritating to the membranes, and gives rise to inflammations of the eye and various forms of catarrh. All these conditions, taken together with the exhaustion consequent upon driving foot-power machines at the highest possible rate of speed, make consumption, either of the lung or intestine, the characteristic malady of the sweaters' victim.

In the minds of the physicians, nurses, and inspectors best acquainted with the sweaters' victims of the nineteenth ward, there is no doubt that the substitution of steam-power for foot-power would do more to change this medical aspect of the case than any other one change that could be made. This is, however, entirely hopeless until tenement-house manufacture is prohibited. Meanwhile, the trade life of the garment worker is probably shorter than prevails in any other occupation; and the employees are always on the verge of pauperism, and fall into the abyss with every illness or particularly bad season.

If the sweaters' victim or any member of his family fall ill, his only hope is in the county doctor and the visiting nurse supported by charity, unless the patient be taken outright to the Michael Reese or County Hospital. If the illness proves a long one, recourse must be had to the various charities; and death brings a funeral ending in the potter's field, unless some prosperous brother of the faith provides for private burial.

A typical example is the experience of a cloakmaker who began work at his machine in this ward at the age of fourteen years, and was found, after twenty years of temperate life and faithful work, living in a rear basement, with four of his children apparently dying of pneumonia, at the close of a winter during which they had had, for weeks together, no food but bread and water, and had been four days without bread. The visiting nurse had two of the children removed to a hospital, and nursed the other two safely through their illness, feeding the entire family nearly four months. Place after place was found for the father; but he was too feeble to be of value to any sweater, and was constantly told that he was not worth the room he took up. A place being found for him in charge of an elevator, he could not stand; and two competent physicians, after a careful examination, agreed that he was suffering from old age. Twenty years at a machine had made him an old man at thirty-four. During these twenty years his earnings had ranged from $260 to $300 per annum.

Even without illness in his family, the sweaters' victim is regularly a pauper during a part of the year. The two seasons of the trade in each year are followed by long pauses, during which nothing can be earned, and debts are incurred. If the "slack" season is phenomenally short, in a year of unusual commercial prosperity, the sweaters' victim may perhaps live through it, by means of the credit given him by the landlord and grocer, without applying for aid to the Charities or the County Relief. But in the ordinary years of merely average prosperity, the sweaters' victim is inevitably an applicant for relief, to supplement, during three to five months, the earnings made during the busy season.

This fact effectively disposes of the favorite humanitarian argument on behalf of tenement-house manufacture; namely, that widows with children to support must be

permitted to work at home. Even if these widows made a sufficient living for themselves and their children, the price paid for their prosperity, in the spread of disease
and the demoralization of a vast trade, might be considered exorbitant. As a matter of
fact, however, no tenement-house garment maker earns a sufficient living for a family,
least of all the widow whose housework and care of her children interrupt her sewing,
and whose very necessities are exploited by the sweater in his doling out of work and
pay. What we really get in the case of the widow is the worst conceivable form of tenement-house manufacture, with full-fledged pauperism thrown into the bargain.

It is preposterous, on the face of it, that a trade employing from 25,000 to 30,000
persons in a single city, with an annual output of many millions of dollars, should
be carried on with the same primitive machines which were used thirty years ago. In
every other branch of manufacture the watchword of the present generation has been
concentration. Everywhere steam, electricity, and human ingenuity have been pressed
into service for the purpose of organization and centralization; but in the garment
trades this process has been reversed, and the division of labor has been made a means
of demoralization, disorganization, and degradation, carried to a point beyond which
it is impossible to go. While the textile mills in which the material for garments is spun
and woven have been constantly enlarged and improved, both as to the machinery
used and as to the healthfulness of the surroundings of the workpeople, the garment
trade has been enriched merely by the addition of the buttonhole machine; and this
lone, lorn improvement has been made the means of deforming the illiterate children
employed at it.

Thirty years ago the shoemaker and the tailor were more or less equally placed.
Each went through the experience of the apprentice, the journeyman, the master,
working for a limited market, and more or less in personal contact with the individual
customer. To-day the shoe industry possesses a wealth of perfected machinery, such
that a tanned hide can be carried through all the processes of manufacture under a
single roof and with incredible speed. The shoemaker's shop, with its little group of
workers, has become the shoemaking town, with a vast organization, both of capital
and of labor, and a very high degree of intelligence and class consciousness pervading
the thousands of employees. The garment worker, on the contrary, still works in his
kitchen, perhaps with the aid of his wife, performing one of the dozen subdivisions
of the labor of making garments. He rarely belongs to an organization, and if he does
it is so weak as to be almost useless to him either for education or defence. If he is an
"all-round garment worker," whatever his skill may be, he has little use for it; since,
in competition with him, the cutter cuts, the operator stitches, the seam-binder binds
seams, the hand-girl fells, the presser presses, the buttonholer makes buttonholes by
the thousand gross. Whatever the disadvantages of the division of labor, the garment
worker suffers them all. Of its advantages he has never had a taste.

A curious example of the isolation of the garment worker is found in a crowded
tenement house in Ewing Street, known as "Poverty Flat," where five different women

were found sewing, each in her own kitchen, five different bundles of knee-pants for the same sweater. The knee-pants were of the same size and quality, with the same amount of work to be done upon them; but the prices paid were five cents, seven cents, nine cents, eleven and thirteen cents per dozen, rising in accordance with the skill in haggling of the home finisher, and with no relation to her skill in sewing on buttons.

A millionnaire philanthropist, at the head of one of the largest clothing-houses in the world, was once asked why he did not employ directly the people who made his goods, and furnish them with steam-power, thus saving a heavy drain upon their health, and reducing the number of sweaters' victims found every winter in his pet hospital. "So far," he replied, "we have found leg-power and the sweater cheaper."

In the shoe industry the products have been cheapened by developing the plant, perfecting the machinery, and employing relatively well-paid, high-grade labor. In the garment trade there is no plant. Under the sweating-system, with the foot-power sewing-machine, cheapness is attained solely at the cost of the victim. Even the inside shops are often located in rented quarters, and frequently the operator is required to supply his own machine, or to pay the rent of a hired one; and even with these niggardly provisions the manufacturers find it profitable to shift the burden of rent upon the sweaters, who, in turn, reduce the size of their shops by giving out garments to the buttonholer and the home finisher.

The intimate connection between this decentralization of the trade and the danger of infecting the purchaser with disease prevalent in tenement-house districts, is too palpable to need comment, and emphasizes the question why the clothing manufacturer should be permitted to eliminate the item of rent from his expenses, at the cost of the trade and of the purchasing community. All other manufacturers have to include rent in their calculations, why not he?

The condition of the sweaters' victim is a conclusive refutation of the ubiquitous argument that poverty is the result of crime, vice, intemperance, sloth, and unthrift; for the Jewish sweaters' victims are probably more temperate, hard-working, and avaricious than any equally large body of wage-earners in America. Drunkenness is unknown among them. So great is their eagerness to improve the social condition of their children, that they willingly suffer the utmost privation of clothing, food, and lodging, for the sake of keeping their boys in school. Yet the reward of work at their trade is grinding poverty, ending only in death or escape to some more hopeful occupation. Within the trade there has been and can be no improvement in wages while tenement-house manufacture is tolerated. On the contrary, there seems to be no limit to the deterioration now in progress.

Merchant Tailors.

It is a fact of which the public has remained curiously ignorant, that the worst forms of danger to the wearers of garments are found in heavier proportion in the manufacture of expensive custom-made clothing than in the ready-made clothing trade; since there are no inside factories for the manufacture of custom-made clothing, and merchant tailors employ only cutters on their premises, and never have any garments completed there, but always give them out to be finished in the sweatershop, or in the individual tailor's own home.

Throughout the agitation carried on for some years past against the sweating-system, the merchant tailors have enjoyed a wholly undeserved immunity from the accusation of spreading infectious and contagious disease by means of the tenement-house manufacture of garments. A striking example may serve to illustrate the point. I have myself found on Bunker Street a brick tenement house filled with Bohemian and Jewish tenants engaged in the tailoring trade and in peddling. In the ground floor, front flat, which was exceedingly clean, I found a tailor at work one Sunday afternoon upon a broadcloth dress-coat belonging to an evening suit of the finest quality, such as sell for from $70 to $100. On a bed about five feet from the table at which the tailor was working, his son lay dying of typhoid fever. The boy died on the following day; and the coat when finished was returned to the merchant tailor, and delivered to the customer without fumigation or other precaution. This was before the passage of the present factory law, and at a time when no authority of the State of Illinois had power to interfere in such a case.

Even where the home tailor, by twenty years of work, has come to own his house, this prosperity is no guaranty of clean goods for the purchaser. At 135 Forquer Street, there stands a two-story frame building swarming with Russian, Jewish, and Italian families, the ground floor occupied by a most disorderly and repulsive grocery. The premises belong to a tailor who lives in a shanty in the rear, where his old mother, dying of cancer, occupies a bed in the kitchen, in which this landlord has been repeatedly found working with his wife upon uniforms for the officers of the Chicago police and the Illinois militia, while his children and a number of chickens swarmed upon the floor. This man, after nineteen years of instalment payments upon his property, is still guilty of all the vices of thrift, in the hope of finally lifting the mortgage indebtedness during the present year.

Law.

The sweating-system in Chicago has been a subject of investigation since 1891, when Mrs. Thomas J. Morgan, on behalf of the Chicago Trades and Labor Assembly, made the first inspection that attracted public attention to the subject, upon the publication in pamphlet form of the results of her investigations.

From 1891 to the passage of the law of 1893 under the leadership of Hull-House, the organizations of garment workers, including the shirtmakers, the men's shop-tailors' union, the women's protective union of cloakmakers, the custom-tailors' union, the cloakmakers and the shoemakers, kept up an unwearied agitation for the abolition by law of the sweating-system, and obtained results proportioned to their good tactics, zeal, and energy, rather than to their numbers.

They urged on every public occasion that tenement house manufacture is a public injury; and they availed themselves of the solidarity of the unions throughout the State, to bring the facts of the case home to legislators with the emphasis of the labor vote. Their claim on behalf of the public health is an unanswerable one; and their appeal for themselves, in their effort to place the garment trades upon the same modern business basis as the factor trades, finds ready response in the minds of intelligent people. Opposition to legislation looking towards the abolition of the sweating-system came from the manufacturers, less than one hundred in number, whose interests are affected, and from a few kind-hearted persons apprehensive of possible injury to the home finishing widow, because they do not know her well enough to judge correctly her present irreparable situation.

In July, 1893, the present Workshop and Factories Act went into effect, and this essay is written after eight months of effort to enforce it. The results obtained may be briefly summed up as consisting of the reduction in number of the small children in shops; the partially successful separation of the homes from the shops, and the partially successful enforcement of the eight-hour day for the women and girls. These results are not wholly unsatisfactory, in view of the fact that the law is not yet a year old; but they indicate that this initial, tentative measure is inadequate for the effective protection of the health of either the public or the employees of the garment trades. Its chief value lies in its use as a transition measure, paving the way for the abolition of tenement-house manufacture.

This should be a comparatively easy matter in a new city where there is no long-standing tradition of generations of handloom weaving in the worker's home, or indeed of home manufacture of any sort. In Chicago, where all industry is on a large scale, and the cheap land available for building factories is ample, there is not even the excuse afforded by the traditions of London or the overcrowding of Manhattan Island. If we tolerate tenement-house manufacture, we do so in the face of the experience of older cities, and in spite of industrial conditions which invite us to its abolition.

Bibliography

Pamphlet on the Sweating-System, published by the Chicago Trades Assembly, 1892.

Investigation of the Sweating-System by Committee of the United States House of Representatives, Sherman Roar, Chairman, 1892.

Report of Illinois Bureau of Labor Statistics, 1892.

Report Joint Special Committee Senate and House of Representatives of Illinois to Investigate the Sweating-System in Chicago, March 1, 1893.

Reports State Factory Inspectors of Illinois.

III

WAGE-EARNING CHILDREN

Florence Kelley and Alzina P. Stevens,
State Inspector and Assistant Inspector of
Workshops and Factories for Illinois

In a discussion of child-labor in Chicago, it may simplify matters to point out, at the outset, what things are not to be looked for. Thus, there is in Chicago virtually no textile industry; and the cotton-mill child of Massachusetts, or the carpet-mill child of Philadelphia, has no counterpart here. There is no industry in which, as in the spinning and weaving of silk, the deft fingers of young children have been for generations regarded as essential. With the large exception of the cigar, tobacco, and paper trades (including both the manufacture of paper boxes and the printing and binding industries), and with the further exception of the utterly disorganized and demoralized garment trades, the industries of Illinois are essentially men's trades. The wood, metal, and food industries employ a heavy majority of men. The vast army of fathers employed in transportation and in the building-trades demand, and as a rule obtain, wages sufficient to support their young children, who are therefore not crowded into factories. As the work of factory inspection in the State is of extremely recent date, and the inspection records are of less than a year's standing, it is impossible to trace the growth of child-labor in Chicago. Its status has, however, been carefully investigated during the present year.

The census of 1880 gave the total number of wage-earning children in the United States in all occupations and industries as 1,118,258. The census of 1890, in sections devoted to "Statistics of Manufactures," gives returns upon child-labor in this division of industry, some of which will be used in this essay. Before any of these are quoted, the reader must be warned that census figures upon the employment of children are invariably too low. They are here used merely as a basis for comparison. The method by which statistics of employees are gathered, leaves it possible for employers and parents to make false returns concerning children. Inclination and interest prompt both to "raise" the age of the child at work; and most employers are so far ashamed of the practice of employing children, that each returns less than the actual number. All

persons who have been officially engaged under municipal, State, or national authority, in gathering statistics of the employed, know that this is true.

In the census bulletin upon manufactures of 1890, the total number of employees
in the United States, of both sexes and all ages, is given as 4,711,831; the total number
of children as 121,494, or a little more than three per cent of all employed. In census
reports, children are all males under sixteen years, and all females under fifteen years.
The table giving manufactures by States shows that it is not where labor is scarce, but
where competition for work is keenest, that the per cent of children is largest in the
total number employed. Thus, 5 children are credited to Wyoming; 9 to Arizona; 1 only
to Nevada; while Pennsylvania has 22,417; New York, 12,413; Massachusetts, 8,877.

Certainly the older and densely populated states report on a greater number of
establishments and employees; but that does not affect the comparison between States
as to the ratio of children to adults. For example: the Nevada report is upon 95 establishments, employing 620 persons, only one a child; while Pennsylvania's report is
upon 39,366 establishments, employing 620,484 persons, of whom 22,417—or about
one in 23—are children.

Child-Labor and the Illinois Law.

The Illinois Bureau of Labor Statistics, established in 1879, which has issued seven
biennial reports, has never furnished any information relative to the employment of
children in the State. The Workshop and Factories Act was enacted by the Thirty-
Eighth General Assembly, and received the signature of Governor Altgeld on July 1,
1893. It provided for the appointment of an inspector, assistant inspector, and ten deputy inspectors, five of whom should be women; and it requires an annual report of
their work, to be submitted to the governor of the State on December 15. From the first
official report, which covers the five months between July 15 and December 15, 1893, the
statistics used in this paper concerning working children in this State are taken.

The census of 1890 reports 20,482 manufacturing establishments in the State, and
gives the total number of children employed in them as 5,426. In five months' work
in 1894 we found 6,576 children in 2,452 establishments employing 68,081 persons, or
about 1 in 10 so employed, a reason for once more challenging census figures; although
in our work girls under sixteen, as well as boys, are counted children. It will be remembered that the census returns place girls over fifteen years among adults, but reckon
boys as children until sixteen years.

The sections of the Illinois law regulating the employment of children are the
following:—

§4. No child under fourteen years of age shall be employed in any manufacturing
establishment, factory, or workshop within this State. It shall be the duty of every
person, firm, corporation, agent, or manager of any corporation employing children,

to keep a register in which shall be recorded the name, birthplace, age, and place of residence of every person employed by him, them, or it, under the age of sixteen years; and it shall be unlawful for any person, firm, or corporation, or any agent or manager of any corporation, to hire or employ in any manufacturing establishment, factory, or workshop, any child over the age of fourteen years and under the age of sixteen years, unless there is first provided and placed on file an affidavit made by the parent or guardian, stating the age, date, and place of birth of said child; if said child have no parent or guardian, then such affidavit shall be made by the child, which affidavit shall be kept on file by the employer, and which said register and affidavit shall be produced for inspection on demand by the inspector, assistant inspector, or any of the deputies appointed under this act. The factory inspector, assistant inspector, and deputy inspectors shall have power to demand a certificate of physical fitness from some regular physician of good standing in case of children who may appear to him or her physically unable to perform the labor at which they may be engaged, and shall have power to prohibit the employment of any minor that cannot obtain such a certificate.

§5. No female shall be employed in any factory or workshop more than eight hours in any one day, or forty-eight hours in any one week.

§6. Every person, firm, or corporation, agent or manager of a corporation, employing any female in any manufacturing establishment, factory, or workshop, shall post and keep posted in a conspicuous place in every room where such help is employed, a printed notice stating the hours for each day of the week between which work is required of such persons; and in every room where children under sixteen years of age are employed a list of their names, ages, and places of residence.

An immediate good result from the enforcement of §4 was that several hundred children under fourteen years of age were taken from the factories after the opening of the school year, September 1. In Chicago, a daily report of these children, giving their names, ages, and places of residence, was forwarded to the compulsory department of the Board of Education, that truant officers might see that the children did not go from the factory to the street, but to school. In "hardship" cases, where there was extreme poverty in the child's family, appeal was made for the child by the inspector to the School-Children's Aid Society, or some kindred organization.[1] Before the law of 1893 took effect, children seeking work in Chicago secured from the city Board of Education permits, the purport of which was that, for reasons deemed sufficient, the child was granted permission to work under fourteen years of age. As these permits were secured on the mere statement of child or parent, false statements were common; and we therefore found hundreds of children in factories who ought to have been in school. The law of 1893 applying only to workshops and factories, the Board of Education still issues permits for children under fourteen years of age to work in other than manufacturing occupations.

A second good result from our system of handling affidavits, and the requirements of the law regarding office registers and wall records, is that the number of children

---

1. No good result having followed these appeals, they are no longer made [1894].

employed between the ages of fourteen and sixteen years is somewhat reduced. Many children to whom age affidavits were issued in the first months of our work, were found to have been employed two, three, and four years, although not yet sixteen. To-day no employer in workshop or factory in Chicago wittingly puts to work a child under fourteen years of age, and some employers are refusing to hire any boy or girl who has not passed the age of sixteen. "They will not be bothered," they say, with employees who come under §§4 and 6 of the law.

The Working Child of the Nineteenth Ward.

The Nineteenth Ward of Chicago is perhaps the best district in all Illinois for a detailed study of child-labor, both because it contains many factories in which children are employed, and because it is the dwelling-place of wage-earning children engaged in all lines of activity.

The Ewing Street Italian colony furnishes a large contingent to the army of boot-blacks and newsboys; lads who leave home at 2.30 A.M. to secure the first edition of the morning paper, selling each edition as it appears, and filling the intervals with blacking boots and tossing pennies, until, in the winter half of the year, they gather in the Polk Street Night-School, to doze in the warmth, or torture the teacher with the gamin tricks acquired by clay. For them, school is "a lark," or a peaceful retreat from parental beatings and shrieking juniors at home during the bitter nights of the Chicago winter.

There is no body of self-supporting children more in need of effective care than these newsboys and bootblacks. They are ill-fed, ill-housed, ill-clothed, illiterate, and wholly untrained and unfitted for any occupation. The only useful thing they learn at their work in common with the children who learn in school, is the rapid calculation of small sums in making change; and this does not go far enough to be of any practical value. In the absence of an effective compulsory school-attendance law, they should at least be required to obtain a license from the city; and the granting of this license should be in the hands of the Board of Education, and contingent upon a certain amount of day-school attendance accomplished.

In this ward dwells, also, a large body of cash-children, boys and girls. Their situation is illustrated by the Christmas experience of one of their number. A little girl, thirteen years of age, saw in an evening paper of December 23d last, an advertisement for six girls to work in one of the best-known candy stores, candidates to apply at seven o'clock the next morning, at a branch store on the West Side, one and a half miles from the child's home. To reach the place in time, she spent five cents of her lunch money for car-fare. Arriving, she found other children, while but one was wanted. She was engaged as the brightest of the group, and sent to a down-town branch of the establishment, at a distance of two and a quarter miles. This time she walked; then worked till midnight, paying for her dinner, and going without supper. She was paid fifty cents, and discharged with the explanation that she was only required for one day.

No cars were running at that hour, and the little girl walked across the worst district of Chicago, to reach her home and her terrified mother at one o'clock on Christmas morning.[2] No law was violated in this transaction, as mercantile establishments are not yet subject to the provisions of the factory act.

Fortunately the development of the pneumatic tube has begun to supersede the cash-children in the more respectable of the retail stores; and a movement for extending the workshop law to the mercantile establishments would, therefore, meet with less opposition now than at any previous time. The need for this legislation will be acknowledged by every person who will stand on any one of the main thoroughfares of Chicago on a morning between 6.30 and 7.30 o'clock, and watch the processions of puny children filing into the drygoods emporiums to run, during nine or ten hours, and in holiday seasons twelve and thirteen hours, a day to the cry, "Cash!"

In the stores on the West Side, large numbers of young girls are employed thirteen hours a day throughout the week, and fifteen hours on Saturday; and all efforts of the clothing-clerks to shorten the working time by trade-union methods have hitherto availed but little. While the feeble unions of garment-makers have addressed themselves to the legislature, and obtained a valuable initial measure of protection for the young garment-workers, the retail-clerks, depending upon public opinion and local ordinances, have accomplished little on behalf of the younger clothing-sellers.

In dealing with newsboys, bootblacks, and cash-children, we have been concerned with those who live in the nineteenth ward, and work perhaps there or perhaps elsewhere. We come now to the children who work in the factories of the nineteenth ward.

The largest number of children to be found in any one factory in Chicago is in a caramel works in this ward, where there are from one hundred and ten to two hundred little girls, four to twelve boys, and seventy to one hundred adults, according to the season of the year. The building is a six-story brick, well lighted, with good plumbing and fair ventilation. It has, however, no fire escape, and a single wooden stair leading from floor to floor. In case of fire the inevitable fate of the children working on the two upper floors is too horrible to contemplate. The box factory is on the fifth floor, and the heaviest pressure of steam used in boiling the caramels is all on the top floor. The little girls sit closely packed at long tables, wrapping and packing the caramels. They are paid by the piece, and the number of pennies per thousand paid is just enough to attract the most ignorant and helpless children in the city.[3] Previous to the passage of the factory law of 1893, it was the rule of this factory to work the children, for several

---

2. Incidentally it is of interest that this firm was one of the most liberal givers of Christmas candy to the poor.

3. The affidavits of the children afford an astonishing collection of unpronounceable names, Polish and Bohemian combinations of consonants, interspersed with Smith. As there is rarely an English-speaking child in this factory, the prevalence of the Smiths was a matter of perplexity, until it transpired that notaries, troubled by the foreign orthography, suggest that the children call themselves by a more manageable name. This widespread custom greatly increases the difficulty of prosecutions for violation of the factory law in establishments in which the employees are drawn from the foreign colonies. And in the caramel works, with its polyglot population, the work of fitting the affidavits to the children is as laborious as it is absurd.

weeks before the Christmas holidays, from 7 A.M. to 9 P.M., with twenty minutes for lunch, and no supper, a working week of eighty-two hours. As this overtime season coincided with the first term of the night-school, the children lost their one opportunity. Since the enactment of the factory law, their working week has consisted of six days of eight hours each; a reduction of thirty-four hours a week.

Health.

It is a lamentable fact, well known to those who have investigated child-labor, that children are found in greatest number where the conditions of labor are most dangerous to life and health. Among the occupations in which children are most employed in Chicago, and which most endanger the health, are: The tobacco trade, nicotine poisoning finding as many victims among factory children as among the boys who are voluntary devotees of the weed, consumers of the deadly cigarette included; frame gilding, in which work a child's fingers are stiffened and throat disease is contracted; buttonholing, machine-stitching, and hand-work in tailor or sweat shops, the machine-work producing spinal curvature, and for girls pelvic disorders also, while the unsanitary condition of the shops makes even hand-sewing dangerous; bakeries, where children slowly roast before the ovens; binderies, paper-box and paint factories, where arsenical paper, rotting paste, and the poison of the paints are injurious; boiler-plate works, cutlery works, and metal-stamping works, where the dust produces lung disease; the handling of hot metal, accidents; the hammering of plate, deafness. In addition to diseases incidental to trades, there are the conditions of bad sanitation and long hours, almost universal in the factories where children are employed.

The power of the Illinois inspectors, so far as they have any power to require that only healthy children shall be employed, and these only in safe and healthy places, is found in §4 of the Workshop and Factories Act, the last clause, already quoted. What may be accomplished under this section is indicated by the following report concerning medical examinations in the inspector's office, made for the boys by Dr. Bayard Holmes, of the College of Physicians and Surgeons; and for the girls by Dr. Josephine Milligan, resident physician at Hull-House:—

During four months 135 factory children were given medical examinations in the office. The inspectors required these children to secure health certificates because they were undersized, or seemed to be ill, or were working in unwholesome shops, or at dangerous occupations. They were children sworn by their parents to be fourteen years of age, or over.

Each child was weighed with and without clothing; had eyes and ears tested; heart, lungs, skin, spine, joints, and nails examined; and forty measurements taken.

Of the 135 children, 72 were found sufficiently normal to be allowed to continue work. Of the 63 refused certificates, 53 were not allowed to work at all, and 10 were stopped working at unwholesome trades, as tobacco-stripping, grinding in cutlery factory, running machines by foot-power, and crimping cans; these were advised to look for more wholesome work.

Of those to whom certificates were refused, 29 were undersized, otherwise normal; i.e., the parents had probably forsworn themselves as to the children's ages.

Certificates were refused because of defects to 34, or 26¹⁄₁₀ per cent of the number examined. Several diseases often exist in the same child. There were 14 children with spinal curvatures, 12 with heart murmurs, 6 with lung trouble, 24 with enlarged glands, 25 with defective sight, 6 with defective hearing, and 56 with defective teeth.

The examination of girls resulted as follows:—

From sweat-shops, 30 examined: 5 had spinal curvature; 1, an organic lesion of the heart (mitral insufficiency); 2, irritable hearts; 2 were anemic, and of these 1 had also incipient phthisis.

From tobacco factories, 11 examined: 1 had spinal curvature; 1, enlarged glands in neck and axilla; 2, defective sight.

From baking-powder factory, 8 examined: 1 had spinal curvature; 1, enlarged glands; 2, defective sight and slight deafness; 1 had sore hands from using crimping-machine; 1 had mutilated forefinger from a swedging-machine.

From feather-duster factories, 7 examined: 2 had enlarged glands in the neck.

From gum factory, 4 examined: 1 had spinal curvature.

From candy factories, 16 examined: 2 had diseases of the skin.

From bookbinderies, 4 examined: 1 was anemic; 1 had enlarged glands in the neck.

From necktie factory, 1 examined: heart murmur.

From yeast factory, 1 examined: normal.

From cracker bakery, 1 examined: undersized, otherwise normal.

From box factory, 1 examined: had organic lesion of the heart.

From popcorn factory, 1 examined: anemic.

Total number of girls examined, 85; certificates granted, 50; certificate refused, 35.
The examination of boys resulted as follows:—

From sweat-shops, 6 examined: 3 had spinal curvature; 1, hernia; 2, enlarged glands.

From cutlery factory, 12 examined: 5 had enlarged glands; 3, tuberculosis; 2, spinal curvature.

From tobacco factories, 9 examined: 4 had enlarged glands.

From metal-stamping factories, 10 examined: 2 had enlarged glands; 1, bronchitis; 1, tuberculosis; 1, spinal curvature; 1, syphilis.

From picture-frame factories, 3 examined: 1 was anemic and had enlarged glands; 1, tuberculosis.

From candy factories, 2 examined: 1 had skin eruption.

From cracker bakery, 1 examined: had phthisis.

From photographic enlargement shop, 1 examined: was anemic and scrofulous.

From glass-sign shop, shoe-shop, cabinet-shop, organ-factory, 1 boy in each: found normal.

Not working, 2 examined: found normal.

Total number of boys examined, 50; certificates granted, 22; certificates refused, 28.

This record, formed in four months by volunteer work done by two busy physicians in the intervals of private practice, indicates an appalling deterioration of the rising generation of the wage-earning class. The human product of our industry is an army of toiling children, undersized, rachitic, deformed, predisposed to consumption, if not already tubercles. Permanently enfeebled by the labor imposed upon them during the critical years of development, these children will inevitably fail in the early years of manhood and womanhood. They are now a long way upon the road to becoming burdens upon society, lifelong victims of the poverty of their childhood, and the greed which sacrifices the sacred right of children to school-life and healthful leisure.

Of the reckless employment of children in injurious occupations the following are examples:—

Jaroslav Huptuk, a feeble-minded dwarf, whose affidavit shows him to be nearly sixteen years of age. This child weighed and measured almost exactly the same as a normal boy aged eight years and three months. Jaroslav can neither read nor write in any language, nor speak a consecutive sentence. Besides being dwarfed, he is so deformed as to be a monstrosity. Yet, with all these disqualifications for any kind of work, he has been employed for several years at an emery-wheel in a cutlery works in the nineteenth ward, finishing knife-blades and bone handles, until, in addition to his other misfortunes, he is now tuberculous. Dr. Holmes, having examined this boy, pronounced him unfit for work of any kind. His mother appealed from this to a medical college, where, however, the examining physician not only refused the lad a medical certificate of physical fitness for work, but exhibited him to the students as a monstrosity worthy of careful observation.

The kind of grinding at which this boy was employed has been prohibited in England for minors since 1863, by reason of the prevalence of grinders' phthisis among those who begin the work young. And no boy, however free from Huptuk's individual disabilities, can grow up a strong man in this nineteenth ward cutlery, because no officer of the State can require the walls to be whitewashed, and the grinding and finishing rooms to be ventilated with suction pipes for withdrawing steel and bone dust from the atmosphere, as it is the duty of the English inspectors to do in English cutleries employing only adults.

Joseph Poderovsky, aged fourteen years, was found by a deputy inspector running a heavy buttonhole machine by foot-power at 204 West Taylor Street, in the shop of Michael Freeman. The child was required to report for examination, and pronounced by the examining physician, rachitic, and afflicted with a double lateral curvature of the spine. He was ordered discharged, and prohibited from working in any tailor-shop. A few days later he was found at work at the same machine. A warrant was sworn out for the arrest of the employer; but before it could be served the man left the State. This boy has a father in comfortable circumstances, and two adult able-bodied brothers.

Bennie Kelman, Russian Jew, four years in Chicago, was found running a heavy sewing-machine by footpower in a sweat-shop of the nineteenth ward where knee-pants are made. A health certificate was required, and the medical examination revealed a severe rupture. Careful questioning of the boy and his mother elicited the fact that he had been put to work in a boiler factory two years before, when just thirteen years old, and had injured himself lifting heavy masses of iron. Nothing had been done for the case; no one in the family spoke any English, or knew how help could be obtained. The sight test showed that the boy did not know his letters in English, though he said that he could read Jewish jargon. He was sent to the College of Physicians and Surgeons for treatment, and forbidden work.

If health certificates are granted to wage-earning children merely *pro forma,* upon the representation of the employer or the child, the object of the law is nullified. The physician who grasps the situation, and appreciates the humane intent of the law, will always find time to visit the factory and see under what conditions the child is working. Otherwise his certificate may be worse than valueless, and work a positive injury to a child whom the inspectors are trying to save from an injurious occupation. Thus, a healthy child may wish to enter a cracker bakery; and unless the physician visits it, and sees the dwarfish boys slowly roasting before the ovens, in the midst of unguarded belting and shafting, a danger to health which men refuse to incur, he may be inclined to grant the certificate, and thereby deprive the child of the only safeguard to health which the State affords him. Similar danger exists in regard to tobacco, picture-frame, box, metal-stamping, and wood-working factories.

The following example of the reckless issuance of certificates is of interest here, the child being a resident of the nineteenth ward, employed in this ward, and receiving the certificates to be subsequently quoted from physicians living and practising in this ward:—

Annie Cihlar, a delicate-looking little girl, was found working at 144 West Taylor Street, in a badly ventilated tailor-shop, in a building in the rear of a city lot, with windows on an alley, and a tenement house in front. The bad location and atmosphere of the shop, and the stooping position of the child over her work, led the inspector to demand a health certificate. Examination at the inspector's office revealed rachitis and an antero-posterior curvature of the spine, one shoulder an inch higher than the other, and the child decidedly below the standard weight. Dr. Milligan indorsed upon the age affidavit: "It is my opinion this child is physically incapable of working in any tailor-shop." The employer was notified to discharge the child. A few days later she was found at work in the same place, and the contractor produced the following certificate, written upon the prescription blank of a physician in good and regular standing: "This is to certify that, I have examined Annie Cihlar, and found her in a physiological condition." A test case was made to ascertain the value of the medical certificate clause, and the judge decided that this certificate was void, and imposed a fine upon the employer for failing to obtain a certificate in accordance with the wording of the law. The child then went to another physician, and obtained the following certificate: "To whom it may concern: This is to certify that I have this day examined

Annie Cihlar, and find her, in my opinion, healthy. She is well-developed for her age; muscular system in good condition; muscles are hard and solid; lungs and heart are normal. The muscles of right side of trunk are better developed than upon the left side, which has a tendency to draw spine to that side. I cannot find no desease [*sic*] of the spine." The sweater, taught by experience, declined to re-engage this child until this certificate was approved by the inspector, and the inspector of course refused to approve it.

Danger of Mutilation and Death.

Not always, however, does the illiteracy of a physician afford an opportunity to have a certificate issued by him declared worthless. If the certificate formally meets the requirement of the law,—the child must be left at work, no matter what the effect upon its health, present and future. The same is true where inspectors have tried to save children from danger to life and limb, by requiring health certificates for them when found working amidst dangerous machinery. There is in the Illinois law no provision for the safeguarding of machinery; and if a physician issues a certificate to a child merely because it is for the moment in good health, with no knowledge of the dangerous occupation of the child, the inspector, under the present law, is powerless. An example is afforded by a stamping-factory of this ward. The inspector called the attention of the head of the firm to the danger to which employees were subjected, because of unguarded shafting and machinery, and required a health certificate for every minor employed there. A week later a deputy inspector went to this factory, and found twenty-five health certificates, in proper form, on file. One of these certificates was already superfluous. The boy for whom it had been obtained had been killed in the factory the day before. Within two years two boys have been killed outright, and several mutilated in this factory. The last boy killed had lost three fingers at his machine only a few months before his death.

One machine used in the stamping-works consists of an endless chain revolving over a trough filled with melted solder. In this trough cans are kept moving in unbroken procession, revolving as they go. At each end of the trough stands a boy with a little iron poker, made for the purpose of keeping the cans in their places and pulling them out at the end. But the poker is not always quick enough, and the boy's hand is apt to get into contact with the melting fluid. In preparation for this danger the lads wrap their hands before beginning work; but this precaution is only good for minor burns, and the real danger to the child is that he may lose a hand outright. This machine has been superseded in the stamping-works of more progressive manufacturers by a self-actor, which may be made free from danger to an employee; but this is expensive, and children of the class employed at the stamping-works are so thoroughly defenceless by reason of poverty and ignorance of the laws and language of the country, that the company finds it cheaper to use the old-fashioned machine, and take the risk of damage suits, than to pay for the more modern solderer. The metal-stamping trade, like the candy, paper-box, and garment trades, is without organization, and the children employed in it suffer accordingly. This company employs a large body of recently immigrated Russian and Bohemian men, boys, and girls, many of whom are wholly illiterate; and even if they can read their own language, this is of little avail for reading the terms of the contract, printed in English, under which they are employed, or the card of directions which each one is required to carry in his or her pocket, in order that the company may prove, in case of injury to an employee, that notice of the danger had been given, and that the injury was therefore no fault of the company, but solely due to the recklessness of the boy or girl.

Of the rules printed on these cards, one reads as follows:—

> 11. All employees are strictly forbidden placing their hands under the dies; and all employees, other than those whose duty it is to repair or clean machines, are strictly forbidden to place their hands or any part of their body in contact with or within reach of those portions of the machinery intended to be in motion when the machinery is in operation, or in contact with, or in reach of the shafting; and this applies to machinery in operation and not in operation. It is dangerous to disobey this rule.

For middle-aged men, self-possessed and cautious, able to read these rules and ponder them, it would still be a grewsome thought that the penalty of violation may be instant death; but where the employees are growing lads, many of them unable to read at all, and all at the age when risk is enticing, and the most urgent warning is often a stimulus to wayward acts, what excuse can be offered for supplying machinery lacking in any most trifling essential of safeguard? Yet these rules themselves announce that the surroundings of these boys are so fraught with danger, that a whole code of fourteen rules and regulations is needful to protect the pockets of the company in the probable event of injury to the children. There are other wealthy corporations and firms in Chicago to-day holding contracts with the parents or guardians of employed children, and with casualty insurance companies, releasing the employers from liability in case of accident to the child. Does any one suppose that an employer would hold such contracts—unless accidents to children in his employ were numerous, and might be made costly?

Ingenious safeguards are a part of the construction of machinery in modern plants; but many factories are operated without such improvements, and expose employees, old and young, to constant danger of death or mutilation. Even where the latest patents in safeguarding are found, accidents are possible if operators are careless. In a factory where accidents are of almost daily occurrence among the children employed, we are told, "They never get hurt till they get careless." This is no doubt true; but if it be offered as an excuse for the mutilation of children, it is an aggravation of, rather than an excuse for, the crime against the child. To be care-free is one of the prerogatives of childhood.

Migration of the Children.

Nothing in our work has been more of a revelation than the migratory method pursued by the children, which forever disposes of the only argument in favor of child-labor that before seemed valid; namely, that the work afforded a sort of industrial education for the boy or girl who must depend upon manual labor for livelihood in adult years. They talk with insufficient knowledge who say it is an advantage to boys and girls to work because they have "a steady occupation," a "chance to learn a trade." The places where boys and girls are learning trades are the exception. The places where fortunes are being built up by employing them in droves are the ones where most of them are found working. In these the condition of work and wages is so unsatisfactory that employment in them is a mere makeshift. One place will be no better than another, and one change will follow another. It is not a trade that is learned in the great workshops where child-labor is the foundation of a company's riches. What the child does learn is instability, unthrift, trifling with opportunity.

On Aug. 23, 1893, an inspection of a candy factory showed 80 children employed under sixteen years. Their affidavits were examined, 63 of them were found correct, and were so stamped; and 17 children unprovided with affidavits were sent home. On September 8 another inspector found 71 children at work in this factory, with 65 affidavits awaiting inspection, only one of which had the stamp of the previous inspection. The 70 children were a new lot, and all but one of those at work there two weeks before had flitted off to other work. In the same factory on September 11, three days later,—and one of these a Sunday,—a third inspector found 119 children at work, and, of course, another lot of affidavits, requiring the employer to make new wall records and a new office register. This candy manufacturer now aims to employ only girls over sixteen years. He will find plenty of them anxious to obtain work; but he cannot get them at four and one-half cents an hour, which is the average wage of the little children employed in this trade.

It is a matter of the rarest occurrence to find a set of children who have been working together two months in any factory. They are here to-day and gone tomorrow; and, while their very instability saves them from the specific poison of each trade, it promises an army of incapables, to be supported as tramps and paupers. The child who handles arsenical paper in a box factory long enough, becomes a hopeless invalid. The boy who gilds cheap frames with mercurial gilding, loses the use of his arm, and acquires incurable throat troubles. The tobacco girls suffer nicotine poisoning; the foot-power sewing-machine girl is a lifelong victim of pelvic disorders. But the boy or girl who drifts through all these occupations, learning no one trade, earning no steady wage, forming no lasting associations, must end as a shiftless bungler, Jack-of-all-trades, master of none, ruined in mind and character, as the more abiding worker is enfeebled or crippled in body.

There are factories in which dissolute adults are employed among children, and sow their moral pestilence unchecked; where petty bosses tempt young girls to evil courses, and the example of trifling favors shown one weak girl who yields demoralizes many more. There are factories where the very sanitary arrangements expose children to temptation and to disease, and the rules violate their natural modesty. There are factories in which children are worked into the late evening hours, and then turned out unprotected, to seek their homes by streets where the immoral side of life is at such hours openly flaunted, and vicious lures draw the unwary feet of tired boys and girls down to moral death. There are factories in which the entire roll of female help is made up of young girls, and these girls are grouped at work with men so vile that the presence of a woman of mature years scarcely serves to check their ribaldry. There are factories where one of the hourly occupations of little boys and girls is to run to a beer saloon with the pails of the older workmen. These are mere outlines of what the factory inspector sees and knows of the environment of a child in the class of factories owned by employers who batten on child-labor.

Causes and Remedies.

While it is true, as has been shown, that the industries of Illinois are essentially men's trades, yet there are here, as in all American industrial communities, occupations employing almost no men, trades known as "baby-trades." These are the candy, the tobacco and snuff, and the paper-box trades. Although in the wood and metal trades, thanks to the powerful organizations of men, the number of children relatively to men is small, yet certain branches, and certain factories within these branches, employ children in peculiarly injurious ways.

It has been found in the case of the cutlery and stamping works that some of the children working for wages are orphans and half-orphans, but a large majority are the children of men employed in industries without strong labor organizations, such as laborers, lumber-shovers, or employees in the garment trades. In an incredibly large proportion of cases, the fathers of young wage-earning children not only do not support the family, but are themselves supported by it, being superannuated early in the forties by the exhaustion characteristic of the garment trades, or the rheumatism of the ditcher and sewer-digger, and various other sorts of out-door workers; or by that loss of a limb which is regarded as a regular risk in the building-trades and among railroad hands. Long years of consumption make hundreds of fathers burdens on their younger children. Some of the children, however, principally Italians, Bohemians, and Germans, are sent to work by their parents out of sheer excess of thrift, perhaps in order to pay off a mortgage upon some tenement house. In hundreds of cases during 1893–1894 the children left school and went to work because the father, previously the sole support of the family, was now among the unemployed. This is a lasting injury wrought by every industrial crisis; for the children so withdrawn from school are ashamed to return, after prolonged absence, to a lower class; and, having tasted the excitement of factory-life and partial self-support, are unfitted for anything else. The growth of child-labor during these months has been very marked, the demand for children increasing in the universal effort to reduce expenses by cutting wages; so that it was a matter of common remark that in any given trade in which children were employed, that factory was busiest which employed fewest adults. In general, however, it remains true, that in the industries of Illinois there is no need in the nature of the work to be performed for any characteristic quality of children. The presence of the children in the industries is more by reason of poverty of their families than of any technical requirements of the industries themselves. Everything done by children under sixteen years of age could be quite as swiftly done by young people between sixteen and eighteen years. As has already been indicated, the question of child-labor in Illinois is primarily a question of the wages of the fathers of families in the unorganized trades; and, secondarily, it is a consequence of the premature disablement of the men upon whom the support of the children would normally fall.

Where a trade is well organized, few children are to be found at work in it. But where a trade is in the hands of women, it is never strongly organized; and the women neither keep the children out of the shops nor demand and obtain wholesome conditions of work. This is conspicuously true in the garment trades, in which women and children outnumber the men by two to one; while hours are longer, sanitary conditions are inferior, and the amount of work required disproportionate to the strength of the workers, to a greater degree than is true in any other occupation. If no child under sixteen were employed after to-morrow, there would be a marked difference in certain limited trades in which the labor of fourteen-year-old children abounds. But it is doubtful whether there would be a perceptible rise in wages, because of the total lack of organization among the girls between sixteen and twenty with whom the children have hitherto competed, and who would merely be somewhat increased in number in consequence of the discharge of the children. It is for the sake of the children themselves that they should be removed from the labor market and kept in school, far more than for the sake of the effect that they have upon the condition of the adults with whom they compete.

If, however, we take this ground, that the prohibition of child-labor is a humanitarian measure, to be adopted in the interest of the children themselves, we must then be consistent, and make provision for them, so that they shall not suffer hardship worse than that from which we aim to shield them. We have seen that the trades in which children abound are the most injurious and least suitable for them. The wages paid children range from 40 cents a week to $4.00 a week, taking the whole 6,576 children together.

In some cases, undoubtedly, in which a young child is withdrawn from work by the law, an older brother or sister steps into the place thus left vacant. But this compensation does not always take place in the same family, and the deficit would have to be made good in many cases. Why should this not be accomplished by means of scholarships in the upper-grade grammar schools and manual-training schools, just as the scholarships are provided to-day in universities and theological seminaries? Would not

CHART I.

MEASUREMENTS OF 154 DEFECTIVE CHICAGO FACTORY-CHILDREN—14-16 YEARS OLD.

The above charts were made by Bayard Holmes, B. S., M.D., from measurements taken in 1893-4, in the office of Mrs. Kelley, State Factory Inspector, of Illinois.

CHART I.

The first fifteen squares in each row, reading from left to right, contain the measurements of ten children each, the sixteenth square contains four. The measurements of the individual child are found directly over each other.

CHART II.

Porter's averages were made on 30,000 school children of St. Louis. The lighter lines represent these averages, and the darker those of the factory children. Both were made in the same year.

CHART II.

Porter's Average, Boys 14-16

is 25 Percentile 14-16 Boys

Weight in Pounds

Porter's Average, 14-16 Boys
His 25 Percentile, Boys 14-16

Height in Inches

Shoulder

Sternum

Porter's Av. Chest of Boys 14-16

Sitting

Chest

Head

Knee

Neck

SUMMARY OF CHART I.

such provision be vastly cheaper in the end than the care of the consumptive young grinders? or than the provision which will be inevitably required for the support of the cripples turned out by the stamping-works? or than the maintenance of the families of those who will be superannuated at thirty-five, because they are now allowed to do in the clothing-shops the work of men, in the years when they ought to be laying up a store of energy to last a normal lifetime?

The key to the child-labor question is the enforcement of school attendance to the age of sixteen, and the granting of such ample help to the poorest of the working children as shall make our public schools not class institutions, but in deed and in truth the schools of the people, by the people, for the people. Only when every child is known to be in school can there be any security against the tenement-house labor of children in our great cities.

The legislation needed is of the simplest but most comprehensive description. We need to have: (1) The minimum age for work fixed at sixteen; (2) School attendance made compulsory to the same age; (3) Factory inspectors and truant officers, both men and women, equipped with adequate salaries and travelling expenses, charged with the duty of removing children from mill and workshop, mine and store, and placing them at school; (4) Ample provision for school accommodations; money supplied by the State through the school authorities for the support of such orphans, half orphans, and children of the unemployed as are now kept out of school by destitution.

Where they are, the wage-earning children are an unmitigated injury to themselves, to the community upon which they will later be burdens, and to the trade which they demoralize. They learn nothing valuable; they shorten the average of the trade life, and they lower the standard of living of the adults with whom they compete.

Bibliography of Child-Labor in the United States.

Third Special Report of United States Commissioner of Labor, 1893, pp. 254–258. References cover official data to Nov. 30, 1892.

Report Chief of Massachusetts District Police, 1893.

New York Factory Inspector's Report, 1893.

Illinois Factory Inspector's Report, 1893.

Report Convention International Factory Inspectors' Association, 1893.

Symposium on Child Labor, *Arena,* June, 1894: Assistant Inspector Stevens of Illinois; Miss Alice L. Woodbridge, Secretary New York Working Women's Society; and Prof. Thomas E. Will.

Factory Children—White Child Slavery, Helen Campbell and others, *Arena,* i. 589.

Prisoners of Poverty, Helen Campbell, Boston, 1887.

Labor of Children, W. F. Willoughby and Clare de Graffenreld, American Economic Association, v. 5.

Our Toiling Children, F. K. Wischnewetzky, pamphlet; Women's Christian Temperance Publishing Association, 1889.

Report of Connecticut Bureau of Labor Statistics, 1889.

IV

RECEIPTS AND EXPENDITURES OF CLOAKMAKERS IN CHICAGO, COMPARED WITH THOSE OF THAT TRADE IN NEW YORK[1]

Isabel Eaton
Dutton Fellow, College Settlements Association

As a basis of comparison in studying the conditions of the cloakmaking trade in the two cities, the New York figures are given first. The information in both cases has been obtained at first-hand from the unions and through a tour of the sweat-shops, as well as by the assistance of certain leading workingmen of unquestionable trustworthiness within these trades.

New York.

The computations in New York were made on one hundred and fifty schedules, indicating the following averages of income and expense of living:—

Regular weekly wage previous to 1893	$11.65
Fallen in 1893–1894 to	4.92
Regular yearly income of family (of 4.4 persons)	323.07
Fallen in 1893–1894 to	127.92
Regular weekly income (distinguished from weekly wage)[2]	6.21
Fallen in 1893–1894 to	2.46

---

1. Taken from material collected during three months' residence at Hull-House.

2. *Weekly wage* should be distinguished from *weekly income,* the first being the average amount earned in a week of the working-season, while the second is $\frac{1}{52}$ of the yearly income. As the working-year seldom lasts more than eight months, the weekly income would range from two-thirds ($\frac{8}{12}$) of the weekly wage downward. This eight months' working-year accounts also for the fact that the yearly income (including wages and other sources of income) appears to be less than a reckoning based on weekly wages alone would show. The apparent discrepancy between the amounts reported as weekly wages and those reported as yearly incomes clears itself up at once, in view of the eight months' working-year.

The one hundred and fifty schedules embraced information as to the number of cloakmakers who increase their income by taking lodgers, or by other methods.

The number thus having increased incomes amounted to 26% of the whole, and the regular yearly income thus increased was, previous to 1893, $455.19; fallen in 1893 and 1894 to $260.04.

Weekly income of this 26%, $8.75; fallen in 1893–1894 to $5.00. Average number in family, 4.4 persons.

The following tabular statement relates to average incomes:—

Average yearly individual income	$73.43
Average weekly individual income	1.41
Average yearly individual income of the 26% having increased incomes, previous to 1893	103.45
Average weekly individual income of the 26% having increased incomes, previous to 1893	1.98
Average yearly income of individual for the year 1893–1894	29.12
Average weekly income of individual for the year 1893–1894	.56

Months in the working year, 6.4.
Daily hours of work (reported), 12.3.[3]

The following shows the cost of living:—

Average yearly cost of food for a family of 4.4 persons ($5.60 a week)	$291.20
Average yearly cost of clothing for a family of 4.4 persons	56.24
Average yearly rent ($10.31 a month)	123.72

Average number of rooms, 2.7.
Percentage of total income spent in rent, previous to 1893, 38%.
Percentage of total income spent in rent during 1893–1894, when practically no cloaks were made, 96%.[4]

Of 150 persons scheduled, 67% reported indebtedness.

Chicago.

In Chicago, Mr. Abram Bisno, for ten years a cloakmaker, at present a State deputy factory inspector, has made a careful study of conditions in his trade, and for that purpose made averages on the wage record-books of 250 cloakmakers in his union. These wage recordbooks give amounts actually paid through an entire year to each of 250 cloakmakers. The yearly incomes so obtained ranged between $408, the lowest, to $450, the highest amount earned in a year by machine-workers in the trade. The

---

3. The Secretary of the Union in New York states that the average of daily hours in the season is more than sixteen.

4. In many cases the computations show $108 yearly rent, and between $75 and $100 yearly earnings, these being, of course, cases of men who have been out of work ten months or more.

average was very near $430. The amount earned by hand-workers is less. Their yearly incomes range between $300 and $350, the average being very near $325. The wages paid to girls employed in the trade are $6.50 or $7.00 weekly. Obtaining from this estimate a mean wage, and computing from it the yearly income, gives $236.25 as the average yearly income of girls in the cloak trade.

The following table gives weekly wage, yearly income, and weekly income, based on the two hundred and fifty wage record-books already referred to:—

CLOAKMAKERS IN CHICAGO.	YEARLY INCOME.	WEEKLY WAGE.	WEEKLY INCOME.
Machine Work	$430.00	$12.28	$8.27
Hand-workers on Cloaks	325.00	9.29	6.25
Girls employed as finishers	236.25	6.75	4.54
Average rec'd by those engaged in the trade	330.42	9.44	6.35

This may properly be followed by a table of computations comparing the yearly income of cloakmakers in Chicago (family men and single men being given together, as they get practically the same wages in this city) with the yearly expenditure of family men and of single men separately:

Yearly income of cloakmakers in Chicago (family men and single men)	$330.42
Yearly expenditure of cloakmakers (family men)	440.04
Yearly expenditure of cloakmakers (single men)	255.44

This table represents current rates paid before the panic of 1893; but during the extreme depression of trade following this panic, the pay of garment workers in nearly every branch of the trade, and in the cloak making trade among others, was cut down about one half. This statement is supported by the following definite enumeration of prices paid to workmen before and after the panic. A plush cloak for which the tailor received $1.25 before the crisis, in August, 1894, brought 65 or 75 cents. A street jacket which formerly brought the tailor 45 cents, brought in August, 1894, 25 cents. One that brought 65 cents, brought in August, 1894, 35 cents. A coat which brought $1.12, brought in August, 1894, 72½ cents; and an overcoat which formerly paid the tailor $2.75, brought in August, 1894, $1.40 to $1.50.

In contrast with these half-rates of 1893–1894, wages in October, 1894, when all the shops resumed work, under unusual pressure, show a rise which is a slight advance even on the usual rate. The following table of averages, based on one hundred records taken in October, 1894, from Hull-House, indicates cloakmakers' wages, rents, and number in debt. The wages will be seen to run slightly in advance even of the regular wages, previous to 1893–1894:—

AVERAGE No. IN FAMILY.	AVERAGE No. OF WORKERS IN FAMILY.	AVERAGE PRESENT WAGE.	AVERAGE YEARLY INCOME AT THIS RATE.	AVERAGE WEEKLY INCOME AT THIS RATE.	HOURS REPORTED.	MONTHS EMPLOYED THIS YEAR.	No. OF ROOMS.	RENT.	AVERAGE NUMBER IN DEBT.
4.77	1.19	$9.59	$335.65	$6.45	11	4.38	3.41	$8.47	52%

Mr. Bisno's estimate that the length of the working year in the cloakmaking trade is "usually about eight months in Chicago, but has only been four months or less during 1893–1894," agrees with this table; and the average wage as here reckoned will also be seen to agree with the average wage which he reports. The yearly incomes also show $330.42 in the case of the two hundred and fifty records taken by Mr. Bisno, and $335.65 in the one hundred schedules taken from Hull-House in October, 1894. Both yearly amounts will be seen to agree quite closely with the New York yearly total of $323.07. The Chicago cloakmaker thus has the advantage of the New Yorker, and a further advantage, as will be seen when rents come under consideration.

Hours of Work.

In this regard there appears to be little difference in the two cities. However, it seems impossible to get the truth. An occasional reckless spirit will tell his real hours, even when contradicted by the sweater; but usually before answering, the workman looks at the sweater, who stands behind the statistician's shoulder (ostensibly interested in examining his record), and from him seems to discover in one glance how to compute his daily hours. They are generally ten or twelve when so given. On coming out of a sweating-establishment in New York, Mr. Glass, who is secretary of the New York Cloakmakers' Union, would frequently say, "That was all right but the hours. They all lie about the hours." Mr. Goldberg, an ex-officer of the United Garment Workers, says, "They won't tell any one, even their neighbors, the hour they begin work, and the amount they take home to do." At another time he said, "If a man (doing task-work) works from five o'clock until midnight, he can do a 'day's work' in a day." He says, "They always begin at five o'clock"; and Mr. Osias Rosenthal, secretary of the Knee Pants Union, says, "If you look into the streets any morning at four o'clock you will see them full of people going to work. They raise themselves up at three o'clock, and are often at their machines at four. The latest is sure to be there at five. The general time is five o'clock all the year around in good times, winter and summer; and if the boss will give them gaslight some will go even earlier than three o'clock."

In regard to extreme cases of long hours Mr. Glass says the following: "I know a man who works in this place we are passing, and the way they do there is this: they work all the week except part of a holiday Saturday; but they come back Saturday afternoon and work until four o'clock in the morning, to make up for the holiday." He says this is the usual thing in this particular Bowery sweat-shop. In speaking of this friend of his he said further: "Once he told me that he had been working thirty-eight hours steady. He went to work Thursday morning at seven, and did not come home until Friday night at nine." In talking to Mr. Jensen, for many years secretary of the Custom Tailors' Union in Chicago, I learned in regard to hours that "It takes from forty-five to fifty hours for a custom-tailor to make a dress coat; but when it has to be done at a certain time they will often work forty-eight hours at a time."—"You don't mean at one sitting, do you?—"Yes."—"Have you ever done that yourself?"—"Yes."—"How often ?"—"I did it the first time when I was fourteen, and I can't tell you how often since,—many times since; but I have not kept account of the times, because it is a common thing."

Mr. Bisno says that in Chicago during the busy season there is no limit; that men frequently work all night, and that even in the slack season there are those who work fifteen and sixteen hours daily,—from 5 A.M. to 9 P.M.

Indebtedness.

Mr. Ehrenpreis of the Chicago Cutters' Union agrees with others in saying that among the Chicago garment workers "every man is in debt." He is "owing the grocer and the butcher, and generally the pawn-shop too." The pawnbroker in Chicago is far worse than in New York, which fact is accounted for by the lack of proper legislation in the former city. The following case came under the notice of a Hull-House resident, during the winter of 1893–1894: a loan of $25 made on household furniture was drawing $2 a week interest, and at the time that Hull-House bought up this mortgage, $42 had already been paid for a little over four months' use of $25; that is to say, the broker was taking interest on the loan at the rate of 416 percent yearly. Those who are familiar with the condition among garment workers in Chicago during the winter of 1893–1894, agree that it is impossible that so small a percentage as 52 percent should be in debt. Statistics on indebtedness must be distrusted, under whatever circumstances they may be given.

Single men in Chicago have not yet resorted in the same degree as in New York to cutting under the family man in the matter of wages, so that their yearly income is practically the same as that of married men; but their living costs are much less, so that it is the exception when the single man is not solvent. For board and lodging, which they customarily engage at the same place, they pay, on the average, $3.95 a week, $17.12 a month, and with the additional item of $50 for clothing, which here, as in New York, appears to be very near the average, amounts to $255.44 for living expenses in the year. Setting this against the single man's yearly income of $330.42, shows a balance to his credit of $74.98. Figuring on the New York basis of expenditure for food and clothing for a family of 4.4, we have for a Chicago family of 4.77, a weekly expenditure for food and clothing amounting to $7.15, which, augmented by the monthly rent paid in Chicago, $8.47, shows a total of $37.07 monthly expense of a family. A comparison of this yearly expenditure with the average yearly income of $330.42, shows the Chicago cloakmaker a bankrupt to the extent of $114.42, while the shortage in the case of the New York cloakmaker is $148.09,—an advantage of about $30 to the Chicagoan.

Rents.

The dwelling-rooms of the cloakmakers in Chicago are better than those in New York in point of size and facilities for light and ventilation. Three hundred and fifty-two records of rent and number of rooms, taken on Bunker and De Koven Streets in Chicago, irrespective of the trades of the occupants, show the average number of rooms to be 3.46. The average rent for this number of rooms is $8.05. The Chicagoan pays $8.05 where the New Yorker pays $10, and gets three and a half rooms where the New Yorker gets two and a half. This would make the percentage of cloakmakers' total income going for rent in Chicago, 29 percent, as opposed to 38 percent in New York. A comparison of these percentages with the approved percentage of income paid for rent in France, and that accepted by our own Labor Department, which is $14\frac{2}{3}$ percent of the total income, leads inevitably to the conclusion that there is something very seriously wrong in the proportion of rent and wages in the cloakmaking trade.

V

THE CHICAGO GHETTO

Charles Zeublin

Two families constituted the Jewish population of Chicago in 1843, when the first refugees from the German persecution of 1830–1840 found their way to Illinois. The Jewish Colonization Society had purchased a hundred and sixty acres of land at Shaumburg, Cook County; but only a few of the settlers took farms. Those who located in Chicago organized the first Jewish religious society in 1845. The history of the religious organizations forms the history of the colony for many years. In 1848 a society was chartered under the name Kehillath Anshé Maariv (Congregation of the Men of Obscurity [Congregation of the Men of the West]). The first religious services were held at the corner of Lake and Wells Streets. In 1849 a synagogue was erected on Clark Street, between Quincy and Jackson. It was from the ranks of the Kehillath Anshé Maariv Congregation that Reform Judaism in Chicago sprung. A few young men in this congregation formed a society called the Reform Association, to introduce changes into the services and doctrines. Unsuccessful in this, they seceded in 1861, and organized the Sinai Congregation, the first Chicago organization of Reform Judaism.

The location of the synagogues marks the region occupied by the Jewish colony. Before the fire they were situated in what is now the chief business district of the city. A whole chapter of social development might be found in the fact that the leading wholesale houses of the prosperous and influential Jews of Chicago mark the former site of the homes of the refugees from Germany; while the earlier "houses of prayer," on South Clark Street, have literally yielded to "dens of thieves." The dispersion, which took place as a result of the fire of 1871, was already presaged by the removal of many of the Jewish families to the West Side, as is indicated by the purchase of a church building on Desplaines Street, between Madison and Washington Streets, in 1864, by the newly organized Zion Congregation, and by their removal in 1869 to an edifice of their own, at the corner of Jackson and Sangamon Streets. Previous to 1871 all of the synagogues, with one exception, were those of German Jews; and the exception was that of a Prussian Polish Congregation, B'nai Sholom (Sons of Peace). Although there were reported to be 12,000 Jews in Chicago in 1868, the recent growth of the present Ghetto is seen when it is remembered that it is composed largely of Russians; while at the time of this estimate of the Jewish population, there were in Chicago but 118 Russians of all faiths. The last item of interest in the present discussion, which relates to the colony before the fire, is the organization in 1868 of the Western Hebrew Christian Brotherhood. This is worthy of passing note, this proselyting propaganda of zealous Christians, because almost every effort to reach the "chosen people" as a people, and not as individuals, has been by narrow-minded theologians, who have been "instant in season and out of season," even to the extent of using the most pernicious methods of bribery in securing converts, thereby producing a social injury which it is within the province of this article to consider. The official report of the "Brotherhood" speaks for itself. In 1869, at the first annual meeting, expenditures to the amount of $1,457 were reported; conversions, four. At the next annual meeting, 1870, the expenditures were reported, $2,375; conversions, none. If anti-Semitism has been escaped by the Jewish refugee, he has not failed to suffer at the hands of his "friends."

At the present time there is a greater and a lesser Ghetto on the West Side of Chicago. The wider circumference, including an area of about a square mile, and a population of perhaps 70,000, contains as nearly as can be estimated 20,000 Jews. This comprises parts of the nineteenth, seventh, and eighth wards, and is bounded by Polk Street on the north, Blue Island Avenue on the west, Fifteenth Street on the south, and Stewart Avenue on the east. The lesser Ghetto is found in the seventh ward, bounded by Twelfth, Halsted, and Fifteenth Streets, and Stewart Avenue, where in a population of fifteen or sixteen thousand, nine-tenths are Jews. There is no record of statistics accessible, either through the federal or local governments. Estimates must be made from election registration, involving much uncertainty.

The extent of the Jewish population has been greatly over-estimated. The present figures are derived by counting the Jewish names on the registration slips, and making the most liberal calculations possible. The number of residents entitled to and using the franchise is limited by the short period of residence of a large part of the population, the ignorance of the language among many of the older residents, and the presence of an anarchistic contingent, which discourages many from voting who are nevertheless not opposed on principle to the ballot.

The physical characteristics of the Ghetto do not differ materially from the surrounding districts. The streets may be a trifle narrower; the alleys are no filthier. There is only one saloon to ten in other districts, but the screens' side-doors, and loafers are of the ubiquitous type; the theatre bills a higher grade of performance than other cheap theatres, but checks are given between the acts, whose users find their way to the bar beneath. The dry-goods stores have, of course, the same Jewish names over them which may be found elsewhere, and the same "cheap and nasty" goods within. The race differences are subtle; they are not too apparent to the casual observer. It is the religious distinction which every one notices; the synagogues, the Talmud schools, the "Kosher" signs on the meatmarkets. Among the dwelling-houses of the Ghetto are found the three types which curse the Chicago workingman,—the small, low, one or two story "pioneer" wooden shanty, erected probably before the street was graded, and hence several feet below the street level; the brick tenement of three or four stories, with insufficient light, bad drainage, no bath, built to obtain the highest possible rent for the smallest possible cubic space; and the third type, the deadly rear tenement, with no light in front, and with the frightful odors of the dirty alley in the rear, too often the workshop of the "sweater," as well as the home of an excessive population. On the narrow pavement of the narrow street in front is found the omnipresent garbage-box, with full measure, pressed down and running over. In all but the severest weather the streets swarm with children day and night. On bright days groups of adults join the multitude, especially on Saturday and Sunday, or on the Jewish holidays. In bad weather the steaming windows show the over-crowded rooms within. A morning walk impresses one with the density of the population, but an evening visit reveals a hive. As has been said before, however, this is not unlike other poor quarters. There are, though, some physical facts startling in their contrast with other districts. An interesting comparison may be made between the vital statistics of the seventh, sixteenth, and nineteenth wards. The figures of the Board of Health are not minute enough to enable one to compare smaller areas than wards, but these are sufficiently instructive. The seventh ward contains the largest Jewish population in the city. The sixteenth ward's population is chiefly Polish and German, which elements are also in the seventh ward; but in the latter they are also Jews. In the nineteenth ward, which adjoins the seventh on the north, and which in a homogeneous population could not be vitally different from it, there are some Jews, some Germans, many Italians, many Irish, and representatives of several other nationalities. The vital statistics ought not to be very different between neighboring wards with similar material characteristics, nor between wards composed of people from the same European countries and of the same social stratum: but the following figures speak for themselves. In each thousand of the population there are:—

	OVER 21 YEARS.	BETWEEN 4 AND 21.	UNDER 4.	DEATH RATE.	
				GENERAL.	UNDER 5 YEARS.
Ward VII.	600	300	100	14.18	7.88
Ward XVI.	550	310	140	19.46	12.24
Ward XIX.	600	310	90	17.13	8.91

Whether it is due to his religious observances or his exclusiveness, the vitality of the Jew is incontestable.

A closer study of the institutions and habits of this community may give us a standard of judgment, a desideratum not only that we may do justice to the Jew in these latter days of anti-Semitism, but also because of the magnitude of the problem forced on the city and the country in the necessity of absorbing these foreign elements. Both by the persistence of their traits when segregated, and the readiness with which they assimilate when encouraged, the Jews furnish the most instructive element in our population. We shall find that although the Jew would be characterized by many Americans in the Shakespearian utterance, "God made him, let him *pass* for a man," the open sesame for the inhabitant of the Ghetto is, "God made him, *let* him pass for a man." Opportunity is what the foreigner in our cities needs.

So much has been written lately on the general features of Jewish life in crowded city quarters, that the reader's familiarity with these facts may be presupposed.[1]

What are the habits and institutions peculiar to the Chicago Ghetto?

Industrial. The features of Jewish industry may be classified under the heads of stores and trades. The usual stores of the meaner sort abound for the supply of the daily necessaries. The provisions of the "orthodox" are bought at "Kosher" (ceremonially clean) shops. It is needless to say that these articles are only ceremonially clean. The more rigidly "fromm" (pious, in the best sense) are very suspicious even of these stores of their own religionists. But one must eat. It is said that at one time the distress of the "orthodox" was great over the inability to secure meat which had certainly been prepared according to the Mosaic code. One of the philanthropic packers of Chicago came to their rescue by hiring Jews to slaughter a certain number of cattle, cutting their throats as the law demands, instead of employing the method usual at the stockyards of striking them on the head with a mallet. He was thus enabled to satisfy the consciences of a large number of his fellow-citizens, and incidentally to sell his toughest meat. "Kosher" restaurants also minister to the wants of the Jewish community. These, when public, are only patronized by the more lax; many even of the indifferent or agnostic class preferring to eat where dishes are prepared according to their inherited tastes. The strict religionists, when not able to eat at home, frequent only private restaurants which can be fully trusted. These are not to be found opening on the street, but in an upper story, where privacy can be had, and the patronage is select.

The proprietor of the down-town clothing-store does not as a rule live in the Ghetto. He, as well as the owner of the pawn-shop, lives over, behind, or near his place of business. This being true, it is hard to find a pawnbroker in the Ghetto. The scarcity of pawn-shops in such a poor district is one of the astonishing features. The greatest enterprise to be placed under the head of stores is the junk-shop. This assumes mammoth and vile proportions. An old storeroom, the cellar or the rear of a house, is made to contain a huge collection of promiscuous pickings which seem useless, but when assorted prove to have a value not to be despised. The pertinacity and vitality of the Jew are seen in his ability to labor in such disagreeable and dangerous surroundings,

---

1. Gregorovius, "Der Ghetto und die Juden in Rom" (Wanderjahre, i); Booth, "Labor and Life of the People in London," vol. i (chap. on the Jews by Beatrice Potter Webb); *Century Magazine,* 1892, "The Jews in New York"; Riis, "How the Other Half Lives," chaps. x, xi; *Forum,* July, 1893, "The Russian Jew"; Zangwill, "Children of the Ghetto," 2 vols; Philipson, "Old European Jewries."

to put his children through such experiences with the waste and filth of a city, and bring himself and them out into a life many grades above the Italian ragpicker. The chief trades in which the Jew is found here, as elsewhere, are peddling, cigarmaking, and tailoring. The last is a sweated trade.

The most pitiable thing about the sweat-shops in this district is the oppression of Jew by Jew. Righteous recompense has disappeared when the trading instinct inherited from centuries of Christian persecution is directed to the crushing of "the weaker brother," instead of turning upon the persecutor. A pedler's license is the ransom of the unskilled Jew. This enables him to spend the day in the open air, though his lodging may be in no way more healthful than the sweater's den to which his fellow is doomed day and night. It makes of him also an independent capitalist, whose hoardings soon lead to an expansion of business, often to the detriment of the small settled traders. Peddling is an individual benefit, but a social ill which can only be excused when contrasted with the slavery of the sweaters' victim.

In this connection must be mentioned the efforts of the Employment Bureau connected with the United Hebrew Charities, by far the most satisfactory and praiseworthy department of that organization. In the ten years, 1883–1893, there were recorded 5,457 applicants for work. Work was provided for 4,596; 711 did not call to know the result of the organization's effort; 120 were not found employment; 857 refused the work offered. These applicants represented thirteen nationalities of Jews, of which 2,733 were Russians, 1,929 from Germany and Austria. In 1893 there were 676 applicants from Russia, as compared with 580 in 1892, 342 in 1891, and 191 in 1890. Among the applicants in 1893, the occupations recorded for which no positions were available were, pedler, 44; merchant, 146; student, 10; distiller, 4; miller and physician each 1. It is to the credit of the unemployed Jews to say that while 191 applied for positions as laborers or porters, 364 accepted such positions. 76 clerkships were provided when there had been 88 applications. Of the applicants as bookbinders, cabinetmakers, coppersmiths, blacksmiths, tinsmiths, locksmiths, machinists, painters, shoemakers, tailors, jewellers, printers, watchmakers, iron-moulders, butchers, and furriers, only 20 out of 224 failed to find the employment they desired. This is not only creditable to the bureau, but shows versatility in the Jew.

In the year 1891 a society was organized to care for the large number of Russian Jews driven to Chicago by the renewed persecutions. For eighteen months the Society in Aid of Russian Refugees succeeded in helping new arrivals, ignorant of language and customs, and without friends. The chief efforts of the society were directed to sending the refugees to homes in smaller cities or in the country. Nearly 1,000 persons were distributed in twenty-four States and Territories, of whom 129 returned unable to find satisfactory employment. The officers of the organization also found employment for over 500 persons during the brief existence of the society. The work thus accomplished during an emergency is a pertinent suggestion of a needful enterprise in Chicago and other large cities. The emigration societies of England accomplish a work which is, if possible, even more needed in the rapidly growing American cities.

The chief labor organizations of the Jews are the Cigarmakers' Union and the Cloakmakers' Union. While these organizations are taxed to keep wages above starvation level, they are composed of an unusually intelligent set of men, when their wages and hours are considered.

Social. The social institutions of the Ghetto are not numerous, but for the most part more helpful than similar institutions in other districts. Perhaps the most interesting is the latest acquisition, the Maxwell Street Settlement. At the suggestion of a prominent Jewish rabbi, two young college-bred Jews have taken up residence in the heart of the Ghetto. Another resident has been added since the work commenced. A private residence of a dozen rooms was secured, which has served their purpose during the initial stages of the work; but its capacity is already taxed. The readiness with which the neighborhood accepted the hospitality of the settlement speaks volumes for the efficiency of the residents and the responsiveness of the Jewish community. The usual social efforts of a settlement are put forth; but, as is natural in a new enterprise, the best work thus far has been educational. Among the more formal social activities may be mentioned three boys' and three girls' clubs, with a total membership of eighty-five, who meet weekly to read juvenile literature; an older girls' club of ten members, and an occasional neighborhood social gathering. Owing to the unusual distress of last winter (1893–1894), some relief-work has been forced upon the settlement; but this has been done by a corps of visitors without in any way encroaching on the time of the other workers. The settlement is demonstrating the faith of a growing number of believers in the Russian Jew, that with the removal of the despotism of his native land his ambition and tenacity will make of him a splendid American, unless he falls a victim to the despotism of commercialism.

One of the indirect benefits of the settlement has been the organization of the Self Educational Club by some of the more intelligent, progressive Jews of the Ghetto, with a view to providing social and educational opportunities for themselves. Club-rooms have been secured at 572 South Halsted Street, and a genuine neighborhood guild is being developed. A musicale every Saturday evening brings the members together weekly for social intercourse. The club is supported by a membership fee of fifty cents, and dues of ten cents a week.

Metropolitan Hall, on Jefferson Street, is the dramatic and operatic centre of the Ghetto. The contrast between this theatre and any other place of amusement in a district of equal poverty is another testimony to the latent tastes of the Jew. It is one of the best places to view the characteristics of the community, if, indeed, the amusements of a people do not always reveal the inner man relaxed as nothing else does. It is a genuine *Volkstheater.* One leaves America almost before entering the theatre. Large signs in Hebrew characters announce the plays, which are given on Wednesday, Saturday, and Sunday evenings. Twenty-five cents admits one to the best seat in the house. The floor is level; the stage quite a little elevated; there are *quasi* boxes on each side, and a well-filled gallery is seen in the rear. The decorations are abominable, but American and not Jewish. The only other American incident is the cat-call, which is periodically heard from the gallery on the appearance of the villain. The play, which gives a large place to the chorus, suggestive rather of the Greek drama than the opera, is genuinely Jewish, and the language, the Jewish jargon (Jüdisch). The better type of play usually narrates the experiences of one of the old Jewish heroes, portraying to the intense satisfaction of the audience his triumphs over one of the historic oppressors of the Jews. The poorer plays, which never descend to the level of the American farce comedy, to say nothing of burlesque, treat, for example, of the experiences of a recent immigrant in adapting himself to the customs of his new home. The delightful unconventionality of the place is well exhibited between the acts when the vendor of cakes and confections and fruits makes his rounds. The munching of these delicacies may then be heard, accompanied by the explosions of pop-bottles. The noise of these latter falling to the floor often disturbs the more sedate in the midst of some very solemn part. To one who looks below the surface, however, there is almost unalloyed delight in the pure, simple amusements of these people, marred only by the regret that they are not hearing their old classic language instead of the frightful jargon. Were a beautiful literature being expounded by these earnest players and singers, the influence on the auditors would be incalculable. As it is, the presence of this theatre is a most hopeful social and educational sign.

Balls are not so numerous in the Ghetto as in other foreign quarters, but they seem to be equally demoralizing. There is a seriousness in the temper of these people which places some damper on amusements. It is also true that the home-life removes the necessity for public amusement so strongly felt by less religious races. The great centre for social influence among the Jews is the home. This is admirably illustrated in the devotion of the children to the home, even after they have lost the religion of their parents. Many of the agnostics observe the religious festivals which centre in the home circle, simply in honor to their parents. It must of course be recognized that it is almost impossible to maintain the old family life in the environment of the factory system, dependent as it is on the surrender of the individual to the division of labor, with its long hours and employment of women. The astonishing fact is the preservation of so much of the tradition of the family in the face of modern social disintegration.

The synagogue is another important social centre. To those whose chief topic of conversation aside from business is the Talmud, it is natural that the Temple should prove a social inspiration, especially on Saturday and Sunday. Even more important, because more modest and more numerous, are the Chevras, or smaller religious congregations. These meet in some private house or storeroom appropriately fitted up for religious services. On Sunday, as well as Saturday and Friday evening, the men of these congregations spend much of their time discussing mooted theological points. These religious bodies are a genuine social factor, although their influence is certainly for the most part negative, keeping the men from the saloon or similar social resort, but also hindering a fuller development of the whole man.

The social influence of the saloon is happily small. It cannot be ignored; but in summer a visitor to the Ghetto is struck by the numerous soda-water fountains, showing the general temperate character of the people. So far as the saloon is gaining strength it is in opposition to the traditions of the Jews.

Educational. The first educational force to be mentioned in an American city is naturally the public school. The school provisions in the Ghetto are lamentably inadequate. The insufficient accommodation and poor instruction of the public schools have been supplemented by a privately endowed manual-training school, the "Jewish Training School," which has already demonstrated the superiority of modern pedagogical methods, and is, in fact, the educational hope of the community. On Judd Street, between Jefferson and Clinton, stands a fine brick building, erected by wealthy Chicago Jews to overcome the chief deficiency of the persecuted Jew, the lack of industrial adaptability. The building, which has a seating capacity of eight hundred, contains twenty-two rooms. The machine-shop accommodates thirty boys, and the joining-shop thirty-five. There are also moulding, drawing, sewing, and kindergarten rooms, and a physical and chemical laboratory. When the school was opened in October, 1890, there were sixteen hundred applicants, of whom eleven hundred were accepted; but lack of accommodation compelled the sending of two hundred of those in better circumstances to the public schools. Since then the enrollment has never been less than nine hundred. The school is not only accomplishing its mission in providing the much-needed manual training, but is doing what the public schools failed to do, destroying the prejudice in favor of the private schools, the "Cheder," conducted by inexperienced teachers, called by the children "Rebbi," but not to be confused with the Rabbis. These Talmud schools, which have not by any means been exterminated, are held in little stuffy rooms, where, with insufficient light, young boys ruin their eyesight over Hebrew characters, distort their minds with rabbinical casuistry, impair their constitutions in unventilated rooms, and defer the hopes of American citizenship by the substitution of Jüdisch for English. The able, progressive superintendent of the Jewish Training-School and his carefully chosen associates are a Godsend to this people.

The Ghetto students who advance to the public high schools are a great credit to the community, one recently taking the highest honors in the gift of the West Division High School. There were formerly night sessions held during the winter at the training-school, but lack of funds compelled their discontinuance. Many Jews attend the public night-schools; and the classes recently organized at the Maxwell Street Settlement are overcrowded, although but a very few deserted the public schools for them. Among the classes at the settlement are civil government, with an attendance of fourteen, meeting twice a week; German, eleven members, twice a week; arithmetic, fifteen members, three times a week; beginning English, twenty-five members, meeting three evenings a week; grammar, fifteen members, twice a week; George Eliot, fourteen members, twice a week; club on questions of the day, ten members, meeting weekly; book-keeping, eighteen members, twice a week; physical culture, eight members, weekly; and American history, ten members, weekly. A literary society meets every Sunday evening; and a concert is given on the first Sunday afternoon of the month, the other Sunday afternoons being devoted to lectures.

The settlement does not monopolize the literary activities of the Ghetto. There are other independent literary societies accomplishing a very desirable work. There is a society for the study of Hebrew literature. Lectures are delivered in pure Hebrew, and the minutes are kept in Hebrew. The Self Educational Club has classes in United States and Jewish history, civil government, English language and literature, French, physiology, bookkeeping, arithmetic, and medical and pharmaceutical Latin.

The synagogue must be mentioned as an educational factor, because the magnificent literature of the Hebrews is there brought before the people, whose literary taste is well nigh annihilated by the frightful jargon of their daily conversation.

The Jewish papers, except the small number published abroad in Hebrew, are even worse in their educational influence than the American dailies, owing to the added demoralization of Jüdisch. All of the Jewish papers have a too foreign tone; but happily with the acquisition of English the Jewish paper loses its interest. There are one or two reading-rooms, where, in addition to the current Jewish papers, much good Hebrew literature is found. These have doubtless a greater social than educational value.

Political. There are several "orthodox" Republican and Democratic clubs in the district, organized mainly through the influence of the ward "heelers." The recent Jewish immigrant seems to choose the Republican party. It is not easy to say whether the idea of protection attracts him, or, as has been suggested, he has become familiar with the term "republican" abroad as contrasted with monarchical, while "democrat" suggests social democracy and atheism. His choice is quite probably a sentimental one. At the opposite pole from these blind followers of the politician are the anarchists. There is quite a body of those whose memories of oppression form their present political creed. An agitation meeting is held every Sunday in some good-sized hall, attracting sometimes several hundred Jews. The anarchism of the leaders is almost purely philosophical, and the majority of the adherents manifest their belief simply by neglecting the polls. The socialists probably outnumber the anarchists by a very small margin. The leaders are blind in their devotion to the Socialist Labor party, and bitter in their antagonism to the anarchists. They seem to be at present the political leaven of the community, because they, at least the leaders, have thought their way to their present position, and they are not merely dreaming, but are engaged in active politics, bringing every election not merely votes from the old parties, but new voters to the polls. They also carry on agitation meetings on Sunday; but their educational influence has been, until this year, limited by their bondage to Continental socialism. During the campaign of 1894 the socialists aided the People's Party. Politics cannot be said to be healthy while they are Jewish; but the great weakness of the Jewish leaders is their ignorance of English. Few of them can make a good address in English. It is some gain, however, to get the civic centre out of the synagogue; and it must be said of the radical political leaders, at least, that they are no longer the abject slaves of tradition.

Religious. The synagogues and chevras conserve the religious life of the majority of the inhabitants of the Ghetto. Their power is not so great as that of the congregations of the old Continental ghettos, or even those of the present London Jewish quarter; but no spark of Reform Judaism has yet entered. The long coats and the curls before the ears, so familiar in Europe, are seldom seen in Chicago; but the Jewish festivals are rigorously maintained, and the ceremonial restrictions observed even in the more prosperous families, where a Christian servant helps to tide over the Sabbath without sin as well as without physical inconvenience. Even the orthodox cannot deny the growing heterodoxy of the Jews of the large city, despite the conservative influence of the Ghetto. On the whole, the religion of the Chicago Ghetto seems to have a hygienic value of a certain kind; but its ethical significance is seen only in its effect on the family life, the larger social duties remaining untouched. One other good thing ought perhaps to be credited to a religious inspiration,—the charity of the poor Jews to their poorer neighbors may originate in religion or in race. At all events, the Ghetto rabbi is in no sense a minister. His functions could as well be performed by a phonograph.

The Hebrew papers also exert a conservative religious influence.

There is a Hebrew Christian Mission of some importance on Margaret Street and Fourteenth, near the western limit of the Ghetto. A neat two-story brick building is devoted to religious meetings, kindergarten, sewing classes, and similar work, while the missionary lives on the second floor. Quite a number of Jews visit this place. The children are attracted by the friendliness and cheer of the house and the workers, as well as by the little forms of bribery that characterize such enterprises; the older Jews, always eager for religious discussion, attend the preaching services. A small number of converts is made, some of them remaining faithful, but others undoubtedly attracted merely by the hope of employment or other reward. There can be no question as to the good intentions of these "friends" of the "chosen people"; but certainly many Jews are pauperized by such efforts, as well as by the counter-deeds of zealous Jews.

The Maxwell Street Settlement and the Self Educational Club are religiously independent.

The evils of the Ghetto may be generalized under two heads,—the environment, including the wretched houses, narrow streets, and the conditions of employment, over which the Jews have little or no control; and the conservatism of the majority of the population. Their conservatism is being slowly undermined. The use of the jargon in their papers, conversation, the Talmud schools, business, and the political organizations, is being counteracted by the social and educational forces already mentioned, as well as by minor influences. The public schools ought to be doing much more than they are. Illiteracy will prevail so long as the municipal conscience slumbers. Nevertheless, the greatest need of the Ghetto is its annihilation. The forces working for good in it are such as are tending to exterminate it. Some of the brightest minds are leaving the community as they advance in professional circles, taking prominent positions as lawyers, physicians, and in the daily press, as well as in business. The Jewish Training-School is making an important contribution in preparing the coming generation for broader fields of industrial activity. The Maxwell Street Settlement is enlarging the social life and consciousness. The socialists are teaching social responsibility. Some of the native qualities of the Jew, such as love of home, seriousness, and ambition, are antagonistic to the existing conditions. It remains to be seen whether external forces will teach him to expand both his personal and social horizon, or lead him, as in the past, to draw himself within his shell. "The poverty of the poor is their destruction." The annihilation of the Ghetto means wealth to the Jew, the wealth of Jesus and Ruskin, that wealth which is life. But the responsibility is not altogether or chiefly his. The qualities he is seen to possess, even under the distressing environment of the Chicago Ghetto, would enable any man to be free were opportunity free. If the versatile, tenacious Jew leads us to apprehend this fact, we may find that even social "salvation is of the Jews."

VI

THE BOHEMIAN PEOPLE IN CHICAGO

Josefa Humpal-Zeman

The neighborhood of Hull-House was once the Prague of the Bohemian people in Chicago. The district extending from Canal to Halsted, and from Ewing to Twelfth Street, was, before the great fire of 1870, the largest and best settlement of Bohemians in the city. When, after that fire, the city began to extend itself beyond the western limits, and new tracts of land were measured off into cheap lots, the Bohemians, who love nature, pure air, and gardens, sold their property in this crowded part of the city, and moved to the new region, where they might invest in more land, and so afford the luxury of a garden. The movement once started, it was not long before the whole community changed its location, and soon there grew up a vast colony, "a city within a city," spreading from Halsted to Ashland Avenue, and from Sixteenth to Twentieth Street, and numbering not less than forty-five thousand Bohemians.

The colony again received a name; and this time it was in honor of the second largest city of Bohemia, Pilzen, or Pilsen. Soon, however, it grew too small for the flood of Bohemians, which reached its highest tide in the years 1884–1885, when the greatest percentage of the Bohemian emigration to the United States poured into the new and prosperous Chicago. It is now estimated that there are from sixty to seventy thousand Bohemians in the city; and Chicago has the distinction of containing within itself the third largest city of Bohemians in the world. The last element of the rapidly growing settlement is now forming west of Douglas Park.

The first Bohemian emigrants came to Chicago in 1851 and 1852, and possibly even earlier. Soon after the revolution in 1848, many of the enthusiastic patriots, young men with large, liberty-loving hearts, forced to flee from their fatherland, sought homes in this country. Among those earlier emigrants were men of cultivation and energy, who loved liberty so well that they were ready to undertake all manner of menial service for her sake; and thus one would often find men of education and high social standing engaged in street-sweeping, cigarmaking, and other humble occupations; and graduates of the University of Prague working for $2.50 and $4.00 per week.

The emigration from Bohemia increased after every Continental war, and especially after the Austro-Italian wars of the '60's. This time not only the political refugees sought new homes, but artisans and peasants also began emigrating. People were tired of constant wars that were sapping the best blood of their nation, wasting their fields, and fastening still more grievous tax burdens upon the shoulders that were already crushed beneath those they had. This was the case in most European countries, and especially in Bohemia.

The social and political upheavals, the exaggerated stories of American wealth, and the natural feeling of self-preservation, were, and still are, the causes of Bohemian emigration. One of the chief causes now is the military law, which drives into this country a steady stream of strong, healthy, and able-bodied men. Bohemia has never sent her "slums," as some politicians assert, because her slums, like the slums of other nations, never like to "move on"; they are too contented in their indolence and filth to be willing to go to work, or to take the trouble of a sea-voyage. Besides, the Austrian money, although exceedingly hard to get in that country, is so depreciated in value, that it takes about one thousand gulden to move a family of eight to America.

Often good artisans were compelled to work for low wages, even $1.25 a day; still, out of this meagre remuneration they managed to lay a little aside for that longed-for possession,—a house and lot that they could call their own. When that was paid for, then the house received an additional story, and that was rented, so that it began earning money. When more was saved, the house was pushed in the rear, the garden sacrificed, and in its place an imposing brick or stone building was erected, containing frequently a store, or more rooms for tenants. The landlord, who had till then lived in some unpleasant rear rooms, moved into the best part of the house; the bare but well-scrubbed floors were covered with Brussels carpets, the wooden chairs replaced by upholstered ones, and the best room received the added luxury of a piano or violin.

In those early days rent was high and flour ten dollars a barrel, but they bought cheap meat at four cents a pound, coffee at twelve cents; and thus by dint of great economy many were able to lay aside money each year, and some of those early settlers now own property ranging in value from fifty thousand to two hundred thousand dollars.

To form at least a small, even if very insufficient, estimate of the value of property owned by the Chicago Bohemians, it may be interesting to note how much the working-people have invested in property within the last eight years. They have saved it in the Bohemian building and loan associations. Before these societies began their activities, the Bohemians had already a large community of not less than fifty thousand inhabitants, and owned property running into hundreds of thousands of dollars in value. The reports are quoted of five Bohemian building and loan associations, out of the forty or more societies that are in existence. From the year 1885 to 1893:—

The society "Borivoj"	has paid $107,795.74
The society "Oul"	" 121,224.34
The society "Bohemia"	" 78,370.00

The society "Domov"	"	80,247.47
The society "Slavie"	"	306,454.24
TOTAL		$694,092.09

We can safely estimate that within the last eight years these societies have disbursed over four millions of dollars, which is all invested in property by the working-people.

Before 1878 the majority of the Bohemians were engaged in the various building-trades, as carpenters, bricklayers, [and] painters; others, again, were tailors, and many ordinary laborers working in the lumber-yards; but after 1878 they began entering as clerks into stores, law offices, and various other business enterprises, so that to-day there is not a profession in which Bohemians are not to be found. The majority of the Bohemians are artisans, and only some of the peasants are contented to be ordinary laborers. The Bohemian business-men command the respect of the very best firms in the city on account of their honesty and integrity in all of their business relations. Business-men dealing with them readily acknowledge the "bad debt" among the Bohemians to be very rare.

The Labor Movement.

The condition of the ordinary workingman is the same as that of his German, Irish, or Swedish brother, the only probable difference being that the Bohemian working-man is frequently more patient, more conservative, and less progressive in reforms. The labor movement, until recently, has made very slow progress among them. This may be accounted for partly by the mistrust which the majority of the people have of strangers who come to agitate among them, and also because certain so-called leaders were neither wise nor honest.

One of the chief reasons for the advance made of late by the Bohemian working-people in Chicago, is the fact that since 1880 some leaders have come from the native land, where the labor movement has been more successful; and many of the immigrants who have arrived here recently are better accustomed to labor unions, and know the power of organization. Then, too, the various newspapers that have been started to agitate reform have grown more popular. The result is, that there are now about twenty-three labor organizations; and, what is more encouraging, the majority of these societies are auxiliary to American labor unions, such as the bricklayers' and other building-trades, or the clothing unions. Two typographical co-operative associations publish dailies; one the Pravo-Lidu ("Rights of the People"), the other, Denni-Masatel ("Daily Herald"), which has the largest circulation of all the Bohemian dailies. The majority of the workingmen favor the eight-hour movement, and many object to child-labor. The wages earned are the same as those paid to other nationalities. There is not a single working-women's union; in fact, nothing whatever has been done for the Bohemian working woman. No one has deemed her worthy of any effort; and with the exception of the few Americanized tailoresses who belong to the Tailors' Union, the whole mass of girls who work in tailor-shops, cigar-factories, and candy-factories have seldom been near a union meeting." This is an interesting fact; for as long as these hundreds and thousands of girls shall be left unorganized and uninformed, they will always be a great stumbling-block in the path of the working-woman of Chicago.

Social Life.

Although the Bohemians have better food and more of it than they had at home, they lack the social life. They miss the free garden concerts that are given in almost every large city in Bohemia; the Sunday walks, the reading-rooms, and various holiday feasts that are almost indispensable to the Bohemian temperament.

This yearning after more social life has led them into various schemes for entertainment which are not always wholesome. The picnics, with uniformed processions, led by brass bands, that are so common and perfectly proper in Bohemia, appear strange and almost ridiculous. The Sunday dances, theatres, and concerts that stand substitute for the walks in the fields; the home entertainments, when families make calls, and amuse themselves by singing, eating, drinking, and telling stories—are to the conservative American desecrations of the Sabbath.

Similar amusements are popular with the newcomers; but as they live here longer, and become more Americanized, this social life changes and becomes more formal, more affected, and gradually becomes a mixture of American and European, something unlike the real Bohemian, and foreign to the American; entirely original, the "Bohemian-American."

The love of social life is the predominating feature in the Bohemian settlement. Almost every Bohemian, man and woman, belongs to some society, and many are members of several orders. Unlike any other Slavonic nation, the Bohemian women have a great many organizations, both educational and benevolent. The secret societies of "Jednota Ceskych Dam" are among the most popular and influential. Their object is at once educational, social, and benevolent; and they pay yearly thousands of dollars to aid the orphan children of their former members. Among the younger women the gymnastic societies, known as "Sokolky," are best organized. Women, like men, also separate their social from their religious life, and have organizations of freethinking and catholic women.

Family Life.

The family life, like that of all Slavonic peoples, is very affectionate. It is a prevailing custom among the working-class that the father and children should give all their wages to the wife or mother. Seldom do the children keep their earnings and pay board; they usually all work and live together, and then at marriage each child receives a portion, or after the death of the parents all is equally divided among the children. The Bohemian women are clean and thrifty, economical housekeepers, and very good cooks. They know the art of making a little go far; and this enables them to feed large families with comparatively meagre sums.

The Illinois State factory inspector has said that of all the children who come to her for medical examination, the Bohemian and Jewish children are the best fed; although these "best-fed" children who work in the factories are usually from the poorest families, where frequently as many as six are fed on less than five dollars a week.

It is not the general custom for the mothers and wives of Bohemians to go out working; but more and younger children go out to work here than in any other Bohemian community. The reason for this is that there is a greater demand for child-labor in Chicago, the supply for which is recruited from the ranks of the needy families of all nationalities. It is a great temptation to all foreigners to sacrifice their children; for the little ones can often get work when grown people, slow to learn a new language, are forced to be idle. The Bohemian press is doing all in its power to discourage this objectionable child-labor, and urges compulsory educational laws.

Religion.

It is estimated that the larger half of the Bohemian population in Chicago is Catholic, while the rest are non-church-goers. The Catholic Bohemians have in Chicago eight parishes, with fine church edifices, of which that of St. Prokopius, corner of Allport and Eighteenth Streets, is the largest and most costly. With the school-buildings, convent, church, and rich farms, it has property the value of which exceeds a million dollars. In every parish there is a Bohemian school, where a half-day is devoted to teaching the English branches, and the afternoon to teaching the Bohemian language, grammar, and catechism. The pupils in these number not less than two thousand seven hundred.

The Bohemian order of Benedictines of St. Prokopius parish has founded a Bohemian College, which is equivalent to the common high school, offering the same curriculum; and it has also a business course, all in the Bohemian language. In each parish there are organizations of men and women, many being benevolent, others more purely social and religious. There are four Catholic Bohemian newspapers published in Chicago,—one daily, one children's paper, the other two weeklies.

The Catholics have their own halls, theatres, schools, and cemetery.

The Protestants have two Bohemian churches: one the Congregational "Bethlehem," and the other the "John Huss" Methodist Episcopal church, and two Methodist Episcopal missions. They publish two papers: one the *Pravda,* Congregational; and the other the *Krestanski Posel,* published by the Bohemian Methodist pastors. These churches have about fifteen hundred members.

One of the many reasons why the Protestant movement has not gained a stronger hold on the Bohemians is that it was initiated by strangers or foreigners; but now that the native Bohemians are taking hold of the work themselves, they are naturally more successful, and their fellow-countrymen are more willing to listen to the message uttered in their own tongue by their own people.

There is a secular society known as the "Svobodna Olbec," which has its speaker, and is pronounced in its agnostic philosophy. One of its chief objects is to publish agnostic literature and arrange anti-religious lectures. This society numbers about one hundred members. The remainder of the Bohemian people are simply non-church-goers, and call themselves "freethinkers," most of them having no definite philosophy, only cherishing antagonism against church institutions. Of these, the greater part merely imitate and repeat the sayings of the newspapers, many of which are edited by agnostics. These people have suffered so much in Bohemia from the state and the clergy, that when they once feel themselves relieved from the "yoke of bondage," they are not afraid to voice their sentiments, and are very bitter in their hatred. They have learned to associate the Roman Catholic Church with the Austrian house of Hapsburg; and the oppressions of these two powers have been the chief reason why so many intelligent people in Bohemia, especially the "Young Czechs," are hostile to the church, and have accepted so readily the materialism of Western Europe.

The freethinkers have four Bohemian-English schools, where both Bohemian and English are taught. They are devoted to the public school, and have the Bohemian schools only as an offset to the parochial schools. The children usually go for a year or two to the Bohemian school, where they learn to read and write in Bohemian, and then enter the public schools. They have separate halls, theatres, and societies. When the priests refused to baptize, marry, or bury the members of these societies, they separated entirely, and now even have their own cemetery. There are one hundred and sixty societies, all of which have some benevolent object, such as paying death-benefits, supporting schools, etc.

Besides these, there are eleven singing and dramatic clubs. The latter clubs give several plays during the season, and the money made is donated to some good cause. There is a great deal of rivalry between these amateur actors, and they do not hesitate to try their abilities on the best of Shakespeare's or Sardou's dramas.

The freethinkers publish three daily newspapers and seven weeklies, so that the Bohemians publish in all sixteen newspapers in Chicago.

Citizenship.

In 1860 several of the Bohemian-Slavonian young men organized a Lincoln Rifle Company, and this was the first regiment that went from Chicago to fight for the Union; and to-day the best monument in the Bohemian cemetery speaks of the patriotism of those early immigrants, who had already learned to love their adopted country so well as to be ready to lay down their lives for its preservation. Year after year their fellow-countrymen gather about this monument, and with flowers and addresses honor the memory of their fallen brethren.

In political life almost all the old settlers, before and after the war, were Republicans. After the year 1880 some began to vote the Democratic ticket; and when in 1883 this party nominated a Bohemian for the office of alderman, it got the first real hold on the people in Chicago. The first political recognition given them was a stroke on the part of the Democratic wire-pullers to win the Bohemian vote. It "took," and the result was that to-day out of the twelve thousand Bohemian votes cast, eight thousand are Democratic. The politicians work on the people's feelings, incite them against the men of the other party as their most bitter enemies; and if this doesn't succeed, they go to work deliberately to buy some. Thus adding insult to injury, they go off and set up a pharisaic cry about the ignorance and corruption of the foreign voters.

As everything in the old country has its price, it is not at all surprising that the foreigners believe such to be the case in this also. But Americans are to blame for this; for the better class of citizens, the men who preach so much about corruption in political life, and advocate reforms, never come near these foreign voters. They do not take pains to become acquainted with these recruits to American citizenship; they never come to their political clubs and learn to know them personally; they simply draw their estimates from the most untrustworthy source, the newspapers, and then mercilessly condemn them as hopeless.

The Bohemian citizens in Chicago have been or are represented in the following offices: alderman, county commissioner, school-board, public-library board, corporation counsel, assessor, and State legislature; while about one hundred and fifty Bohemians are employed in the service of the city government, engaged in almost every department.

Since 1874 there has been a Bohemian department in the Public Library, which now numbers four thousand books.

The Bohemian Republican League publishes a very good politico-economic journal called the *American Citizen;* and many of the younger politicians are men of culture, who take vital interest in social and economic questions, and are thoroughly Americanized. This is very cheering, and promises better things for the future.

The Bohemian people in Chicago are called "clannish." They may deserve that epithet; but who is to be blamed for that? In the early days it was natural that they should settle near their kinsmen or relations. Their language, being Slavonic, was unlike any other about them; and they were at a disadvantage as compared with the Germans, whose native tongue is so closely allied to the English that they learn the latter readily, and thus appear superior to their Bohemian brethren. Then, too, the Germans, being their traditional enemies, took no pains to enlighten the American in regard to them, but rather tried to disparage them in every way, until the poor inoffensive Bohemian was insulted by all around him; so that in time he began to regard everyone non-Bohemian as his enemy. As was said before, a goodly portion of the blame for this rests upon the American press; for in times of political campaigns it heaps insult or flattery without discrimination. We ought not to cater to the foreigners at the cost of truth, any more than we would do so to our own children; yet we should not allow our own prejudices to undermine the future good of this republic. Left alone, the foreigners are harmless, for they are too divided by their petty traditional national hatreds; but this constant aimless baiting of the American press gives these great masses one theme, one bond of sympathy, on which they can all unite; and that is,—hatred of Americans.

So far, the Bohemians are free from any such feeling, and, to the sorrow of their European brothers, Americanize almost too rapidly; so that frequently the second and third generations do not even speak their own native language. They constitute only a drop in the mighty artery of foreign blood in America; but their leaders are anxious that this shall be pure and healthy, and in its way contribute the very best to the life of this new and mighty nation.

VII

REMARKS UPON THE
ITALIAN COLONY IN CHICAGO

Alessandro Mastro-Valerio

Italians do not come to America to find a home, as do the British, Teutons, Slavs, and Scandinavians, but to repair the exhausted financial conditions in which they were living in Italy, or to make more money if they were well-to-do. They leave the mother-country with the firm intention of going back to it as soon as their *scarsellas* shall sound with plenty of *quibus*. And if they remain here, they do so as a result of unforeseen circumstances which surprise even themselves, and which they finally accept.

At their embarkation for America they might be classified as temporary immigrants; but when they are here, in the majority of cases they become permanent ones. The sons of Italy in emigrating do not sell the home, but mortgage it for money to pay for the passage, because they dream of a return home with plenty of money. They plan the improvements they will make and that they will spend the remainder of the happy life there. How different from the people of other nationalities, who sell everything before emigrating! Italians leave the members of the family behind, with the promise that they will send money to them to live on, to pay debts, to raise the mortgage. But after some years they send for the family, and settle in America permanently, sometimes becoming American citizens, but always remaining Italians. Their children, though American-born, will always be "incorrigible" Italians because of their distinct individuality, and of their sonorous and difficult Italian names.

On arriving in this country they swear to impose upon themselves all sorts of sacrifices, by limiting their personal expenses to the minimum, in order to hasten the realization of the dream of a happy and moneyed return. Therefore, if their way of living in the crowded tenement houses of the American cities has been found objectionable, it is to be ascribed to this proposed economy, which is carried to the extreme limit of the possible or the imaginable. I must state, before going farther, that I am writing of the Italians of the peasant class, and particularly of the provinces of Southern Italy, which furnish the bulk of the Italian immigration; also that I make honorable exceptions, and that I do not wish to offend against the Italian name, since there is not in

America an Italian more incorrigible than I, and a Southern Italian too. The Italian immigrants, in the majority of instances, are regarded as unskilled laborers, and are employed, accordingly, in building railroads, and in earthwork, such as excavation, bedding, etc.; and as carriers. For this reason they find work during only a portion of the year, when the clemency of the weather allows such work to be done. The rest of the year they remain idle in the American towns whither they have floated, and where they sometimes find work, incidentally, as snow and street sweepers. During these winter months they sometimes experience hardship, and particularly when work begins very late; so much so that a great many of them leave for Italy in time to be there for Christmas, and return in March or April, ready to work as before. This last year, owing to the financial conditions which afflicted this country, the exodus of Italians has been great. It is also partly due to the fact that the price of passage on the half-dozen steamship lines which carry Italian immigrants has been very low, owing to competition.

Here I beg to be allowed to defend the Italian immigrants from the classification to which they are condemned; viz., of unskilled laborers. In America they might be very good farmers, vine-growers, gardeners, olive and fruit growers, and stock-farmers, just as they were in Italy, in their own home, which comprised a field for grain and a vineyard, a fruit orchard, and a little stockyard. Or they may have been employed in the same capacity by large farmers, as vine-growers, fruit-raisers, olive-growers, and stock-farmers. In certain parts of Southern Italy, owing to the large emigration of peasants, these farmers find it at present difficult to carry on their industries, But the Italian immigrants, unfortunately, when they arrive in America do not continue the work to which they were used in Italy. They do not apply themselves to tilling the soil, in which they would not only prove skilful laborers, but examples to other nationalities (Frenchmen excepted), as those who have happily followed this practice have fully demonstrated. It would be a fortunate movement, that of inducing the Italian immigrants to leave American towns for farming pieces of land in a climate congenial to them and like that of their native country, and where the land would yield a variety of crops all the year round. Then their instinct of picking would have full sway in a more decent manner than now, when many of them, finding in the American towns nothing comely to pick, pick rags, cigar-stumps, bones, and other filthy things from alleys and ash and garbage boxes.

It must be added that such filthy trades are practised with ingenuousness and nonchalant persistence worthy of a better cause. The Italian instinct for picking is notable. In Italy they are used to pick wood from the forest, weeds from the fields, wheat and grain after the mowers, fruit from the trees, insects from the bark of the trees and vines, for which they are paid so much per hundred; herbs, beans, pease, and other truck-farm products from the plants; the seeds of weeds from wheat, oats, rye, etc.; herbs from the woods, and many other things which the average American would never think of using in any way.

In my opinion the only means for the regeneration of the Italian immigrants from the state in which they nowadays find themselves in the crowded districts of the American cities, is to send them to farming. All other means are mere palliatives. Then they will begin to belong to the same class of citizens to which they did at home, the first producers; that class which is the backbone of the country, and most worthy of respect. The result of the present combination of circumstances of the Italian peasant is in Chicago the same as in any other American town, except on the Pacific coast.

The Italians of Chicago number 25,000, mostly belonging to the peasant class. Those who have grown with the town are in prosperous circumstances; and, with few exceptions, they came from the north of Italy, and particularly from the Riviera. They do not, for the most part, form an intelligent class. They are neither *entrepreneurs* nor producers. They have not been identified with the wonderful, intelligent progress of the city; but they have grown rich with it from the increase in value of real estate, or from their business of selling fruit. The children are no better than their parents. A case was discovered recently of a young Italian worth $100,000 who was contented to be simply a policeman. Behind bar-room counters, there are young Italians who are worth even more money. Some of the present generation deserve praise because they have entered the liberal professions or legitimate manufacturing enterprises. The Italian colony consists of professional men,—newspaper-men, bankers, publicans, employment agents, lawyers, interpreters, midwives, musicians, artisans, laborers, sweaters' victims, grocers, bakers, butchers, barbers, merchants, etc., all of which are necessary one to another, and cannot bear separation without disorganization. It is a town within a town, a stream, a rivulet in the sea, of such intense force of cohesion that it cannot be broken, as the mighty ocean cannot break the Gulf Stream.

The immigrant Italians are lodged by Italian innkeepers, and fed by Italian *restaurateurs*. Italian publicans quench their thirst. Italian employment agents or "bosses" find them work, and group them and take them to the country, where, in the majority of cases, they board them, and act as interpreters between the contractor and them. Italian agents or bankers send their money to their families in Italy, and sell them tickets for the latter when they come to join them in America. Italian doctors are called in case of sickness, and Italian druggists furnish the curative drugs, which must bear Italian names in order to be trusted. Italians manufacture macaroni as nearly as possible like that of Italy; and Italian grocers furnish cheese, oil, olives, bologna, bread, and many other Italian delicacies or necessaries. Their priests must be Italians; also their lawyers and their undertakers. These streams and rivulets run into the midst of the *mare magnum* Chicago, about South Clark Street, and Third, Fourth, Pacific and Sherman Avenues, and Dearborn Street between Harrison and the Twelfth Street viaduct; about Illinois, Michigan, Indiana, and La Salle Streets, where the Italian Church of the Assumption is located; about West Indiana, Ohio, Huron, Sangamon, and North Halsted Streets, and Milwaukee and Austin Avenues; about South Halsted, Ewing, Forquer, DeKoven, and Twelfth Streets and the river.

Smaller streams run in other directions. Each is well marked, and bears, more or less, a reputation of its own.

The charge of filthiness, so often made against Italians of this class, is to be attributed partly to their special condition of life in the crowded tenement houses of our American towns, which are the reverse of hygienic in their construction, both in regard to the material used, which is poor and easily impregnable, and as to the disposition of space, which does not conduce to healthful living. The accusers ought to consider that those Italian immigrants come from the open country, or from villages where the houses are built of stonemasonry less easily heated and cooled, and having wide corridors differently disposed with doors and windows, which give room for plenty of light and air. The promiscuity of sex and of strange people force sighs from the hearts of Italian women, mothers of girls, on first setting foot into the "infernal bolges" of South Clark Street and Fourth Avenue. "*Madonna mia, qui debbo vivere?*" I have heard sigh an Italian woman on one of these occasions, looking at her girls, while her heart was full of dismay. It is the custom of my part of Italy to whitewash the houses with lime in September, and before Easter, or in May, at the time of moving. It is also the custom that, on the Saturday before Easter, the priest goes in *pompa mayna* to bless the houses of the district assigned to him, one by one. For such an occasion the houses of even the poorest people are made clean from roof to cellar in honor of the sanctity of the visitor who comes to bless the buildings, the persons, and the animals in the stable, in the name of God; therefore he is received with marked and religious reverence. Presents of eggs and money are made to him; the eggs are taken care of by the priest's servant maid, who attends in her picturesque peasant's costume, and puts them in a straw basket. A boy responds to the Latin prayers, and puts the money into a silver bucket containing the blessed water and the sprinkler. When a boy, I often attended to act in this capacity, and I remember with pleasure the neat appearance of the poorest houses. When I found myself in an American tenement house, inhabited by Italians, at the sight of the filth that appeared before me I could not help thinking with a sense of *ripianto amarissimo* of the houses of the same people as I have seen them on those good Saturdays. Most certainly the same conditions would not exist among these people on a farm in the country.

The greed of gain which has developed among the Italians causes most of the women to employ all their spare time in sewing clothing, in order to add their little share to the earnings of the husband and sons. This is a serious detriment to them, and is one cause of their filthy homes, which they have no time to care for. By reason of the same greed, boys and girls are sent to sell newspapers in the streets, and sometimes to beg. The skilled Italian in Chicago gets as much money as the American skilled laborer. The unskilled Italian laborer gets from $1.00 to $1.75 a day. As I have stated before, they economize in every way they can; but when the occasion arises which pleases them, they spend their money like water. They are hard workers, and not inclined to be vicious. Their women are notably virtuous.

L'Italia, the leading Italian newspaper of Chicago, inaugurated with its first number a veritable crusade against the two offences of ragpicking and sending boys and girls in the streets, and was instrumental in holding a mass-meeting for compulsory education in Chicago, which was part of a movement in the course of which the principle of compulsory education was adopted by the Board of Education, led by the late Charles Kominsky. The mass-meeting ended in the appointment of a committee of prominent Italians to call upon Mayor Cregier and upon the council, requesting the interference of the police in the ragpicking of the Italians. Briefly speaking, an ordinance was passed and enforced; but the ragpickers formed a sort of political association, and let the party in power understand that they were voters who would vote against that party at the next election if the interference of the police in their occupation was not stopped. Immediately the police, by secret orders, let the ragpickers alone. No lobbyists at Washington could have worked the scheme more effectually. This will answer the question whether Italians have Americanized themselves, and to what extent.

VIII

THE COOK COUNTY CHARITIES

Julia C. Lathrop,
Member of the Illinois State Board of Charities

As the study of these maps reveals an overwhelming proportion of foreigners, and an average wage-rate so low as to render thrift, even if it existed, an ineffective insurance against emergencies, we are led at once to inquire what happens when the power of self-help is lost. This district was chosen by the government for investigation because it was believed to represent fairly the most untoward conditions of life in Chicago; it was selected as a "slum," and is that portion of the city containing on its western side the least adaptable of the foreign populations, and reaching over on the east to a territory where the destructive distillation of modern life leaves waste products to be cared for inevitably by some agency from the outside. The preponderance of unskilled labor necessarily means the weakness of trade unions and mutual benefit societies; in short, the inability to organize and co-operate. When we inquire, then, what provision is made to meet sickness, accident, non-employment, old age, and that inevitable accident, death, we are asking what some outside agency performs. Here is a foreign population, living in every sort of mal-adjustment,—rural Italians, in shambling wooden tenements; Russian Jews, whose two main resources are tailoring and peddling, quite incapable in general of applying themselves to severe manual labor or skilled trades, and hopelessly unemployed in hard times; here are Germans and Irish, largely of that type which is reduced by drink to a squalor it is otherwise far above. Here amongst all, save the Italians, flourishes the masculine expedient of temporary disappearance in the face of non-employment or domestic complexity, or both; paradoxically enough the intermittent husband is a constant factor in the economic problem of many a household. In this region west of the river, and stretching on into the seventh, eighth, and eighteenth wards, there are many streets where foreign tongues are more spoken than English; thousands of people who, having their own shops and churches and theatres and saloons, may be said hardly to come in touch with the commonwealth of which some immigration company has made them an unconscious part until they are given over as the wards of its charity. To meet the needs of such a city population, a whole system of charitable institutions has grown up; though they are carried on, not by the city of Chicago, but by the county of Cook. It is true, of course, that much private charity supplements the county's efforts, or rather that the county's provision is accepted when all the resources of private charity and of neighborly aid have been exhausted. Indeed, one may as well admit in starting, that the capacious bosom of the county is sought with much reluctance, even by the population of which we speak; and while this population represents the last degree of social submergence, the county is in turn its *dernier ressort*. There is, doubtless, a certain satisfaction to the philanthropist and the sociologist alike, in having touched bottom, reached ultimate facts; and this in a sense we have done when we have reached the county institutions. These are the infirmary, the insane asylum, the hospital, the detention hospital, and the county agency. The county maintains at Dunning, just across the city limits line on the northwest, the infirmary and the insane asylum, together constituting the poorhouse; the infirmary with an average population of about 1,500, and the asylum with from 800 to 1,000 inmates. To show the relation of the infirmary population to the population of this district, it is enough to state that of its 5,651 admissions during the year 1893, there were 3,563 persons of foreign birth. The nativity records show that of this number Ireland furnishes 1,457; Germany, 727; England, 299; Sweden, 202; Canada, 183; Scotland, 135; Norway, 116; Poland, 80; Bohemia, 53; Austria, 61; Denmark, 53; Switzerland, 41; Italy, 40; Russia, 37; France, 28; Holland, 23; the balance being made up from thirteen countries.

The infirmary is a great brick building, with many well-lighted wards, steam-heated and clean. It is fronted by a grass plat, with trees and flower-beds, and the open country stretches back for miles, giving a good sweep for air and sunshine. There is a separate maternity ward, an attractive and comfortable brick cottage, at a distance of several hundred feet from the main building.

A very little work is required of each inmate to keep the place in order. There is a hired attendant in every ward, and over the men a supervisor, and over the women a supervisoress. The infirmary and the insane asylum are both under the control of one superintendent; and there is a corps of book-keepers and clerks who are necessary to keep accounts and registers, and do the office work required in carrying on the affairs of a community of this size.

The head cooks are regular employees, as are all the directing powers; but most of the work of the laundry, the wards, the bakery, the dining-room, the sewing room, is performed by the inmates. In the work of the farm of one hundred and sixty acres, as many men inmates as possible of both the infirmary and the insane asylum are utilized. Divided among such numbers, there are still many hours of listless idleness for hundreds of these people, men and women alike. It is to be noted at once that there are no shops, no provision for industries. The clothing is the usual cotton found in such institutions; and that, together with the bedding furnished, is under ordinary circumstances abundant for warmth in buildings well heated by steam as are these.

The women's wards are never crowded as are the men's. By some curious law of pauperism and male irresponsibility, whose careful study offers an interminable task to any loving collector of data, men are in a great majority in poorhouses. In the Cook County infirmary we find the following proportions:—

> January 4, 1894, 1,455 men and 396 women.
> January 4, 1893, 1,156 men and 380 women.
> January 4, 1892, 1,108 men and 321 women.
> January 4, 1891, 1,021 men and 469 women.

A curious indication of the effect of hard times is shown in the sudden increase of 299 in the male population, and of only 16 among the women,—nearly 25 percent in the first case, and a little over 4 percent in the second, from January, 1893, to January, 1894.

There is a chapel, in which a kindly old Catholic priest and various Protestant clergymen alternately officiate. The solemn little room is always open; and after the early winter supper, old people clamber painfully upstairs to say their evening prayers before its altar. For one instant the visitor is hushed as he stands before the door, watching the straggling little procession of human wastage entering the dim apartment, and feels a thrill of thankfulness that these poor evidences of defeat and failure cherish a belief in some divine accounting more individual and generous than that of the sociologist and statistician.

In a winter so unprecedented as that of 1893–1894, the men's wards are always full, many of them fearfully over-crowded, and certain of the hallways are some times nightly filled with straw ticks for sleepers who cannot be accommodated in the wards. In the men's and women's wards alike, the beds are set closely, and at best allow only a chair and a few feet by the window for each occupant. Ward 3 B, with beds crowded together, others made on the floor, and filled with a melancholy company of feeble and bedridden men and idiot children, must haunt the memory of whoever has seen it.

The surgical wards are of course less crowded, and are clean. The men's and women's consumptive wards are sunny and clean, and not painfully crowded. There are two resident physicians, a man and a woman, and their services are needed for the chronic and hopeless cases sent to the infirmary from the Cook County Hospital, and these would alone fill a small hospital. There are here usually from fifty to seventy-five children, of whom a large proportion are young children with their mothers, and very few of whom are for adoption. The remainder, perhaps a third, are the residuum of all the orphan asylums and hospitals, children whom no one cares to adopt because they are unattractive or scarred or sickly. These children are sent to the public school across the street from the poor-farm. Of course they wear hideous clothes, and of course the outside children sometimes jeer at them; and then if they are stout little lads like Jim Crow, they doubtless, as did he one day, teach courtesy to their tormentors with their fists.

And now what impression does the visitor receive who sees the infirmary, not as to the great problems of pauperism and crime, for the study of which this place offers infinite opportunity; not upon the value or efficiency of our system of caring for the dependent, but simply as to whether the work undertaken is adequately and reasonably performed? Do we have difficulty in understanding the universal dread of the "County"?[1]

Let us leave to quite one side considerations as to the moral deserts of these people, admitting even that most are brought here by their own misbehavior or that of those responsible for them. The county of Cook has them as wards. The determining standard of treatment is not "what they have been accustomed to," but what experience and modern science show to be essential to the proper care of such a mass. The absolute lack of privacy, the monotony and dulness, the discipline, the enforced cleanliness,—these are the inevitable and, in the opinion of some, the wholesome disadvantages of the infirmary from the standpoint of the inmate. There is not a common sitting-room for men or for women in the whole great place; the supply of books and papers is so small as scarcely to be visible. Occasionally one may see a group of men playing cards upon a bed in one corner of a ward, and the old fellows have a tobacco allowance; but any provision for homely comfort, for amusements or distractions from themselves and their compulsory neighbors, is wanting alike for the most decent and the most worthless.

If husbands and wives are obliged to come to the infirmary, they are always separated, no matter how aged and infirm, nor how blameless. How painful this separation may be, is indicated by the attitude of an old Irish couple of my acquaintance. They are past the power of self-support; their only child, a son, is an incurable lunatic, confined at Dunning. At one time they held title to a house and lot—"worth $6,000 now," the old woman says with mournful pride,—and are, to judge from internal evidence, and from the testimony of the neighbors, honest, decent people. When Dunning was suggested to them they were panic-stricken; and the old woman; who is ninety odd, said, "Oh, he'll have to go in with the men; I'll have to go in with the women, and all our own clothes will be taken away from us. I can somehow sort o' do for myself; but he is somehow sort o' shiftless like, and he can't. I'll feel sorrier for him than for me. I am older than he is, but I can get along better'n he. Let us stay here."

The meals are served three times daily, in a common dining-room, from bare tables scrubbed white, and the seats are backless benches. The room is so small that the benches are filled and refilled, first with the women and then with the men, until all have eaten. The food is perhaps more nourishing than many had at home, but that has nothing to do with the case. Its original quality is, in fact, good or aggressively bad, depending upon the administration. The cooking is bad,—tea boiled forty-five

---

1. The one exception in the range of my acquaintance to this dislike of the infirmary is on the part of a little Irish woman, a soldier's widow, who is lame and feeble, but who by the aid of a small pension is able to fee the attendants a bit, and who moves from the infirmary to some humble friend in the city and back again with the elegance and dignity which only leisure and money can bestow.

minutes, mushes cooked very hard, three-quarters of an hour, cheap cuts of meat kept madly jumping in the pot for an hour or less, fats almost eliminated, such cooking cannot give from the materials employed a wholesome dietary.

But in the infirmary, as in the three other county institutions, the pivot upon which turns the question of sweet or tainted meat, as well as the care and nursing of all these feeble beings, is the change in the *personnel* of the county board, which annually, and hereafter biennially, means a change in practically all the officers of this institution. Is it strange that now and again grave scandals reach even the deaf ear of the indifferent public, when we realize that the appointment of all the persons who have charge of this community is made and changed solely according to political preference? "Not fitness, but 'pull,'" is necessarily their motto. It is this irresponsible supervision which must entail the greatest hardship upon this feeble-minded and irresponsible population.

The insane hospital is upon the same grounds as the infirmary, about a thousand feet distant. Here are gathered usually about eight hundred men and women, paupers, incurably insane. Can words express a more pitiable condition? Certainly there are no creatures in a state of more painful helplessness. Here, as in the infirmary, all appears immaculately clean, and fortunately so, for the construction of the wards is such that only their perfect cleanliness makes them tolerable. Many are long, dark tunnels, in which it is the simple truth to say that sunshine can never penetrate, save for a short distance at either end. The plan is the old one of long interior corridors, from which open the sleeping-rooms on either side, with a dining-room also off the corridor. These rooms, together with bath-room and clothes-room, constitute the usual ward. On some of the wards the corridor broadens out transversely into a sitting-room, and on a few there is only a single row of sleeping-rooms, thus giving outside windows for the corridor; but the usual arrangement is the dark, narrow inside corridor. In this the patients must spend their waking hours. In such a hospital, there are a large proportion of patients sunk in various stages of dementia, who are dead to any save the most primal physical sensations; but, on the other hand, there are unfortunately a proportion of curable patients even here, and there are chronic cases not demented. For the year 1893, there are reported seventy-two recoveries, which is in itself a proof that the county is obliged to care for more than its legal charge; i.e., the incurable insane.

The admissions to the insane asylum for the year 1893 were 442, of whom 109 are entered as born in the United States; of the remaining three-quarters, Germany is charged with 96; Sweden and Norway with 45; Ireland, 74; Poland, 13; Bohemia, 8; Russia, 5; Austria, 8; unknown, 20; while the others are contributed from fifteen different countries. Here, as in the infirmary and other institutions where birthplace only is entered, without lineage, it is not possible to state from the records how many are Jewish; but it is certain that a considerable proportion are, probably, for instance, all of those born in Russia. Of the admissions for 1893, 288 were men and 154 were women, a preponderance of men far beyond the usual proportion in insane hospitals. In the

State hospitals, in 1892, out of a total population of 5,177, there were only one-tenth more men than women.

Two physicians, a man and a woman, have charge of the medical side of the asylum. In addition to the main building, there are already four cottages, two for men and two for women, receiving about fifty patients each. Two of these are used as infirmary wards, and the others for quiet inmates. The Wines cottage has the lightest and most spacious sitting-room, and the darkest and most unattractive cellar dining-room imaginable. This is an illustration of the irregularity with which work is done for public purposes; for there is a still unexecuted conception of a great general dining-room, lacking which, this honest cellar is made to do duty. The ward dining-rooms have many disadvantages, and a general dining-hall would be a most wholesome improvement. It is intended that the food of the asylum shall be somewhat more liberal than that of the infirmary; but here, as there, the cooking methods are absolutely unscientific. The chief additional items are, that butter is allowed for all meals, and that pudding is given for dinner. There is mush for breakfast; for dinner, beef and potato and another vegetable—often cabbage; for supper, stewed apples or rice; with coffee or tea for breakfast and dinner, and tea for supper, and bread and butter for all meals. Unfortunately, this sounds better than it is in fact. Few persons could see the food as prepared and served (excepting the bread) without a sense of physical revolt.

The attendants are too few in number to give the patients proper out-door exercise, which they especially need, because of the darkness of the wards and the fact that they are seriously overcrowded according to modern hospital standards. There is no system of employment here for the patients, save some work in keeping the wards in order and about the house. The monotony and idleness, the unutterable dreariness, dull the faculties of those not already beyond change.

But if the constant succession of new attendants is prejudicial to the proper work of the infirmary, what must it be here, where insane people are to be cared for? A man or a woman overcome with an infirmity, which the laws of Illinois at last recognize as a disease, is placed in constant care night and day of nurses trained for such care? Not at all. But of some one who has a "pull." I chanced to be standing in the asylum corridor one day just after there had been a revolution of the county wheel, when a stout, aggressive and excited Irish woman, evidently an attendant, bore down upon one of the commissioners present, who was also of foreign birth, and said, "Mr. Blank, I want to see you." To which he replied with a helpless gesture, "Well, I hope you don't want anything, because I haven't got anything left."—"Aw, don't tell that to me, Mr. Blank! Do you know I live only two blocks from your house, and we've got nine men in our house that worked mighty hard for you?"—"Well, I can't help it; I haven't got anything left. Can't you see I am busy talking now?" To which the attendant replied more imperatively than ever, "Well, I want to see you; I want to see you alone. Where is Mr. So-and-So?" with which she flounced on, to return later. The remarkable thing with our present system of appointments is, not that abuses occur, but that more do not occur. It gives one, after all, a new confidence in human nature, that the demands of helplessness and insanity develop in unpromising material such excellent qualities of patience and self-control as are sometimes shown.

Down in the city of Chicago the county carries on its remaining charitable undertakings. Out on Harrison Street, a little over two miles from the lake, stands the Cook County Hospital, to which were admitted in the year 1893 more than eleven thousand cases, while more than two thousand were dressed and sent home. It is due to the substitution of trained nurses for the former political-appointee attendants, that this hospital now stands in the front rank of American public hospitals, so far as the nursing care of the wards is concerned. Its benefits are given free of charge. The position of an interne in this hospital is only obtained after competitive examination, and it is much coveted. One reason why it is coveted may be found in the statement of an interne, whose naivete can no more be questioned than his truthfulness. "I like my position. In fact, I much prefer it to a similar place in a New York hospital. There about all an interne can do is to follow after the outside doctors on their rounds, and watch them, and hear what they say, and see their prescriptions. But here the outside doctors do not visit regularly, and do not interfere with the interne's treatment." There may be carpers who would pick a flaw in the county's method of educating doctors by self-instruction; but it would seem that no paternalist could question its care—for the medical profession. Yet just at this point the paternalist and the man of medical science do agree in questioning this care, and that on the ground of the best service for the hospital wards. They say that the attending physicians, who are now forbidden to bring students upon the wards, should be allowed to do so, on the same principle that the surgeons bring the students into the amphitheatre; that if the physician had this privilege, they would give the wards all due attention, and the education of the interne and the student would be better in proportion to the skill the attending physician could offer the patient. Neither the physicians nor the surgeons of the Cook County Hospital staff are salaried; and the appointments are valued for prestige, and for clinical advantages. As the physician and surgeon gain prestige through the reputations of their clinics, and as the forbidding of students upon the wards practically forbids the physician having any clinical advantages from the hospital, it is easy to understand why the salaried internes have full sway. Moreover, there can be no doubt that the practitioner feels himself spurred to his best efforts by the presence of students, the most mercilessly critical beings in existence; and thus incidentally the patient might be benefited. We are told that the opening of the wards of the free hospital of New Orleans to students resulted in a diminished death-rate. The great foreign free hospitals are open, and it would be difficult to find any sound reason for the closing of Cook County.

Here again, the food problem is unsolved, save that here, again, the bread is of the average baker's quality. The ward cooking, done by convalescents, cannot be satisfactory. The old kitchen is unwholesome in odor and appearance, and the whole culinary department shows an inattention to scientific methods more painful in a hospital than anywhere else. The constant change in the business management entailed by the constant succession of administrative officers of course makes it expensive and really impossible to carry on the business side of this hospital in the best manner.

Unfortunately the hospital is obliged to discharge many patients before they are strong enough to work, and oftentimes patients who are without money or home. The only place where a person without money or a home can go is Dunning; and self-respecting people decline that, and stagger along, beginning work too soon. This is, in the long run, financially expensive to the county, as it destroys or impairs the power of the individual to support himself. A proper convalescents' home would lengthen the working-life of many a man and woman, to say nothing of its increasing their comfort. And an establishment of this sort in country surroundings would be justified by the success of the Boston Convalescents' Home.

The detention hospital stands upon the same plat of ground with the hospital. Here the insane are brought and confined for periods of from twenty-four hours to eight days (in exceptional cases even two or three weeks), pending the weekly hearing of insane cases. The court sits in this building, so that no exposure is necessary in carrying patients to and from a down-town courtroom. This building, too, is immaculately clean. Indeed, it sometimes seems as though this were the age of institutional tidiness; and that in itself is a cheering sign of advancing care, though the polished outside of cup and platter may be delusive.

Through this detention hospital must pass in turn the insane persons of Cook County; and she now contributes more than twenty-five hundred to the insane population of the State. When this hospital was built, it was fondly hoped that many hysterical and recent cases might be cured by a few days or weeks of its tender care; but the facts, as shown by the investigation of the winter of 1894, prove how far from curative the institution is, and must be so long as it is managed upon its present basis. The attendants are political appointees. It is useless to enter into brutal particulars; it is enough to say that they are and must be ill-fitted for the care of insane patients who are received here at the most critical and violent periods of their malady. The detention hospital should be treated as a ward of the Cook County hospital, and trained nurses with specific teaching in the care of the insane placed in charge.

There is at present no training-school for nurses for the insane in this State; and if one could be thus established, which should have in charge the detention hospital, it would be a starting-point for better work everywhere. In connection with the training-school for nurses, which has in charge most of the wards of the Cook County hospital, this is an entirely feasible plan. In fact, it only requires the taking of twelve appointments out of politics, and some changes in the medical attendance, not requiring more money, to make this hospital as nearly a model as its cramped quarters will allow.

The most spectacular proof of the poverty entailed upon Chicago by the general business depression of 1893, and locally by the inevitable human *débris* left by the

World's Fair, could be daily seen during all the severer months of the winter of 1893 and 1894. It was a solid, pressing crowd of hundreds of shabby men and shawled or hooded women, coming from all parts of a great city whose area is over one hundred and eighty-six square miles, standing hour after hour with market baskets high above their heads, held in check by policemen, polyglot, but having the common language of their persistency, their weariness, their chill and hunger. This crowd stood daily, unsheltered from the weather, before 130 South Clinton Street. Now and again a woman was crushed,—in one instance it is reported was killed, and the ambulance was called to take her away. Once a case of smallpox was discovered, and a sign hung out, and the office closed for a day or two; but this did not frighten away the crowd outside. It only served to give the clerks inside a little chance to get their work up. When once the applicant penetrates the office, he is in the great dingy waiting-room of the Cook County Agency, from whence is dispensed out-door relief. He furnishes his name and address, and is called upon later by a paid visitor, upon whose report the fuel and ration are allowed or refused. Or, if the application has been granted, the market basket discloses its *raison d'être*, and the allowance of food and one bar of hard soap is carried hence, the coal being sent later from the contractor.

It is hard to go to the infirmary, hard to get relief from the county; but it is esteemed hardest of all to be buried by the county. The abhorrence of a pauper burial cannot be better indicated than by the fact that of the 607 inmates who died at Dunning in 1893, the funerals of 251 were provided by friends. Indeed, the one general effort at saving in this district is that sorry speculation in futures called burial-insurance. Of course there are numberless lapses of the policies, which make the business profitable. The dread of pauper burial is twofold. First, the lack of religious ceremony, and, secondly, the loss of a great social function, far exceeding in magnificence a wedding or a christening. The necessary cost of sickness and death is vastly increased by absolutely unnecessary items on the undertaker's bill. It is the hope of this anticipated pageantry which makes the burial-insurance collector a constant figure, threading in and out among the tenements, and collecting his weekly premiums. "And to think," exclaimed a mother, in a spasm of baffled prudence and grief, "that this child I've lost was the only one that wasn't insured!"

There is a constant criticism of the county relief office from the recipient's point of view. He says the coal is delivered slowly and in scant measure, that favoritism is shown by visitors, that burials are tardy and cruel; and the facts justify him. But any one acquainted with the daily work of this office must feel that the wonder is that the $100,000 allotted for its work is really as fairly divided as we find it. The methods of this office, with its records kept as each changing administration chooses, its doles subject to every sort of small political influence, and its failure to co-operate with private charities, are not such as science can approve.

These institutions cost the county for running expenses alone, nearly $700,000 annually, providing salaried positions for five hundred persons or more, and of course do in some degree meet the necessities of a great dependent population which is at present an unavoidable factor in our social problem. Yet such a state of irresponsibility as investigation now and again discloses must discourage us. We are impressed with the lack of system and classification among the beneficiaries of the infirmary and the county agency for outdoor relief. We are shocked by the crudeness of the management which huddles men, women, and children, the victims of misfortune and the relics of dissipation, the idle, the ineffective criminal, the penniless convalescent, under one roof and one discipline. On purely economic grounds we need a children's home, or some provision so that no child shall be in a poorhouse. We need a home for convalescents. Both humanity and economy demand that there be workshops provided at Dunning for the sane and the insane paupers. Then there is that small remnant of blameless poor for whom we can surely make more dignified provision without pauperizing society. It is painful enough to see "desert a beggar," without seeing her thrust in to die disgraced by the association of a public poorhouse. Yet these measures, unfortunately, will be considered primarily only as furnishing certain "places" to be filled by political preferment. The comfort, the recovery, the lives, of all these thousands of dependent people, hang upon the knowledge, the kindliness, the honesty, and good faith of those hired to care for them. How are these people hired,—in the open labor market, for fitness, by examination? Not even an Altrurian would waste words on such a question. These places are scheduled, with the salaries attached, and each commissioner disposes of his share of the patronage. Commissioners are not responsible for this method; it is not unlawful, and it is convenient for them. They act from the pressure of public opinion translatable into votes, and modify their actions according to the strength of such pressure. How many persons in the city of Chicago whose incomes make them safe from the possibility of a personal interest in these places ever visit them, or perhaps know where they are ? More, how many of them realize that their visits, their intelligent interest, are all that is necessary to make these institutions give really good service? There is no mal-administration so strong that it can persist in the face of public knowledge and attention. The public now has and will have exactly such institutions as it demands, managed exactly as its discrimination requires. It is as tiresome as that Carthage must be destroyed, but it is as true, that the charities of Cook County will never properly perform their duties until politics are divorced from them.

IX

ART AND LABOR

Ellen Gates Starr

To any one living in a working-class district of a great city to-day, the question must arise whether it be at all worth the cost to try to perpetuate art under conditions so hopeless, or whether it be not the only rational or even possible course to give up the struggle from that point, and devote every energy to "the purification of the nation's heart and the chastisement of its life." Only by re-creation of the source of art can it be restored as a living force. But one must always remember the hungering individual soul which, without it, will have passed unsolaced and unfed, followed by other souls who lack the impulse his should have given. And when one sees how almost miraculously the young mind often responds to what is beautiful in its environment, and rejects what is ugly, it renews courage to set the leaven of the beautiful in the midst of the ugly, instead of waiting for the ugly to be first cleared away.

A child of two drunken parents one day brought to Hull-House kindergarten and presented to her teacher a wretched print, with the explanation, "See the Lady Moon." The Lady Moon, so named in one of the songs the children sing, was dimly visible in an extreme corner of the print otherwise devoted to murder and sudden death; but it was the only thing the child really saw.

The nourishment to life of one good picture to supplant in interest vicious story-papers and posters; of one good song to take the place of vulgar street jingles, cannot, I believe, be estimated or guessed. A good picture for every household seems unattainable until households can produce, or at least select, their own; but certainly a good one in every schoolroom would not be unattainable, if the public should come to regard it as a matter of moment that the rooms in which the children of the land spend their most impressionable days be made beautiful and suggestive, instead of barren and repellant.

Mr. T. C. Horsfall, of Manchester, England, who has developed a system of circulating collections of pictures in the schools[1] of that unhappy city, says that the decision

---

1. The principles and plan of Mr. Horsfall's beneficent work may be found in his papers entitled, "The Use of Pictures in Schools," "Art in Large Towns," and "The Work of the Manchester Art Museum." J. E. Cornish, St. Ann's Square, Manchester.

as to whether art shall be used in education is, to modern communities, a decision as to whether the mass of the people shall be barbarian or civilized. Assuredly it has a direct bearing upon the art-producing possibilities of the communities in question.

Let us consider what is the prospect for an "art of the people" in our great cities. And first let us admit that art must be of the people if it is to be at all. We must admit this whether we look into the life of the past or into our own life. If we look to any great national art, that of Athens or of Venice or of Florence, we see that it has not been produced by a few, living apart, fed upon conditions different from the common life; but that it has been, in great part, the expression of that common life. If it has reached higher than the common life, it has done so only by rising through it, never by springing up outside it and apart from it. When Florence decked herself with reliefs of the Madonna and the Infant, the life of Florence was a devotion to these shrines. Giotto and Donatello only expressed with a power and grace concentrated in them what all the people felt; and more than that, had not the people felt thus, there could have been no medium for that grace and power.

If we are to have a national art at all, it must be art of the people; and art can only come to a free people. The great prophet of art in our day, John Ruskin, has said that "all great art is praise," showing man's pleasure in God's work; and his disciple, William Morris, expresses another side of the same truth when he says that "to each man is due the solace of art in his labor, and the opportunity of expressing his thoughts to his fellows through that labor." Now, only a free man can express himself in his work. If he is doing slave's work, under slavish conditions, it is doubtful whether he will ultimately have many thoughts worth the name; and if he have, his work can in no wise be their vehicle. It is only when a man is doing work which he wishes done, and delights in doing, and which he is free to do as he likes, that his work becomes a language to him. As soon as it does so become it is artistic. Every man working in the joy of his heart is, in some measure, an artist. Everything wrought with delight in the work itself is, in some measure, lovely. The destructive force of the ugly is its heartlessness. The peasant's cottage in the Tyrol, built with its owner's hands, decorated with his taste, and propounding his morals and religion in inlaid sentences under its broad eaves, blesses the memory with a beauty but half obliterated by daily sight of dreary parallelograms and triangles, joylessly united, which make up the streets of our working-people. The streets of Venice, of Verona, of Rouen, were built by men working in freedom, at liberty to vary a device or to invent one. They were not built by lawlessness or caprice, but under a willing service, which alone is perfect freedom.

The same men who built so nobly the cathedrals and council-halls of Rouen and Venice, built as harmoniously, though more simply and modestly, as was fit, their own dwellings. Had they been capable of making their own houses ugly, they would have been incapable of housing beautifully the rulers of their city or the King of kings.

This is the fatal mistake of our modern civilization, which is causing it to undo itself and become barbarous in its unloveliness and discord. We have believed that we could force men to live without beauty in their own lives, and still compel them to make for us the beautiful things in which we have denied them any part. We have supposed that we could teach men, in schools, to produce a grace and harmony which they never see, and which the life that we force them to live utterly precludes. Or else we have thought—a still more hopeless error—that they, the workers, the makers, need not know what grace and beauty and harmony are; that artists and architects may keep the secrets, and the builders and makers, not knowing them, can slavishly and mechanically execute what the wise in these mysteries plan.

The results should long ago have taught us our mistake. But only now are we learning, partly from dismal experience of life barren of beauty and variety, and partly from severe but timely teaching from such prophets as Ruskin and Morris, that no man can execute artistically what another man plans, unless the workman's freedom has been part of the plan. The product of a machine may be useful, and may serve some purposes of information, but can never be artistic. As soon as a machine intervenes between the mind and its product, a hard, impassable barrier—a non-conductor of thought and emotion—is raised between the speaking and the listening mind. If a man is made a machine, if his part is merely that of reproducing, with mechanical exactness, the design of somebody else, the effect is the same. The more exact the reproduction, the less of the personality of the man who does the work is in the product, the more uninteresting will the product be. A demonstration of how uninteresting this slavish machine-work can become may be found in the carved and upholstered ornamentation of any drawing-room car—one might also say of any drawing-room one enters.

I have never seen in a city anything in the way of decoration upon the house of an American citizen which he had himself designed and wrought for pleasure in it. In the house of an Italian peasant immigrant in our own neighborhood, I have seen wall and ceiling decorations of his own design, and done by his own hand in colors. The designs were very rude, the colors coarse; but there was nothing of the vulgar in it, and there was something of hope. The peasant immigrant's surroundings begin to be vulgar precisely at the point where he begins to buy and adorn his dwelling with the products of American manufacture. What he brings with him in the way of carven bed, wrought kerchief, enamel inlaid picture of saint or angel, has its charm of human touch, and is graceful, however childish.

The peasants themselves secretly prefer their old possessions, but are sustained by a proud and virtuous consciousness of having secured what other people have and what the world approves. A dear old peasant friend of Hull-House once conceived the notion that the dignity of his wife—whom he called "my lady"—required that she have a dress in the American mode. Many were the mediatorial struggles which we enacted before this "American dress" was fitted and done. And then, by the mercy of Heaven, her courage gave out, and she never wore it. She found it too uncomfortable, and I know that in her inmost heart she found it too ugly.

Could men build their own houses, could they carve or fresco upon casing, door, or ceiling any decoration which pleased them, it is inconceivable that, under conditions of freedom and happiness, they should refrain from doing so. It is inconceivable that, adorning their own dwellings in the gladness of their hearts, they should not develop something of grace, of beauty, of meaning, in what their hands wrought; impossible that their hands should work on unprompted by heart or brain; impossible then, as inevitable now, that most men's houses should express nothing of themselves save a dull acceptance of things commercially and industrially thrust upon them.

A workingman must accept his house as he finds it. He not only cannot build it, he cannot buy it, and is usually not at liberty to alter it materially, even had he the motive to do so, being likely to leave it at any time. The frescoed ceiling to which I have referred, as the only example within my experience of any attempt at original decoration, was in a cottage tenement. If the author had any affection for the work of his hands, he could not take it away with him. He would probably not be permitted, were he inclined, to carve the doorposts; and the uncertainty of tenure would deter him from yielding to any artistic prompting to do so. It would be disheartening to find one's belongings set into the street, and be obliged to leave one's brave device half finished.

A man's happiness, as well as his freedom, is a necessary condition of his being artistic. Ruskin lays it down as a law that neither vice nor pain can enter into the entirely highest art. How far art can be at all co-existent with pain, ugliness, gloom, sorrow, slavery, concerns very vitally the question of an art of the people.

No civilized and happy people has ever been able to express itself without art. The prophet expands his "All great art is praise" into "The art of man is the expression of his rational and disciplined delight in the forms and laws of the creation of which he forms a part." A rational and disciplined delight in the forms and laws of the creation of which a denizen of an industrial district in one of our great cities forms a conscious part is inconceivable. Some of the laws which govern its conscious life may be traced in their resultant forms.

Its most clearly manifested law is "the iron law of wages." Of the workings and products of this law in squalor, deformity, and irrecoverable loss of health, many examples are given in the accompanying article on child-labor.

Of the law of love manifested in the harmonious life of the universe, these little toilers know nothing. Of the laws of healthy growth of mind and body by air, sunlight, and wholesome work, neither they nor their children can know anything. Of the laws of heredity they know bitterly, and of the law of arrested development.

It is needlessly painful to say here in what forms these laws have made themselves known to them, and to all who look upon them. It is equally needless to say that they can have no delight in these forms, no wish to reflect and perpetuate them. Need it be said that they can have no art?

The Greek was compelled by his joy in his own and his brother's beauty and strength to make it abiding, and a joy to all who should look upon it. It was a not unreasonable pride which offered to the gods as a religious act the feats of those strong and perfect bodies; and Greek sculpture smiles forth the gladness of the Greek heart blithely in its graceful runners and wrestlers, solemnly in its august deities, whose laws the people obeyed, and rejoiced in obeying. It may not be quite profitless, though altogether painful, to think sometimes of the weak, small, ugly frames produced by the life we force men and little children to live, and of which we would not dare make an offering to an offended God, whose laws we have neither rejoiced in nor obeyed.

Obedience to physical law results always in forms of physical beauty; love of these forms and happy activity, in artistic expression. From disobedience to law follows physical ugliness, which inspires nothing but apathy or distaste, and results in no artistic utterance. A higher art is born of delight in spiritual beauty, consequent upon obedience to law above the physical. It remains to determine how far the disharmony of disobedience can have expression through art. Discord has place in music only as a negative, to give accent to the positive good. Variety is good, but the eye and ear crave occasional monotony in art-form to make the good of multiform life keenly felt. Beyond that need monotony and discord are both painful. This is the limit of the purely artistic use of these negative values.

The expression of the negative in art-form has, however, within limits, another legitimate use, which bears the same relation to art in its strict sense which pamphleteering bears to literature proper.

Against the infliction or willing permission of pain, there is a gospel to be preached; and for the effectual preaching of this gospel, literature, art, every language in which it can be couched, may be pressed into service.

> "We're made so that we love
> First when we see them painted, things we've passed
> Perhaps a hundred times nor cared to see;
> And so they are better, painted,—better to us,
> Which is the same thing. Art was given for that."

So it was,—to make us love the lovable. But if we are made so, too, that we hate for the first time as it deserves to be hated, and dread as we ought to dread it when we see it painted, the destruction of the lovable and the beautiful by the impious hand of man, then art must descend from her altar service to that hard work of discipline.

As long as we inflict or supinely permit the wilful destruction of life by rapid process or slow, we need to be shocked into the realization of our guilt. But we cannot grow by a series of shocks; and only in so far as we are conceivably responsible for any measure of this woe, and most assuredly only in so far as the sight of it is awful and unbearable to us, can it be anything but harmful to us to see it. So far as it gives any pleasure it blunts or degrades. It is only the faith that God wills that not one of His children should perish, and that with Him all things are possible, in His eternity, which makes it endurable to look for one moment upon the starvation and degradation of mind and soul, the defacement of the image of God by man, in Millet's "Laborer." Strange that we can bear so constantly the sight of the real laborer; that the back bent, never to stand erect in the true figure of a man, the stolid and vacant face, should be looked upon with such equanimity and apathetic acceptance.

The pictures of Jean François Millet illustrate well the limit beyond which art cannot go into the realm of gloom and wrong. They are entirely true always. They reflect perfectly the life and work of the people he knew best, and of whose life he was part. They are beautiful and artistic, or painful and inartistic, just in the degree in which naturalness, the joy, the rightness, or the unnaturalness, severity, gloom and slavery of that life predominate. From the child carrying a lamb in her arms, and followed by the loving mother and whole docile flock; the father stretching out his arms to his baby, graceful in his love through the clumsiness of his excessive toil; all the dreary distance to that heartbreaking image of man's desecration he passes, through every step of increasing backache and stolidity, fearless and, indeed, helpless. It is the awful record of a soul seeing things as they are, and recording them as he must in his art language, which ceases to be artistic and becomes ugly, inartistic, inarticulate, and finally refuses to go farther into the discord of man's desolate, stifled, degraded life. Behind the laborer with the hoe stretch God's earth and sky. "With these open witnesses, you have done that, O man! What you have done in darkness, away from the face of these witnesses, my art cannot say." No true art can. Into the prison-houses of earth, its sweat-shops and underground lodging-houses, art cannot follow.

Whatever the inspiring motive of art, though there be in it pain and struggle, the result must be one of triumph, at least of hope. Art can never present humanity as overborne. It cannot let the hostile principle, pain, sorrow, sin, at the last conquer. Just where it begins to smother and snuff out the flame of life, art turns away.

When life reaches a point at which it can furnish no more material for art, we cannot look to it for an artistic people. If in all the environment of a man's life, there is nothing which can inspire a true work of art, there is nothing to inspire a true love of it, could it be produced. The love of the beautiful grows by what it feeds on; and the food must be the common bread of life. That which makes the art-loving people, makes the artist also. Every nation which has left a great art record has lived an artistic life. The artist is not a product of spontaneous generation. Every Athenian, every Florentine boy, saw daily in the street the expression of the most perfect thought of his people, reflecting their thought of God; and he saw it, side by side with God's own thought, undefaced and undefiled. He saw column and tower and statue standing against a sky, the pure, serene, tender, infinite mirror of the divine intelligence and love; and hills, the unswerving image of divine steadfastness. He saw them unpolluted by the smoke, and undistracted by the din of commercial strife. Poor or rich, the best his nation wrought was his. He must be taught his art as a craft, if he were to follow it; and he did learn it precisely as a craft which must be honestly and industriously practised. But first and always he lived it, as a life, in common with the life of his nation.

The boy of our great cities, rich or poor (we are so far democratic), has this common inheritance. He sees from his earliest years the mart;—not the *mereato vecehio* of Florence, where the angel faces of Della Robbia looked down above the greengrocer's wares in the open booth, from out wreaths of fruit and flowers that vied with those below; but our *mereato nuovo.* He sees there walls high and monotonous; windows all alike (which he who built had no pleasure in); piles of merchandise, not devised with curious interest and pleasant exercise of inventive faculty, but with stolid, mechanical indifference; garish wares, and faces too harassed and hurried to give back greeting. These belong to rich and poor alike. But here the lots diverge. The poor lad goes, not to his sheep, like Giotto, nor to keeping his feet warm, like Luca, in a basket of shavings, while he works cheerily at his art and saves fire; he goes home to the dreary tenement, not fireless, but with closed windows to keep its heat within, dingy plaster, steam of washing and odors of cooking, near discordant voices, loneliness of a crowded life without companionship or high ideals; and for view of hills and sky, the theatre bills on the walls across the street, and factory chimneys.

The son of the rich man goes home to his father's house. Through plate glass and lace curtains he looks across at his neighbor's father's house, with its lace curtains,— perhaps a little less costly, perhaps a little more. Up and down the street he compares the upholstery, the equipages, the number and formality of the servants belonging to the establishments which represent his social life. He has flowers in a greenhouse; he has fine clothes; he has books; he has pictures. Does he live an artistic life? Can we look to him for the great art of the future? Alas! "The life of the poor is too painful; the life of the rich too vulgar." Rather, is not the life of each both painful and vulgar to a degree which seems almost beyond hope? "The haggard despair of cotton-factory, coal-mine operatives in these days is painful to behold; but not so painful, hideous to the inner sense, as that brutish, God-forgetting, Profit-and-loss Philosophy and Life-Theory which we bear jangled on all hands of us, from the throats and pens and thoughts of all-but all men."[2] Happily, at least for art, there remains that "all-but" modicum,—be tenaciously impractical and unbusiness-like, the incorrigibly unconvinced as to the supreme importance of "selling cotton cheaper." Else "vacuum and the serene blue" would, indeed, "be much handsomer" than this our civilization. For the children of the "degraded poor," and the degraded rich as well, in our present mode of life, there is no artistic hope outside of miracle.

There is one hope for us all,—a new life, a freed life. He who hopes to help art survive on earth till the new life dawns, must indeed feed the hungry with good things. This must he do, but not neglect for this the more compassionate and far-reaching

---

2. Carlyle, *Past and Present.*

aim, the freeing of the art power of the whole nation and race by enabling them to work in gladness and not in woe. It is a feeble and narrow imagination which holds out to chained hands fair things which they cannot grasp,—things which they could fashion for themselves were they but free.

The soul of man in the commercial and industrial struggle is in a state of siege. He is fighting for his life. It is merciful and necessary to pass in to him the things which sustain his courage and keep him alive, but the effectual thing is to raise the siege.

A settlement, if it is true to its ideal, must stand equally for both aims. It must work with all energy and courage toward the rescue of those bound under the slavery of commerce and the wage-law; with all abstinence it must discountenance wasting human life in the making of valueless things; with all faith it must urge forward the building up of a state in which cruel contrasts of surfeit and want, of idleness and overwork, shall not be found. By holding art and all good fruit of life to be the right of all; by urging all, because of this their common need, to demand time and means for supplying it; by reasonableness in the doing, with others, of useful, wholesome, beneficent work, and the enjoyment, with others, of rightful and sharable pleasure, a settlement should make toward a social state which shall finally supplant this incredible and impious warfare of the children of God.

Whatever joy is to us ennobling; whatever things seem to us made for blessing, and not for weariness and woe; whatever knowledge lifts us out of things paltry and narrowing, and exalts and expands our life; whatever life itself is real and worthy to endure, as there is measure of faith in us, and hope and love and patience, let us live this life. And let us think on our brothers, that they may live it too; for without them we cannot live it if we would; and when we and they shall have this joy of life, then we shall speak from within it, and our speech shall be sweet, and men will listen and be glad. What we do with our hands will be fair, and men shall have pleasure therein. This will be art. Otherwise we cannot all have it; and until all have it in some measure, none can have it in great measure. And if gladness ceases upon the earth, and we turn the fair earth into a prison-house for men with hard and loveless labor, art will die.

X

THE SETTLEMENT AS A FACTOR IN THE LABOR MOVEMENT

Jane Addams

One man or group of men sometimes reveal to their contemporaries a higher conscience by simply incorporating into the deed what has been before but a philosophic proposition. By this deed the common code of ethics is stretched to a higher point.

Such an act of moral significance, for instance, was John Burns's loyalty to the dockers' strike of East London. "The injury to one" did at last actually "become the concern of all"; and henceforth the man who does not share that concern drops below the standard ethics of his day. The proposition which workingmen had long quoted was at last incarnated by a mechanic, who took his position so intelligently that he carried with him the best men in England, and set the public conscience. Other men became ashamed of a wrong to which before they had been easily indifferent.

When the social conscience, if one may use the expression, has been thus strikingly formulated, it is not so hard for others to follow. They do it weakly and stumblingly perhaps; but they yet see a glimmer of light of which the first man could not be sure, and they have a code of ethics upon which the first man was vague. They are also conscious of the backing of a large share of the community who before this expression knew not the compunction of their own hearts. A settlement accepts the ethics of its contemporaries that the sharing of the life of the poor is essential to the understanding and bettering of that life; but by its very existence it adopts this modern code somewhat formally. The social injury of the meanest man not only becomes its concern, but by virtue of its very locality it has put itself into a position to see, as no one but a neighbor can see, the stress and need of those who bear the brunt of the social injury. A settlement has not only taken a pledge towards those thus injured, but it is placed where the motive-power for the fulfilment of such a pledge is constantly renewed. Propinquity is an unceasing factor in its existence.

A review of the sewing-trades, as seen from a settlement, will be sufficient to illustrate this position.

Hull-House is situated in the midst of the sweaters' district of Chicago. The residents came to the district with the general belief that organization for working-people was a necessity. They would doubtless have said that the discovery of the power to combine was the distinguishing discovery of our time; that we are using this force somewhat awkwardly, as men use that which is newly discovered. In social and political affairs the power to combine often works harm; but it is already operating to such an extent in commercial affairs, that the manufacturer who does not combine with others of his branch is in constant danger of failure; that a railroad cannot be successfully projected unless the interests of parallel roads are consulted; and that working-people likewise cannot be successful until they too, learn, skillfully to avail themselves of this power.

This was to the residents, as to many people, an accepted proposition, but not a working formula. It had not the driving force of a conviction. The residents have lived for five years in a neighborhood largely given over to the sewing-trades, which is an industry totally disorganized. Having observed the workers in this trade as compared to those in organized trades, they have gradually discovered that lack of organization in a trade tends to the industrial helplessness of the workers in that trade. If in all departments of social, political, and commercial life, isolation is a blunder, and results in dreariness and apathy, then in industrial affairs isolation is a social crime; for it there tends to extermination.

This process of extermination entails starvation and suffering, and the desperate moral disintegration which inevitably follows in their train, until the need of organization in industry gradually assumes a moral aspect. The conviction arrived at entails a social obligation.

No trades are so overcrowded as the sewing-trades, for the needle has ever been the refuge of the unskilled woman. The wages paid throughout the manufacture of clothing are less than those in any other trade. In order to meet the requirements of the workers, lack of skill and absence of orderly life, the work has been so subdivided that almost no skill is required after the garment leaves the cutter. It is given practically to the one who is at hand when it is ready, and who does it for the least money. This subdivision and low wage have gone so far, that the woman who does home finishing alone cannot possibly gain by it a living wage. The residents of Hull-House have carefully investigated many cases, and are ready to assert that the Italian-widow who finishes the cheapest goods, although she sews from six in the morning until eleven at night, can only get enough to keep her children clothed and fed; while for her rent and fuel she must always depend upon charity or the hospitality of her countrymen. If the American sewing-woman, supporting herself alone, lives on bread and butter and tea, she finds a Bohemian woman next door whose diet of black bread and coffee enables her to undercut. She competes with a wife who is eager to have home finishing that she may add something to the family comfort; or with a daughter who takes it that she may buy a wedding outfit.

The Hebrew tailor, the man with a family to support, who, but for this competition of unskilled women and girls, might earn a wage upon which a family could subsist, is obliged, in order to support them at all, to put his little children at work as soon as they can sew on buttons.

It does not help his industrial situation that the woman and girl who have brought it about have accepted the lower wages in order to buy comforts for an invalid child, or to add to the earnings of an aged father. The mother who sews on a gross of buttons for seven cents, in order to buy a blue ribbon with which to tie up her little daughter's hair, or the mother who finishes a dozen vests for five cents, with which to buy her children a loaf of bread, commits unwittingly a crime against her fellow-workers, although our hearts may thrill with admiration for her heroism, and ache with pity over her misery.

The maternal instinct and family affection is woman's most holy attribute; but if she enters industrial life, that is not enough. She must supplement her family con-science by a social and an industrial conscience. She must widen her family affection to embrace the children of the community. She is working havoc in the sewing-trades, because with the meagre equipment sufficient for family life she has entered industrial life.

Have we any right to place before untrained women the alternative of seeing their little children suffer, or of complicating the industrial condition until all the children of the community are suffering? We know of course what their decision would be. But the residents of a settlement are not put to this hard choice, although it is often dif-ficult to urge organization when they are flying to the immediate relief of the underfed children in the neighborhood.

If the settlement, then, is convinced that in industrial affairs lack of organization tends to the helplessness of the isolated worker, and is a menace to the entire com-munity, then it is bound to pledge itself to industrial organization, and to look about it for the lines upon which to work. And at this point the settlement enters into what is more technically known as the labor movement.

The labor movement may be called a concerted effort among the workers in all trades to obtain a more equitable distribution of the product, and to secure a more orderly existence for the laborers. How may the settlement be of value to this effort?

If the design of the settlement is not so much the initiation of new measures, but fraternal co-operation with all good which it finds in its neighborhood, then the most obvious line of action will be organization through the trades-unions, a movement already well established.

The trades-unions say to each workingman, "Associate yourself with the fellow-workers in your trade. Let your trade organization federate with the allied trades, and they, in turn, with the National and International Federation, until working-people become a solid body, ready for concerted action. It is the only possible way to prevent cuts in the rate of wages, and to regulate the hours of work. Capital is organized, and has influence with which to secure legislation in its behalf. We are scattered and feeble because we do not work together."

Trades-unionism, in spite of the many pits into which it has fallen, has the ring of altruism about it. It is clearly the duty of the settlement to keep it to its best ideal, and to bring into it something of the spirit which has of late characterized the unions in England. This keeping to the ideal is not so easy as the more practical work of increasing unions, although that is difficult enough. Of the two women's unions organized at Hull-House, and of the four which have regularly held their meetings there, as well as those that come to us during strikes at various times, I should venture to say of only one of them that it is filled with the new spirit, although they all have glimpses of it, and even during times of stress and disturbance strive for it.

It was perhaps natural, from the situation, that the unions organized at Hull-House should have been those in the sewing-trades. The shirtmakers were organized in the spring of 1891. The immediate cause was a cut in a large factory from twenty-five cents a dozen for the making of collars and cuffs to twelve cents. The factory was a model in regard to its sanitary arrangements, and the sole complaint of the girls was of the long hours and low rate of wages. The strike which followed the formation of the union was wholly unsuccessful; but the union formed then has thriven ever since, and has lately grown so strong that it has recently succeeded in securing the adoption of the national labels.

The cloakmakers were organized at Hull-House in the spring of 1892. Wages had been steadily falling and there was great depression among the workers of the trade. The number of employees in the inside shops was being rapidly reduced, and the work of the entire trade handed over to the sweaters. The union among the men numbered two hundred; but the skilled workers were being rapidly supplanted by untrained women, who had no conscience in regard to the wages they accepted. The men had urged organization for several years, but were unable to secure it among the women. One apparently insurmountable obstacle had been the impossibility of securing any room, save one over a saloon, that was large enough and cheap enough for a general meeting. To a saloon hall the women had steadfastly refused to go, save once, when, under the pressure of a strike, the girls in a certain shop had met with the men from the same shop, over one of the more decent saloons, only to be upbraided by their families upon their return home. They of course refused ever to go again. The first meeting at Hull-House was composed of men and girls, and two or three of the residents. The meeting was a revelation to all present. The men, perhaps forty in number, were Russian-Jewish tailors, many of whom could command not even broken English. They were ill-dressed and grimy, suspicious that Hull-House was a spy in the service of the capitalists. They were skilled workers, easily superior to the girls when sewing on a cloak, but shamefaced and constrained in meeting with them. The American-Irish girls were well-dressed, and comparatively at ease. They felt chaperoned by the presence of the residents, and talked volubly among themselves. These two sets of people were held together only by the pressure upon their trade. They were separated by strong racial differences, by language, by nationality, by religion, by mode of life, by every possible social distinction. The interpreter stood between the two sides of the room, somewhat helpless. He was clear upon the economic necessity for combination; he realized the mutual interdependence; but he was baffled by the social aspect of the situation. The residents felt that between these men and girls was a deeper gulf than the much-talked of "chasm" between the favored and unfavored classes. The working-girls before them, who were being forced to cross such a gulf, had a positive advantage over the cultivated girl who consciously, and sometimes heroically, crosses the "chasm" to join hands with her working sisters.

There was much less difference of any sort between the residents and working-girls than between the men and girls of the same trade. It was a spectacle only to be found in an American city, under the latest conditions of trade-life. Working-people among themselves are being forced into a social democracy from the pressure of the economic situation. It presents an educating and broadening aspect of no small value.

The Woman's Cloakmakers' Union has never been large, but it always has been characterized by the spirit of generosity which marked its organization. It feels a strong sense of obligation toward the most ill-paid and ignorant of the sweaters' victims, and no working-people of Chicago have done more for abolition of the sweating-system than this handful of women.

But the labor movement is by no means so simple as trades-unionism. A settlement finds in the movement devoted men who feel keenly the need for better industrial organization, but who insist that industrial organization must be part of the general re-organization of society. The individualists, for instance, insist that we will never secure equal distribution until we have equality of opportunity; that all State and city franchises, all privilege of railroad, bank, and corporation, must be removed before competition will be absolutely free, and the man with his labor alone to offer will have a fair chance with the man who offers anything else; that the sole function of the State is to secure the freedom of each, guarded by the like freedom of all, and that each man free to work for his own existence and advantage will by this formula work out our industrial development. The individualist then works constantly for the recall of franchise and of special privilege, and for the untrammelled play of each man's force. There is much in our inheritance that responds to this, and he has followers among workingmen and among capitalists; those who fear to weaken the incentive to individual exertion, and those who believe that any interference would work injuriously. The residents of a settlement hear the individualist pleading in many trades assemblies. Opposite to him, springing up in discussion every time he speaks, is the socialist in all varieties. The scientific socialist reads his Karl Marx, and sees a gradual and inevitable absorption of all the means of production and of all capital by one entity, called the community. He makes out a strong case because he is usually a German or a Russian, with a turn for economic discussion, and widely read. He sees in the present tendency towards the concentration of capital, and in the growth of trusts and monopolies, an inevitable transition to the socialistic state. Every concentration of capital into fewer hands but increases the mass of those whose interests are opposed to the maintenance of its power, and vastly simplifies the final absorption. He contends that we have already had the transformation of scattered private property into capitalistic property, and that it is inevitable that it should be turned into collective property. In the former cases we had the ex-propriation of the mass of the people by a few usurpers; in the latter we have the ex-propriation of a few usurpers by the mass of people. He points with pride to the strong tendency towards State regulation of the means of transportation, and of many industries, and he urges legislative check and control at every point.

Between these two divergent points of view we find many shades of opinion and many modifications of philosophy; but perhaps a presentation of these two, as heard many times from earnest workingmen, will illustrate how difficult a settlement finds it to be liberal in tone, and to decide what immediate measures are in the line of advantage to the labor movement and which ones are against it.

It has been said that the imagination in America has been seized in due turn by the minister, the soldier, and the lawyer, who have successively held the political appointments; but that it is now the turn of the economist; that the man who would secure votes and a leadership in politics is the one who has a line of action to propose which shall bring order out of the present industrial chaos. This may be illustrated by the marvellous growth of the single-tax movement, which offers a definite remedial measure. Is it not true that our knotty theological difficulties as matters for prolonged discussion are laid aside? Is it not true that the interpretation of the Constitution, and the standard of action for the lawabiding and upright citizen, are well determined in men's minds? But that the moral enterprise of each man, not by any means his morality, but his moral enterprise, has to be tested by his attitude toward the industrial problem? The crucial question of the time is, "In what attitude stand ye toward the present industrial system? Are you content that greed and the seizing upon disadvantage and the pushing of the weaker to the wall shall rule your business life, while in your family and social life you live so differently? Are you content that Christianity shall have no play in trade?" If these questions press upon all of us, then a settlement must surely face the industrial problem as a test of its sincerity, as a test of the unification of its interests with the absorbing interests of its neighbors. Must it, then, accept the creeds of one or the other of these schools of social thought, and work for a party; or is there some underlying principle upon which the settlement can stand, as in its Christianity it endeavors to stand on something more primitive than either Catholicism or Protestantism? Can it find the moral question involved? Is there a line of ethics which its action ought to follow? Is it possible to make the slow appeal to the nobler fibre in men, and to connect it with that tradition of what is just and right?

A glance at the labor movement shows that the preponderating force has been given to what may be called negative action. Unions use their power to frustrate the designs of the capitalist, to make trouble for corporations and the public, such as is involved, for instance, in a railroad strike. It has often seemed to be the only method of arresting attention to their demands; but in America, at least, they have come to trust it too far.

A movement cannot be carried on by negating other acts; it must have a positive force, a driving and self-sustaining motive-power. A moral revolution cannot be accomplished by men who are held together merely because they are all smarting under a sense of injury and injustice, although it may be begun by them.

Men thus animated may organize for resistance, they may struggle bravely together, and may destroy that which is injurious, but they cannot build up, associate, and unite. They have no common, collective faith. The labor movement in America bears this trace of its youth and immaturity. As the first social organizations of men were for purposes of war; as they combined to defend themselves, or to destroy their enemies, and only later they united for creative purposes and pacific undertakings, so the labor organizations first equip themselves for industrial war, and much later attempt to promote peaceful industrial progress. The older unions have already reached the higher development, but the unions among the less intelligent and less skilled workmen are still belligerent and organized on a military basis, and unfortunately give color to the entire movement.

It is doubtless true that men who work excessively certain weeks in the year, and bear enforced idleness, harassed by a fear of starvation, during certain other weeks, as the lumber-shovers and garment-workers do, are too far from that regulated life and sanity of mind in which the quiet inculcation of moral principle is possible. It is also doubtless true that a more uniform leisure and a calmer temper of mind will have to be secured before the sense of injury ceases to be an absorbing emotion. The labor movement is bound, therefore, to work for shorter hours and increased wages and regularity of work, that education and moral reform may come to the individual laborer; that association may be put upon larger principles, and assume the higher fraternal aspect. But it does not want to lose sight of the end in securing the means, nor assume success, nor even necessarily the beginnings of success, when these first aims are attained. It is easy to make this mistake. The workingman is born and reared in a certain discomfort which he is sure the rich man does not share with him. He feels constantly the restriction which comes from untrained power; he realizes that his best efforts are destined to go round and round in a circle circumscribed by his industrial opportunity, and it is inevitable that he should over-estimate the possession of wealth, of leisure, and of education. It is almost impossible for him to keep his sense of proportion.

The settlement may be of value if it can take a larger and steadier view than is always possible to the workingman, smarting under a sense of wrong; or to the capitalist, seeking only to "quiet down," without regard to the historic significance of the case, and insisting upon the inalienable right of "invested capital," to a return of at least four per cent, ignoring human passion. It is possible to recall them both to a sense of the larger development.

A century ago there was an irresistible impulse, an upward movement, among the mass of people to have their share in political life,—hitherto the life of the privileged. The universal franchise was demanded, not only as a holy right, but as a means of entrance into the sunshine of liberty and equality. There is a similar demand at the close of this century on the part of working-people, but this time it is for a share in the results of industry.

It is an impulse to come out into the sunshine of Prosperity. As the leaders of political democracy overestimated the possession of the franchise, and believed it would obtain blessings for the working-people which it has not done, so, doubtless, the leaders of the labor movement are overestimating the possession of wealth and leisure. Mazzini was the inspired prophet of the political democracy, preaching duties and responsibilities rather than rights and franchises; and we might call Arnold Toynbee the prophet of the second development when we contend that the task of the labor movement is the interpretation of democracy into industrial affairs. In that remarkable exposition called "Industry and Democracy," Toynbee sets forth the struggle between the masters and men during the industrial revolution. Two ideals in regard to the relationship between employer and employee were then developed. Carlyle represented one, pleading passionately for it. He declared that the rich mill-owner's duty did not end with the "cash nexus"; that after he had paid his men he should still cherish them in sickness, protect them in misfortune, and not dismiss them when trade was bad. In one word, he would have the rich govern and protect the poor. But the workers themselves, the mass of the people, had caught another ideal; they dreamed of a time when they should have no need of protection, but when each workman should stand by the side of his employer—the free citizen of a free state. Each workingman demanded, not class protection, but political rights. He wished to be a unit; not that he might be isolated, but that he might unite in a fuller union, first with his fellow-workers, and then with the entire people. Toynbee asks who was right, Carlyle or the people. And replies that the people were right—"The people who, sick with hunger and deformed with toil, dreamed that democracy would bring deliverance." And democracy did save industry. It transformed disputes about wages from social feuds into business bargains. It swept away the estranging class elements of suspicion and arrogance. "It gradually did away with the feudal notion among the masters that they would deal with their men one at a time, denying to them the advantages of association." It is singular that in America, where government is founded upon the principle of representation, the capitalist should have been so slow to accord this right to workingmen; that he should refuse so steadily to treat with a "walking delegate," and so long maintain that no "outsider" could represent the men in his shop.

We must learn to trust our democracy, giant-like and threatening as it may appear in its uncouth strength and untried applications. When the English people were demanding the charter, the English nobility predicted that the franchise would be used to inaugurate all sorts of wild measures, to overturn long-established customs, as the capitalist now sometimes assumes that higher wages will be spent only in the saloons. In both cases there is a failure to count the sobering effect of responsibility in the education and development which attend the entrance into a wider life.

The effort to keep the movement to some consciousness of its historic value in the race development is perhaps no more difficult than to keep before its view the larger ethical aims. There is doubtless a tendency among the working men who reach leadership in the movement to yield to individual ambition, as there is among capitalists to regard class interests, and yield only that which must be yielded. This tendency on one side to yield to ambition, and on the other to give in to threats, may be further illustrated.

The poor man has proverbially been the tyrant of poor men when he has become rich. But while such a man was yet poor, his heart was closed to his fellows, and his eyes were blinded to the exploitation of them and himself, because in his heart he hoped one day to be rich, and to do the exploiting; because he secretly approved the action of his master, and said, "I would do the same if I were he."

Workingmen say, sometimes, that the rich will not hear the complaint of the poor until it rises into a threat, and carries a suggestion of ruin with it; that they then throw the laborers a portion of the product, to save the remainder.

As the tendency to warfare shows the primitive state of the labor movement, so also this division on class lines reveals its present undeveloped condition. The organization of society into huge battalions with syndicates and corporations on the side of capital, and trades-unions and federations on the side of labor, is to divide the world into two hostile camps, and to turn us back into class warfare and class limitations. All our experience tells us that no question of civilization is so simple as that, nor can we any longer settle our perplexities by mere good fighting. One is reminded of one's childish conception of life—that Right and Wrong were drawn up in battle array into two distinct armies, and that to join the army of Right and fight bravely would be to settle all problems.

But life itself teaches us nothing more inevitable than that right and wrong are most confusedly mixed; that the blackest wrong is by our side and within our own motives; that right does not dazzle our eyes with its radiant shining, but has to be found by exerting patience, discrimination, and impartiality. We cease to listen for the bugle note of victory our childish imagination anticipated, and learn that our finest victories are attained in the midst of self-distrust, and that the waving banner of triumph is sooner or later trailed to the dust by the weight of self-righteousness. It may be that as the labor movement grows older and riper, it will cease to divide all men so sharply into capitalists and proletarians, into exploiter and exploited.

We may live to remind its leaders in later years, as George Eliot has so skilfully reminded us, that the path we all like when we first set out in our youth is the path of martyrdom and endurance, where the palm branches grow; but that later we learn to take the steep highway of tolerance, just allowance, and self-blame, where there are no leafy honors to be gathered and worn. As the labor movement grows older its leaders may catch the larger ethical view which genuine experience always gives; they may have a chance to act free from the pressure of threat or ambition. They should have nothing to gain or lose, save as they rise or fall with their fellows. In raising the mass, men could have a motive-power as much greater than the motive for individual success, as the force which sends the sun above the horizon is greater than the force engendered by the powder behind the rocket.

Is it too much to hope that as the better organized and older trades-unions are fast recognizing a solidarity of labor, and acting upon the literal notion of brotherhood, that they will later perceive the larger solidarity which includes labor and capital, and act upon the notion of universal kinship? That before this larger vision of life there can be no perception of "sides" and no "battle array"? In the light of the developed social conscience the "sympathetic strike" may be criticised, not because it is too broad, but because it is too narrow, and because the strike is but a wasteful and negative demonstration of ethical fellowship. In the summer of 1894 the Chicago unions of Russian-Jewish cloakmakers, German compositors, and Bohemian and Polish butchers, struck in sympathy with the cause of the American Railway Union, whom they believed to be standing for a principle. Does an event such as this, clumsy and unsatisfactory as its results are, prefigure the time when no factory child in Chicago can be overworked and underpaid without a protest from all good citizens, capitalist and proletarian? Such a protest would be founded upon an ethical sense so strong that it would easily override business interests and class prejudices.

Manifestations of the labor movement are erratic and ill-timed because of the very strength of its motive power. A settlement is not affrighted nor dismayed when it sees in labor-meetings, in caucuses, and turbulent gatherings, men who are—

> "Groping for the right, with horny, calloused hands,
> And staring round for God with bloodshot eyes,"

although the clumsy hands may upset some heavy pieces of convention, as a strong blindman overturns furniture, and the bloodshot eyes may be wild and fanatical. The settlement is unworthy of its calling if it is too timid or dull to interpret this groping and staring. But the settlement should be affrighted, and bestir itself to action, when the groping is not for the right, but for the mere purpose of overturning; when the staring is not for God, but for Mammon—and there is a natural temptation towards both.

A settlement may well be dismayed when it sees workingmen apathetic to higher motives, and thinking only of stratagems by which to outwit the capitalists; or when workingmen justify themselves in the use of base measures, saying they have learned the lessons from the other side. Such an attitude at once turns the movement from a development into a struggle, and the sole judge left between the adversaries must in the end be force. Class interests become the governing and motive power, and the settlement can logically be of no value to either side. Its sympathies are naturally much entangled in such a struggle, but to be of value it must keep its judgment clear as to the final ethical outcome—and this requires both perceptions and training.

Fortunately, every action may be analyzed into its permanent and transient aspects. The transient aspect of the strike is the anger and opposition against the employer, and too often the chagrin of failure. The permanent is the binding together of the strikers in the ties of association and brotherhood, and the attainment of a more democratic relation to the employer; and it is because of a growing sense of brotherhood and of democracy in the labor movement that we see in it a growing ethical power.

Hence the duty of the settlement in keeping the movement from becoming in any sense a class warfare is clear. There is a temperamental bitterness among workingmen which is both inherited and fostered by the conditions of their life and trade; but they cannot afford to cherish a class bitterness if the labor movement is to be held to its highest possibilities. A class working for a class, and against another class, implies that within itself there should be trades working for trades, individuals working for individuals. The universal character of the movement is gone from the start, and cannot be caught until an all-embracing ideal is accepted.

A recent writer has called attention to the fact that the position of the power-holding classes—capitalists, as we call them just now—is being gradually undermined by the disintegrating influence of the immense fund of altruistic feeling with which society has become equipped; that it is within this fund of altruism that we find the motive force which is slowly enfranchising all classes and gradually insisting upon equality of condition and opportunity. If we can accept this explanation of the social and political movements of our time, then it is clear that the labor movement is at the bottom an ethical movement, and a manifestation of the orderly development of the race.

The settlement is pledged to insist upon the unity of life, to gather to itself the sense of righteousness to be found in its neighborhood, and as far as possible in its city; to work towards the betterment not of one kind of people or class of people, but for the common good. The settlement believes that just as men deprived of comradeship by circumstances or law go back to the brutality from which they came, so any class or set of men deprived of the companionship of the whole, become correspondingly decivilized and crippled. No part of society can afford to get along without the others.

The settlement, then, urges first, the organization of working people in order that as much leisure and orderly life as possible may be secured to them in which to carry out the higher aims of living; in the second place, it should make a constant effort to bring to bear upon the labor movement a consciousness of its historic development; and lastly, it accentuates the ultimate ethical aims of the movement.

The despair of the labor movement is, as Mazzini said in another cause long ago, that we have torn the great and beautiful ensign of Democracy. Each party has snatched a rag of it, and parades it as proudly as if it were the whole flag, repudiating and not deigning to look at, the others.

It is this feeling of disdain to any class of men or kind of men in the community which is dangerous to the labor movement, which makes it a class-measure. It attacks its democratic character, and substitutes party enthusiasm for the irresistible force of human progress. The labor movement must include all men in its hopes. It must have the communion of universal fellowship. Any drop of gall within its cup is fatal. Any grudge treasured up against a capitalist, any desire to "get even" when the wealth has changed hands, are but the old experiences of human selfishness. All sense of injury must fall away and be absorbed in the consciousness of a common brotherhood. If to insist upon the universality of the best is the function of the settlement, nowhere is its influence more needed than in the labor movement, where there is constant temptation towards a class warfare.

Appendix: Outline Sketch Descriptive of Hull-House

List of Residents Who Have Been in Residence for Six Months or Longer.

Jane Addams	Annie Fryar
Ellen G. Starr	Josefa Humpal Zeman
Julia C. Lathrop	Margaret M. West
Florence Kelley	Jeannette C. Welch[1]
Mary A. Keyzer	Enella Benedict
Anna M. Farnsworth	Clifford W. Barnes[1]
Agnes Sinclair Holbrook	Alex. A. Bruce[1]
Josephine Milligan, M.D.	Edward L. Burchard[1]
Wilfreda Brockway	Henry B. Learned[1]
Rose M. Gyles	Chas. C. Arnold[1]
Gertrude Barnum	John Addams Linn
Ella Raymond Waite	Edwin A. Waldo

The settlement, Jan. 1, 1895, numbers twenty, including those who are in residence now but have not yet resided for six months.

Hull-House: A Social Settlement.

The two original residents of Hull-House are entering upon their sixth year of settlement in the nineteenth ward. They publish this outline[2] that the questions daily asked by neighbors and visitors may be succinctly answered. It necessarily takes somewhat the character of a report, but is much less formal. It aims not so much to give an account of what has been accomplished, as to suggest what may be done by and through a neighborhood of working-people, when they are touched by a common stimulus, and possess an intellectual and social centre about which they may group their various organizations and enterprises. This centre or "settlement," to be effective, must contain an element of permanency, so that the neighborhood may feel that the interest and fortunes of the residents are identical with their own. The settlement must have an

---

1. No longer in residence.
2. This outline was originally issued as a pamphlet, Feb. 1, 1893. It is here revised to Jan. 1, 1895.

Hull-House with Reading-Room and Studio Building

enthusiasm for the possibilities of its locality, and all ability to bring into it and develop from it those lines of thought and action which make for the "higher life."

The original residents came to Hull-House with a conviction that social intercourse could best express the growing sense of the economic unity of society. They wished the social spirit to be the undercurrent of the life of Hull-House, whatever direction the stream might take. All the details were left for the demands of the neighborhood to determine, and each department has grown from a discovery made through natural and reciprocal social relations.

The College Extension Courses

grew thus from an informal origin. The first class met as guests of the residents. As the classes became larger and more numerous, and the object of the newcomers more definitely that of acquisition of some special knowledge, the informality of the social relation was necessarily less; but the prevailing attitude toward the house of the two hundred and fifty students now enrolled is that of guests as well as students. Many new students, attracted and refreshed by the social atmosphere, come into the classes who would not be likely to undertake any course of study at an evening high school, or any school within their reach. These students, the larger proportion of whom are young women, represent a great variety of occupations. Among them are teachers in the public schools, employees of factories and shops, typewriters and cashiers. The College Extension Course aims not to duplicate, but to supplement, the advantages offered by evening high schools and business colleges. Hence in these classes the emphasis is laid upon the humanities, and no attempt is made to supply means for earning a livelihood. The most popular and continuous courses have been in literature, languages, music, art, history, mathematics, and drawing. The saving grace of all good things, and the developing power of the love of them, have been proved to the satisfaction of the residents of Hull-House. A prospectus of the College Extension classes is published at the beginning of each term for ten weeks.

The College Extension classes are so called because the instructors are mostly college men and women. These classes were established at Hull-House before the University Extension movement began in Chicago, and are not connected with it. The faculty numbers thirty-five, mostly college men and women, some of whom have taught continuously for three years. No charge is made for the teaching, which is gratuitous

Library in Hull-House

on the part of the faculty; but the students pay fifty cents a course, which covers the printing of the prospectuses and other incidental expenses. Any surplus is expended upon lectures and reference books. Three University Extension Courses have been given at the centre formed at Hull-house—two in the drawing-room and one in a neighboring church. The lecturers were from the University Extension Department of the University of Chicago.

Summer School.

A helpful supplement of the College Extension Courses has been the summer school held for three years in the buildings of Rockford College, at Rockford, Ill. Half the students were able to attend. The sum of three dollars a week paid by each student for board, covered the entire expenses of the school—the use of the buildings, including gymnasium and laboratories, having been given free of rent. Much time was devoted to out-door work in botany and the study of birds, and the month proved a successful combination of a summer vacation and a continuation of the year's study. The *esprit de corps,* fostered by the intimacy of the month's sojourn in college quarters, bore its first fruits in a students' association formed at the close of the summer's term.

The Students' Association.

The Students' Association, now including a good proportion of the attendants of the class, is divided into the literary, the dramatic, and the musical sections. The society meets once a month, and each section in turn is responsible for an evening's entertainment. The programme is followed by an informal dance in the gymnasium. Each term's course is opened by a students' reception given by the residents.

Reading-Room.

A reading-room in the lower floor of the Hull-House Art Gallery was maintained by the Chicago Public Library Board for three years, with two city librarians in charge. The room was supplied with English and foreign magazines and papers, as well as several hundred books. All the books of the Public Library are accessible to the neighborhood through the excellent system of sub-station delivery. This library has now been moved to a neighboring block.

Exhibitions of Pictures.

Owing partly to the limited space available for the purpose, the picture exhibits have been necessarily small. An effort has been made to show only pictures which combine, to a considerable degree, an elevated tone with technical excellence; and at no time can a very large assortment of such pictures be obtained. There is an advantage on the side of a small exhibition carefully selected, especially to an untrained public. The confusion and fatigue of mind which a person of no trained powers of selection suffers in passing his eyes wearily over the assortment of good, bad, and indifferent which the average picture exhibit presents, leave him nothing with which to assimilate the good when he finds it, and his chances of finding it are small. Frequently recurring exhibitions of a few very choice pictures might do more toward educating the public taste of the locality in which they occur than many times the number less severely chosen and less often seen. Hull-House has had two exhibits every year since the gallery was built, which were well attended. They were omitted during the World's Fair, and an effort was made to supply their place by assisting as many people as possible to see the pictures of the fair intelligently. Parties formed for the purpose were conducted regularly by a resident.

The first residents of Hull-House held strongly to the belief that any compromise in the matter of excellence in art was a mistake. They hung their own walls only with such pictures as they felt were helpful to the life of mind and soul. Very much of the influence of the House they believed to be due to the harmony and reasonableness of

Studio, with View into Art Exhibit Room

the message of its walls. One of the residents has been much interested in pictures in the public schools, and has aroused sufficient interest in the subject to result in providing good sets of pictures and casts for several schools in the poorest localities. With the means at her disposal she has been able to put a number of good pictures into each room of the school nearest Hull-House, and one or more into five of the public kindergartens. A society has been organized for carrying on the work.

Working-People's Chorus.

The same principles the House is striving to carry into effect in regard to the music it provides.

The director of the World's Fair choruses has undertaken the training of a chorus of five hundred working-people. He believes that working-people especially need the musical form of expression, their lives being shorn on the art side. He further holds that musical people need for their art's sake the sense of brotherhood; that art is hollow and conventional unless it is the utterance of the common and universal life.

Sunday Concerts.

A free concert is given in the gymnasium every Sunday afternoon. The concerts, at first given with the motive of entertaining, are now conducted with the development of musical taste and understanding as the object in view. This may be illustrated by selections from the programme.

Sunday Concerts, 5 P.M.
Beethoven Concert . . . Mrs. H. L. Frank.
(Beethoven's Birthday.)

Christmas Music.—Songs and carols of Eleanor Smith Reineke, Cornelius, and others.
Miss Eleanor Smith and the Senior Singing-Class.

Music.—From Wagner's Opera of "Lohengrin,"
with interpretation . . . Mrs. James Hunt.
(In preparation for the music Miss Starr will read
Tennyson's "Holy Grail," at four o'clock.)

Concert.—Choral . . . Led by Mr. W. L. Tomlins.
(Solos and choruses from "The Messiah" and "Elijah")

Concert.—Organ and String Quartette.
To be given at the house of Mrs. John C. Coonley,
620 Division Street (and Lake Shore Drive), by
Mr. W. Middleschulte and the Spiering Quartette.

Jane Club Parlors

The oldest singing-class is now pursuing its third year of study under the instruction of a composer and teacher of vocal music who has never compromised her severe musical standards here or elsewhere. The comparatively small number of students whose intellect and perseverance have survived the test have had the advantage of an unusual training.

The Paderewski Club.

A club of twenty children, calling themselves the Paderewski Club, has had a year of instruction on the piano, together with Sunday afternoon talks by their teacher on the lives of the great musicians. Six of the most proficient have obtained scholarships in the Chicago Conservatory.

The Jane Club.

The Jane Club, a co-operative boarding-club for young working-women, had the advice and assistance of Hull-House in its establishment. The original members of the club, seven in number, were a group of trades-union girls accustomed to organized and co-operative action. The club has been from the beginning self-governing, without a matron or outside control, the officers being elected by the members from their own number, and serving for six months gratuitously. The two offices of treasurer and steward have required a generous sacrifice of their limited leisure, as well as a good deal of ability from those holding them. This being given, together with a considerable *esprit de corps* in the increasing number of members, the club has thriven both substantially and socially. The weekly dues of three dollars, with an occasional small assessment, have met all current expenses of rent, service, food, heat, and light, after the furnishing and first month's rent was supplied by Hull-House. The club now numbers fifty members, and the one flat is increased to five. The members do such share of the housework as does not interfere with their daily occupations. There are various circles within the club for social and intellectual purposes; and while the members are glad to procure the comforts of life at a rate within their means, the atmosphere of the club is one of comradeship rather than thrift. The club holds a monthly reception in the Hull-House gymnasium.

The Phalañx Club.

A similar co-operative club has been started by nine young men at 245 West Polk Street, most of the members of which are members of the Typographical Union. The club has made a most promising beginning.

The Labor Movement.

The connection of the House with the labor movement may be said to have begun on the same social basis as its other relations. Of its standing with labor unions, which is now "good and regular," it owes the foundation to personal relations with the organizer of the Bindery Girls' Union, who lived for some months in the House as a guest. It is now generally understood that Hull-House is "on the side of unions." Several of the women's unions have held their regular meetings at the House, two have been organized there, and in four instances men and women on strike against reduction in wages met there while the strike lasted. In one case a strike was successfully arbitrated by the House. It is most interesting to note that a number of small and feeble unions have, from the very fact of their weakness, been compelled to a policy which has been their strength, and has made for the strength of their cause. In this policy it has been the privilege of Hull-House to be of service to them. The stronger unions, such as the carpenters' and bricklayers', trusting in their own strength and the skill of their members, have too often adopted a course of exclusiveness and self-centred effort. The weak ones, as those in the clothing trades, finding it impossible to accomplish much alone, betook themselves to the constant urging of concerted action. The most important illustration of this highly useful policy is in the action of the unions in urging the factory inspection law passed by the Legislature of Illinois during the spring of 1893. The initiative toward the introduction of the measure in the legislature was taken by a resident of Hull-House; and a Committee of Investigation sent from Springfield to inspect sweat-shops, and decide upon the necessity for legislation, was piloted by her upon its tour. The same resident, who was at that time conducting in Chicago a so-called "slum investigation" for the Department of Labor at Washington, was, after the passage of the law, appointed inspector of factories in the State of Illinois. The work of the inspector and her assistants and deputies can be found in the annual report of the Illinois State Factory Inspector, the first of which has already been issued.

Hull-House is situated in the midst of the sweat-shop district of Chicago, and it was natural that the first effort of the House to procure legislation against an industrial evil should have been directed against the sweating-system.

A ward book has been kept by the residents for two years in which have been noted matters of sociological interest found in the ward. Many instances of the sweating-evil and child-labor have been recorded, as well as unsanitary tenements and instances of eviction.

Eight-Hour Club.

After the passage of the factory and workshop bill, which includes a clause limiting women's labor to eight hours a day, the young women employees in a large factory in the near neighborhood of Hull-House formed an eight-hour club for the purpose of encouraging women in factories and workshops to obey the eight-hour law. This club has maintained its position, and done good missionary work for the cause. They have developed a strong sense of obligation toward employees in shops where the wages are low, and the employees much less favored than themselves. Their enthusiasm has carried them across a caste line. This club meets at Hull-House, and makes full use of the social factor so essential in fusing heterogeneous elements.

The Working-People's Social Science Club

was formed during the first year of residence at Hull-House, and has met weekly ever since, with the exception of the two summer months. In the summer of 1893, however, owing to the number of interesting speakers to be secured from the World's Fair Congresses, the club met without interruption. The purpose of the club is the discussion of social and economic topics. An opening address of forty-five minutes is followed by an hour of discussion. The speakers in the latter represent every possible shade of social and economic view. Working men and women are in the majority, although professional and business men are to be found at every meeting. The attendance averages seventy-five; the discussion is always animated and outspoken. The residents believe that one of the offices of the settlement is to provide that people of various creeds and class traditions should meet under a friendly and non-partisan roof, and discuss differences fairly. Following is a list of ten speakers and their subjects, selected from the programme of 1893:

"The English Labor Movement"
Mr. Wm. Clarke

"Woman's Suffrage"
Miss Susan B. Anthony

"The Economic and Social Conditions of India"
Swami Vivehañañde.

"The Unemployed"
Dr. Charles R. Henderson

"The London County Council"
Mr. Percy Alden

"The New Trades-Unionism"
Mrs. Robt. A. Wood

"Charity Organization"
Dr. Seth Low

"The Neighborhood Guild"
Dr. Stanton Coit

"The Conscience of the State"
Dr. Bayard Holmes

"The Chicago City Council"
Mr. Wm. T. Stead

The programme for the fall of 1894 is possibly more typical:—

"Socrates"
Prof. Charles F. Bradley, Northwestern University

"Epictetus"
Dr. John Dewey, University of Chicago

"Marcus Aurelius"
Prof. J. H. Tufts, University of Chicago

"St. Francis"
Miss Eliza Allen Star

"Savonarola"
Rev. F. W. Gunsaulus, D.D.

"Sir Thomas More"
Mr. Charles Zeublin, University of Chicago

The Arnold Toynbee Club meets at Hull-House.

The objects of the club are: 1. To offer lectures upon economic subjects. 2. To ascertain and make known facts of interest to working-people in the fields of economics and legislation. 3. To promote legislation for economic and social reform, especially to secure greater public control over natural monopolies. Membership is by invitation. Members of the club offer a list of free lectures on economic and social questions. It is especially desired to aid in the educational work of trades' unions and young people's societies.

The Chicago Question Club

meets in the Hull-House Art Gallery at two o'clock every Sunday afternoon. The club was fully formed before it asked for the hospitality of Hull-House. It is well organized, and each meeting is opened by presentation of two sides of a question. Occasionally the various economic clubs meet for a common discussion. One of the most successful was led by Father Huntington, on the subject, "Can a Freethinker believe in Christ?" An audience of four hundred people followed closely the two hours' discussion, which was closed by Mr. Henry George.

The Nineteenth Ward Improvement Club.

The Nineteenth Ward Improvement Club meets at Hull-House the second Saturday evening of each month. The president is the district representative in the Illinois State Legislature, and one of the ward aldermen is an active member. The club is pledged to the improvement of its ward in all directions. It has standing-committees on street-cleaning, etc., and was much interested in the efforts of the Municipal Order League to secure public baths. Through the solicitation of the league the City Council in 1892 made an appropriation of $12,000 for public baths. Hull-House was able to offer the use of a lot which had been given it by the owner rent free for two years. He transferred the lease to the city, with a satisfactory arrangement for its sale at the expiration of the lease, and a free public bathhouse has been erected upon it, which is now in daily use. It contains seventeen shower-baths, a swimming-tank, and a tub. The Nineteenth Ward Improvement Club has formed a co-operative association, the first officers of

A Hull-House Interior

which are the same as its own. It has opened a co-operative coalyard near Hull-House. The purchaser of a ton of coal becomes a member of the Co-operative Association. At its first meeting the members voted that their dividends be employed in establishing a bushel trade to meet the wants of the poor people of the neighborhood. The purchaser of each bushel receives a ticket, six of which entitle him to a rebate in coal. The association hopes in time to deal in other commodities.

Civic Federation Ward Council.

In the fall of 1894 a ward council of the Civic Federation was organized at Hull-House for the nineteenth ward. The active members of the Nineteenth Ward Improvement Club are naturally working together under this new name.

A full set of committees have been organized—Municipal, Philanthropic, Industrial, Educational, Political, and Moral.

The Hull-House Women's Club

which now numbers ninety of the most able women in the ward, developed from a social meeting for purposes of tea drinking and friendly chat. Several members of this club have done good work in street and alley inspecting through the Municipal Order League. The club has also presented to a public school in the neighborhood a fine autotype of Millet's Knitting Shepherdess, and hopes to do more in the future for the art-in-schools movement. They have been active in the visiting and relief work which has taken so large a share of the energies of the settlement during the hard times. One winter they purchased a ticket to the lectures given to mothers in the Kindergarten College. One member attended each week, and reported to the club. They are in touch with some of the vigorous movements of the city, and have frequent lectures on philanthropic and reform questions.

A Reception for Germans

has been held every Friday evening in Hull-House for four years. Two hours are spent in singing, reading, games, etc., and the habituees have all the comradeship of a club. They give an occasional coffee-drinking and entertainment. They are a good illustration of the social feeling too often wasted in a cramped neighborhood for lack of space and encouragement.

During the first two years of Hull-House the residents held receptions for Italians each week, which were largely attended. These were for a time discontinued, as their success depended mainly upon an Italian philanthropist, who has since started an agricultural colony in Alabama. Immigration societies, such as are successfully operated in London, are needed properly to place the Italian immigrants, who might do as much for the development of the Southern States as they have done for South America. Hull-House has not been able to inaugurate such a society, but sincerely hopes that one may be formed, as well as an association for improving tenement houses, those occupied by the Italians being overcrowded and unsanitary.

Children's Clubs.

Since its foundation, Hull-House has had numerous classes and clubs for children. The fortunes and value of the clubs have varied, depending very much upon the spirit of the leaders. An effort has always been made to avoid the school atmosphere. The children are received and trusted as guests, and the initiative and control have come from them as far as possible. Their favorite occupation is listening to stories. One club has had a consecutive course of legends and tales of chivalry. There is no doubt that the more imaginative children learn to look upon the house as a gateway into a magic land, and get a genuine taste of the delights of literature. One boy, after a winter of

Charlemagne stories, flung himself, half-crying, from the house, and said that "there was no good in coming any more now that Prince Roland was dead." The boys' clubs meet every Tuesday afternoon at four o'clock, and clubs of little girls come on Friday. The latter are the School Girls' Club and the Pansy Club, the Story-Telling Club and the Kindergarten Club. They sew, paint, or make paper chains during the story-telling, and play games in the gymnasium together before they go home at five o'clock. A club of Bohemian girls, called "Libuse," meets every Monday, and studies the heroic women in history. The little children meet one afternoon in the week for advanced kindergarten work. There are various children's classes for gymnastics and dancing; and two children's choruses, of two hundred and fifty each, meet weekly under the direction of Mr. William Tomlins. Dinners are served to school-children upon presentation of tickets which have been sold to their mothers for five cents each. Those children are first selected whose mothers are necessarily at work during the middle of the day; and the dinner started with children formerly in the Hull-House *crèche*. While it is desired to give the children nutritious food, the little diners care much more for the toys and books and the general good time than they do for the dinners. It has been found, too, that the general attractiveness performs the function of the truant-officer in keeping them at school; for no school implies no dinner. The House has had the sympathetic and enthusiastic co-operation of the principal of the Polk Street public school.

Savings-Bank.

A branch of the New York Penny Provident Savings-Bank has been sustained for two years. There are six hundred depositors.

Sewing-School.

One hundred and twenty Italian girls meet every Monday afternoon in the gymnasium, directed by a superintendent and fifteen teachers. The children make garments, which they may purchase for the price of the material. An effort is made to follow up each new garment with lessons in tidiness. There are smaller classes in darning, knitting, and simple embroidery among the English-speaking little girls.

Cooking-Classes.

Three cooking-classes for adults are held each week. The cooking-class for Italian girls has been very gratifying in its results. There is also a cooking-class every week for American children, and a nature class, which meets every Saturday morning. The young members are very happy when the weather permits them to go with their teacher to the park in pursuit of their subject. When it does not, they are most content with the simple microscopes at their disposal.

Summer Excursions.

A systematic effort is made during the summer to have each of the four hundred children connected with the clubs spend at least one day in the country or parks. Excursions in small groups are more satisfactory than the time-honored picnic method. Each summer from fifty to a hundred children are sent from Hull-House to the fresh-air homes and country-houses. The residents were able, through the generosity of World's Fair enthusiasts, to assist fifteen hundred children to see the fair.

Playground.

During the last year the use of a piece of ground near Hull-House measuring 326 × 119 was given rent free for a year, and in case it should not be sold in the meantime, for a longer period. The owner permitted the houses upon it, which were in bad sanitary condition, to be torn down; the ground was graded, fenced, provided with swings and other enticing apparatus, an officer was supplied from the city force, and a playground was thrown open to the juvenile public. Through the summer evenings many parents came with their children. Several of the residents spent much time there teaching the children games, and regulating the use of the fifty buckets and shovels which were active in the sand-piles. The music furnished by an organ-grinder every afternoon often brought forth an Italian tarantella or an Irish jig with curious spontaneity.

Free Kindergarten and Day Nursery.

From the first month of its existence Hull-House has had a free kindergarten, and for three years a day nursery, where mothers who are obliged to work leave their children for the day, paying five cents for each child, The *crèche* averages in summer fifty children, and in winter between thirty and forty. A friend of the House, who makes herself responsible for the financial support of the *crèche,* gives largely of her time in directing and assisting in the work. This nursery is like others in most respects, differing chiefly, perhaps, in the attention paid to the matter of pictures and casts. The Madonnas of Raphael, in the best and largest photographs, are hung low, that the children may see them, as well as casts from Donatello and Della Robbia. The children talk in a familiar way to the babies on the wall, and sometimes climb upon the chairs to kiss them. Surely much is gained if one can begin in a very little child to make a truly beautiful thing truly beloved. An experienced kindergartner is in charge of the nursery. She has the constant assistance of two women.

Nursery

Men's Club Room

Gymnasium.

The last building added to the equipment of Hull-House includes a public coffee and lunch room, a New England kitchen, a gymnasium, with shower-baths, and men's club-room, supplied with billiard and card tables. The use of the gymnasium is divided between men and women, girls and boys, at different hours. The evening hours are reserved more especially for men. The gymnasium, being now the largest room in the possession of the settlement, is necessarily used on certain evenings as an audience room, and as a reception and ball room by the various clubs.

The Hull-House Men's Club

holds a reception there once a month, and an occasional banquet. This club, which rents a room in the front of the building, is composed of one hundred and fifty of the abler citizens and more enterprising young men of the vicinity. Their constitution commits them among other things, to the "cultivation of sobriety and goodfellow-ship." They are not without political influence in the ward, and are a distinct factor in its social life, as all of their social undertakings have been remarkably spirited and suc-cessful. They are in sympathy with the aims of Hull-House, and are prompt to assist and promote any of its undertakings. Business meetings are held on the first and third Friday evenings of each month, and on alternate evenings the Literary and Debating Sections hold meetings.

Hull-House Mandolin Club

consists of twelve members of the Men's Club, who have successfully sustained an orchestra of mandolin and guitars for a year. They are most generous with their ser-vices to the entertainments of the House.

Young People's Clubs.

The Lincoln Club is a debating-society of young men, whose occasional public debates are always heard by a large and enthusiastic audience. In their weekly meeting they have a carefully prepared debate, usually upon current political events. They meet once a month with the Hull-House Social Club. This is composed of young women of the neighborhood, many of whom have met every week for four years. Their pro-grammes are literary and social. They give an occasional play. The last one presented was the court scene from the "Merchant of Venice."

Among the other clubs of young people, the Young Citizens boasts the oldest club-life. Their programmes alternate between discussions and readings. An effort is made in both for civic and municipal education.

The Anfreda Club of thirty young girls meets the same evening. After the literary programme is concluded, the two clubs have half an hour of dancing or games together before going home.

Henry Learned Club, Hull-House Glee Club, Jolly Boys' Club, Good-Fellowship Club, Lexington Club, Bohemian Garnet Club, Longfellow Club, Laurel Club, Harrison Club, and others, are composed of young people from fourteen to twenty-five years of age. Alumni associations of the neighboring public schools hold their meetings at the House. An effort is being made toward school extension.

The Hull-House Coffee-house and Kitchen.

The Hull-House coffee-house was opened July 1, 1893. The room itself is an attractive copy of an English inn, with low, dark rafters, diamond windows, and large fireplace. It is open every day from six in the morning to ten at night. An effort has been made to combine the convenience of a lunch-room, where well-cooked food can be sold at a reasonable rate, with cosiness and attractiveness. The residents believe that substitution is the only remedy against the evils of the saloon. The large kitchen has been

Coffee-house and Gymnasium Building

carefully equipped, under the direction of Mrs. Ellen Richards, with a New England kitchen outfit, including a number of Aladdin ovens. The foods are carefully prepared, and are sold by the quart or pound to families for home consumption. Coffee, soups, and stews are delivered every day at noon to the neighboring factories. By means of an indurated fibre can, it is possible to transport and serve the food hot. The employees purchase a pint of soup or coffee with two rolls for five cents, and the plan of

Noon Factory Delivery

is daily growing in popularity. The kitchen during the winter of 1893–1894 supplied hot lunches at ten cents each to the two hundred women employed in the sewing-room established by the Emergency Committee of the Chicago Women's Club. This room supplied work to unemployed women during the stress of the last winter. Hull-House has also superintended a temporary lodginghouse, for the use of unemployed women for some months.

A physician is in residence at Hull-House, and another who lives near is most constant and generous with her professional services. A nurse of the Visiting Nurses' Association has her headquarters, and receives her orders, at the House.

A Public Dispensary

was undertaken in 1893. It is open every day from three until four, and every evening from seven to eight o'clock. A small charge is made when possible for drugs. In the same house, 247 Polk Street, is the

Hull-House Labor Bureau,

necessarily small at present from the extreme difficulty of finding work for men or women. Hull-House has always undertaken a certain amount of relief work, the records of which are kept with those of the Labor Bureau. One of the residents served for a winter as a visitor on the Cook County staff, all the cases of destitution within a certain radius of Hull-House being given to her for investigation. She also has established and maintained with all the charitable institutions of the city a cordial and sympathetic relationship, which has been most valuable to the neighborhood. She has more recently been appointed a member of the State Board of Charities. The House has been active in the movement to organize the charities of Chicago, and has recently united its relief office with the ward office established by the new organization.

Residents.

No university or college qualification has ever been made for residence, although the majority of residents have been college people. The organization of the settlement has been extremely informal; but an attempt has been made during the last winter to limit the number of residents to twenty. The household, augmented by visitors, has occasionally exceeded that number. Applicants for residence are received for six weeks, during which time they have all privileges, save a vote, at residents' meeting. At the end of that period, if they have proved valuable to the work of the House, they are invited to remain, if it is probable that they can be in residence for six months. The expenses of the residents are defrayed by themselves on the plan of a cooperative club under the direction of a house committee. A limited number of fellowships has been established, one of them by the Chicago branch of the Inter-Collegiate Alumnae Association.

All the residents of Hull-House for the first three years were women, though much valuable work has always been done by non-resident men. During the last year men have come into residence in a cottage on Polk Street, dining at Hull-House, and giving such part of their time to the work of the settlement as is consistent with their professional or business life.

It is estimated that two thousand people come to Hull-House each week, either as members of clubs or organizations, or as parts of an audience. One hundred of these come as teachers, lecturers, or directors of clubs. The house has always had much valuable assistance from the citizens of Chicago. This voluntary response to its needs perhaps accounts for the fact that it has never found it necessary to form an association with chapters in colleges, as other settlements have done.

Finances.

Hull-House and the adjacent lots are given by the owner rent free until 1920. Two buildings have been built upon these by friends of the House. Three other buildings are to be erected in 1895. One is an addition to the coffee-house, a second is designed for general class and audience rooms, while the third is to be known as the children's house. The superintendence and teaching of the settlement are volunteered by residents and others, and are unpaid. The running expenses of the settlement proper are therefore reduced to a minimum. Large sums are constantly needed, however, for the initiation of new departments and the expenses of those branches, such as the nursery, which can never be self-supporting. These are constantly defrayed by generous friends of the House, many of whom are active in its service.

Index

Abbott, Edith: background and career of, 13–14; as HH resident, 14; social science and advocacy, 13–14

Abbott, Grace, 13

Addams, Jane: background of, 10–11; Civic Federation of Chicago, 29; on class warfare, 147–49; as clubwomen, 15; on ethical aims of labor, 149; friendship with Ellen Gates Star, 11; head resident, 1; HH Association, 17; HH donors and, 17; HH incorporation, 16; *HHM&P*, 4; HH trustees and, 17; Italian Institute, 9; Italian neighborhood, 8; on life experience, 12; Plymouth, Mass., conference, 12; on Pullman Strike (1894), 29; research, 13; residency, 14; on settlement as factor in labor movement, 138–49; on settling, 12; on sewing-trades, 138–39; "slumming," 13; slums, 7; and social claim, 14; as social reformer, 4; social work of, 3; sociological investigation, 5; as sociologist, 3; at Toynbee Hall, 12; on trades-unions, 140; on working people's demands, 145

African Americans, 19

agricultural colonies, 8, 163

Aladdin ovens, 169

alleys, 53, 54

Altgeld, John Peter, 5, 74; on Julia C. Lathrop to State Board of Charities, 8

American Economic Association, 3

Americanization, 101, 114, 119, 132

American Journal of Sociology, 3

American Railway Union, 14

Americans, 62

anarchists, 32m 104

Anfreda Club, 168

anti-clericalism, 9

anti-sweatshop campaign, 5, 18, 33, 70, 142, 159

Arabians, 60

Arnold Toynbee Club, 161

art: Christian, 11; for the masses, 29; in working-class districts, 17, 130–37

art exhibits (at HH art gallery), 154–55

arts and crafts movement, 11, 29

assimilation, 19, 26, 28

Austrians, 59

Barnett, Henrietta, 12

Barnett, Samuel, 12, 45

Beard, Charles, 1

Bemis, Edward, 16

Bindery Girls' Union, 158

Bisno, Abraham: and Illinois Factory and Inspection Act, 6; as labor leader, 7; as state deputy factory inspector, 2

blacks, 20, 62

Board of Charities, 8

Board of Education, 75, 119

boarders, 3, 61

Board of Health, 26, 98

boarding and lodging houses, 61

Bohemian chapter, Women's Christian Temperance Union, 9

Bohemian College, 111

Bohemian committee, Columbian Exposition, 9

Bohemian Garnet Club, 168

Bohemian Republican League, 113

Bohemians, 9, 34, 59, 61, 85; becoming American, 114; building and loan associations, 27, 108; as businessmen, 109; as Catholics, 111; in Chicago, 10; child labor and, 111; family and social life, 110–11; as freethinkers, 112; *HHM&P*, 19; immigration of, 108; labor organizations of, 109, 110; newspapers, 109, 111, 112; occupation of, 109; in Pilsen, 107; politics, 113; population of, 107; property investment of, 109; as Protestants, 111–12; refugees of 1848, 107; sweating-system and, 18; tenement shops, pre-1870 settlement, 107

bootblacks and newsboys, 76, 77

Booth, Charles: *Life and Labour of the People of London,* 2, 17; maps of London, 9, 18–19, 45, 57

Bowen, Joseph T., 17

Bowen, Louise de Koven: as benefactor of HH,

RIMA LUNIN SCHULTZ is assistant director of the Jane Addams Hull-House Museum and editor of the education Website *Urban Experience in Chicago: Hull-House and Its Neighborhoods, 1889–1963.* She is the coeditor, with Adele Hast, of the award-winning *Women Building Chicago, 1790–1990: A Biographical Dictionary* (2001).

The University of Illinois Press
is a founding member of the
Association of American University Presses.

—————————————————————

Composed in 11/13.5 Adobe Garamond
by Jim Proefrock
at the University of Illinois Press
Designed by Paula Newcomb
Manufactured by Thomson-Shore, Inc.

University of Illinois Press
1325 South Oak Street
Champaign, IL 61820-6903
www.press.uillinois.edu